The Basics of Hebrew Poetry

The Basics of Hebrew Poetry

Theory and Practice

SAMUEL T. S. GOH

Foreword by Tremper Longman III

CASCADE *Books* · Eugene, Oregon

THE BASICS OF HEBREW POETRY
Theory and Practice

Cascade Books
An Imprint of Wipf and Stock Publishers
199 W. 8th Ave., Suite 3
Eugene, OR 97401

www.wipfandstock.com

PAPERBACK ISBN: 978-1-5326-0190-3
HARDCOVER ISBN: 978-1-5326-0192-7
EBOOK ISBN: 978-1-5326-0191-0

Cataloguing-in-Publication data:

Names: Goh, Samuel T. S., author | Longman, Tremper, III, foreword.

Title: The basics of Hebrew poetry : theory and practice / Samuel T. S. Goh ; foreword by Tremper Longman III.

Description: Eugene, OR: Cascade Books, 2017 | Series: if applicable | Includes bibliographical references and index.

Identifiers: ISBN 978-1-5326-0190-3 (paperback) | ISBN 978-1-5326-0192-7 (hardcover) | ISBN 978-1-5326-0191-0 (ebook).

Subjects: LCSH: Hebrew poetry, Biblical | Bible. Old Testament—Language, style | Hebrew language—Parallelism.

Classification: BS1405.2 G66 2017 (print) | BS1405.2 (ebook).

Manufactured in the U.S.A.   09/27/17

To

my beloved wife

our lovely children

Contents

Foreword

THE OLD TESTAMENT CONTAINS many poems. Some books are written total-ly in poetic form (Psalms, Proverbs, Song of Songs, Isaiah, and many Minor Prophets), while other books are largely poetic (Job, Jeremiah, Ezekiel). Indeed, virtually every book of the Old Testament contains some poetry. If one gathered all the poetry of the Old Testament into a single place, the resulting compilation would be longer than the whole New Testament.

Realizing the extent of poetry in the Old Testament presses upon us the need to know how to read and interpret Hebrew poetry and this entails becoming knowledgeable in the various poetic conventions utilized by the ancient poets. Familiarity with poetry written in Chinese, in English, or any other language only gets the reader so far. What Robert Alter, the renowned literary scholars with special interest in the Hebrew Bible, tells us about the stories of the Old Testament is equally true of poetry:

> Every culture, even every era in a particular culture, develops distinctive and sometime intricate codes for telling its stories, involving everything from narrative point of view, procedures of description and characterization, the management of dialogue, to the ordering of time and the organization of plot.[1]

We need to familiarize ourselves with the "distinctive and intricate codes" that Hebrew authors use to compose their poems. This includes, among other features, parallelism, imagery, acrostics, and more.

Thus, we should all be thankful to Dr. Samuel Goh for producing this insightful guide to the conventions of Hebrew poetry. In addition, he not only gives us the principles, but also outstanding examples of poetic analysis from passages in Psalms, Ecclesiastes, and Job. I was privileged to have Dr. Goh as a student when I taught at Westminster Theological Seminary in

---

1. R. Alter, "A Response to Critics," *JSOT* 27 (1983) 113-17.

Philadelphia in the 1990s and have been pleased to see how he has gone on to establish himself as a leading scholar in Old Testament studies.

This book is thus important for every serious student of the Hebrew Bible who wants to uncover the message that God, through his human authors, intended us to learn from the fascinating and powerful poems of the Old Testament.

Tremper Longman III
Robert H. Gundry Professor of Biblical Studies
Westmont College

Preface

THERE ARE MANY MEANS to represent reality (physical or conceptual). Some people do it by painting, photography, others do it by narrative, yet some others by versification (poetry). Among the four, poetry is arguably the least popular, because it is not easy to appreciate. This situation may change, however, when words of poetic nature appear in pop songs. One may raise the question: why when "poetry" and "melody" are put together, do they become popular? The reason could be that the music element has a stronger appeal than the poetic element. When a pop song has a "catchy" melody and rhythm, it is usually better appreciated.

To my limited knowledge, not many Christians appreciate biblical poetry. The reason is simple: the Hebrew poetry in the Old Testament has only "lyrics," no music. For various reasons, the ancient songs (such as those in the Psalter and Song of Songs) in the present Hebrew Bible (the Masoretic Text) have lyrics but not the original music. To many Bible readers, this poses an obstacle to their Bible reading. Poetry is an unfamiliar genre to them; its expressions are not part of their daily language; consequently, it is not easy to understand.

To Christians who are interested in knowing the Bible, the problem is compounded by the fact that more than fifty percent of the Old Testament is poetic in nature: the Psalter, the wisdom books, and most prophetic books. Poetry is even found in the narratives (such as the Song of the Sea in Exodus 15, the Song of Deborah in Judges, and the Song of Hannah in 1 Sam 2:1–10). In other words, a huge portion of the Bible is inaccessible to them. Consequently, most lay Christians, even preachers, can only read selected passages, leaving behind a huge portion of the Bible undiscovered. This in turn hampers the church's understanding of God's word, leading to weak or even bad theology.

For reason of the foregoing problems, this book's goal is not to offer an introduction to the poetic books in general. Issues such as background, social setting, genre classification of poetry are not the concerns of this book. Instead, its focus is primarily on the literary aspects of the Hebrew poetry in the Old Testament. Our interest is in how biblical poets get their theological message across by versification. We will begin with a brief introduction to the definition of biblical poetry and the literary elements involved. This will be followed by three chapters which discuss the key poetic elements of Hebrew poetry, parallelism, rhythm (meter) and figurative language respectively. To illustrate how the elements work, the last three chapters provide three examples. Each example features a poetic analysis of a text, respectively Psalm 1, Eccl 1:3–8, and Job 42:2–6. The reason for three examples is that since Hebrew poetry is a complex art, more examples are necessary to demonstrate the diversity of biblical poetic artistry. This in turn would remind us not to study the poems mechanically. As will be shown, every one of the three texts has its own uniqueness. While the poets use the same set of literary devices, the way they appropriate them showcases the beauty of their artistry.

The publication of this book is made possible by the support and assistance of many. I'm grateful to Singapore Bible College for its one year sabbatical leave (2013), which allowed me to work on this project. A word of appreciation is also due to Princeton Theological Seminary, where I was a visiting scholar and had the privilege to use its facilities, attend colloquiums, as well as interact with its professors. Special thanks to Professor Choon-Leong Seow for being instrumental in getting me into the visiting scholar program and for scholarly insights learned in his class as well as our personal conversations. Special thanks also to my former professors, Professor Tremper Longman III for his foreword and Dr. Desmond Alexander for his endorsement.

Some parts of this book were written in Taiwan Theological Seminary, for whose facilities and great hospitality I am grateful. Thanks are also due to a few of my colleagues and students at Singapore Bible College for their helpful comments and suggestions. I would like to thank my student Leow Wen Pin for proofreading, indexing and his pedagogical perspective (such as the need for diagrams in chapters 2 and 4).

A special thanks to my wife, Joyce, and our children for their understanding and support. Most importantly, I'm grateful to God for providing all this. I hope this modest effort can help the reader know and appreciate Old Testament poetic texts, and that in doing so they can deepen their understanding of the theology of the texts and the God they speak about.

Abbreviations

AB	Anchor Bible
ABD	*Anchor Bible Dictionary*
AnBib	Analecta Biblica
AOTC	Abingdon Old Testament Commentaries
BASOR	*Bulletin of the American Schools of Oriental Research*
BBC	Blackwell Bible Commentaries
BBR	*Bulletin for Biblical Research*
BCOT	Baker Commentary on the Old Testament
BDB	Francis Brown, S. R. Driver, and Charles A. Briggs, *A Hebrew and English Lexicon of the Old Testament*. Oxford: Clarendon, 1907
BETL	Bibliotheca Ephemeridum Theologicarum Lovaniensium
BHK	Biblia Hebraica Wurttembergensia
BHS	Biblia Hebraica Stuttgartensia
Bib	*Biblica*
BibInt	*Biblical Interpretation*
BibRev	*Bible Review*
BJS	Brown Judaic Studies
BLS	Bible and Literature Series
BRLAJ	Brill Reference Library of Ancient Judaism
BZ	*Biblische Zeitschrift*
CBQ	*Catholic Biblical Quarterly*
CC	Continental Commentaries

CESJ	*China Evangelical Seminary Journal*
CBET	Contributions to Biblical Exegesis & Theology
CJT	*Canadian Journal of Theology*
CritInq	*Critical Inquiry*
CTR	*Criswell Theological Review*
DBI	*Dictionary of Biblical Imagery.* Edited by Leland Ryken, James C. Wilhoit, and Tremper Longman III. Downers Grove, IL: InterVarsity, 1998
EBib	Etudes Bibliques
EncAes	*Encyclopedia of Aesthetics*
EncJud	*Encyclopedia Judaica*
EPP	*Encyclopedia of Poetry and Poetics.* Edited by Alex Preminger. Princeton: Princeton University Press, 1965
ErIsr	*Eretz-Israel*
FOL	*Foundations of Language*
GKC	*Gesenius' Hebrew Grammar.* Edited and enlarged by E. Kautzsch. Translated by A. E. Cowley. Oxford: Clarendon, 1910
HBM	Hebrew Bible Monographs
HSM	Harvard Semitic Monographs
HSS	Harvard Semitic Studies
HTR	*Harvard Theological Review*
HUCA	*Hebrew Union College Annual*
IBC	Interpretation Bible Commentary for Teaching and Preaching
IBT	Interpreting Biblical Texts
ICC	International Critical Commentary
Int	*Interpretation*
ITC	International Theological Commentary
JANES	*Journal of the Ancient Near Eastern Society*
JBL	*Journal of Biblical Literature*
JBQ	*Jewish Bible Quarterly*

Joüon	Paul Joüon, *The Grammar of Biblical Hebrew*. 2 vols. Revised by T. Muraoka. Reprinted with corrections. SubBi 27. Rome: Editrice Pontificio Istituto Biblico, 2006
JPhil	*The Journal of Philosophy*
JPS	Jewish Publication Society
JSNT	*Journal for Studies of the New Testament*
JSOT	*Journal for Studies of the Old Testament*
JSOTSup	Journal for the Study of the Old Testament Supplement
JSS	*Journal of Semitic Studies*
JTAK	*Journal of Theta Alpha Kappa*
JTI	*Journal of Theological Interpretation*
LCL	Loeb Classical Library
NCB	New Century Bible Commentary
NEA	*Near Eastern Archaeology*
NICNT	New International Commentary on the New Testament
NICOT	New International Commentary on the Old Testament
NJPS	New Jewish Publication Society (translation of the Hebrew Bible)
NPEPP	*The New Princeton Encyclopedia of Poetry and Poetics*. Edited by Alex Preminger and T. V. F. Brogan. Princeton, NJ: Princeton University Press, 1993
OTL	Old Testament Library
PJ	Prace Jezykoznawcze
PMLA	*Pacific Ancient and Modern Language Association*
PRS	*Perspectives in Religious Studies*
Proof	*Prooftexts*
PT	*Poetics Today*
ResQ	*Restoration Quarterly*
RvExp	*Review and Expositor*
SBEC	Studies in Bible and Early Christianity
SBLAB	Society of Biblical Literature Academia Biblica
SPSM	Studia Pohl Series Maior

1

Hebrew Poetry
The Art of Versification

POETRY: VERSIFICATION OF REALITY

It is universally acknowledged that the Greek philosopher Aristotle is the first person who provides an extended philosophical treatment of poetry in his *Poetics*.[1] For Aristotle, poetry is an artistic representation (mimesis) of reality. By this he means the poet mimics real life experience through poetry.[2] In other words, poetry is a representation of reality by *versification*.

People employ many means to represent their real life experience. Some choose to narrate it (hence we have stories); others paint it (paintings); yet others film it (movies). The poet, naturally, versifies it (i.e., turning it into poetry). The English poet William Blake (1757–1827) versified spring as an angelic male figure:

> O thou with dewy locks, who lookest down;
> Through the clear windows of the morning, turn
> Thine angel eyes upon our western isle,
> Which in full choir hails thy approach, O Spring![3]

---

1. Johnson, "Introduction," 5. Aristotle's *Poetics* is a rare surviving Greek theory of drama and poetry.

2. Aristotle, *Poetics*, 1447a, 1447b, 1448b.

3. Quoted in Yeats, *Poems of William Blake*, 3.

Elsewhere, in ancient China, the Chinese poet Meng Haoran (689–740), versified his experience of spring:

Sleeping in spring oblivious of dawn
Everywhere I hear birds
After the wind and rain last night
I wonder how many petals fell[4]

We have similar examples from the Old Testament. The final author of Exodus first narrates God's deliverance of the Israelites in Exodus 14 then versifies the same event in Exodus 15. Elsewhere, a psalmist versifies his experience of God's providence (Ps 23:1–2):

Yahweh is my shepherd,
I lack nothing.
In green pastures he makes me lie down,
beside still waters he leads me.[5]

The biblical poets versify all sorts of reality: natural and supernatural; physical and spiritual. Their art of versification has produced various kinds of poetry: praises, lament, complaints (Psalms), wisdom teaching (aphorisms and wise sayings in Proverbs), discourse, dialogue (Ecclesiastes and Job), and love songs (Song of Songs). All these various versifications reflect the diverse human experiences and real life phenomena behind the poetic texts.

THE DIFFICULTIES OF UNDERSTANDING HEBREW POETRY

To understand a poet's work, one needs to know the literary conventions by which they versify reality. Unfortunately, in this matter the student of Hebrew poetry is less privileged than the student of Greek poetry. The reason is we have inherited from the biblical poets their versification but not their poetic conventions. Whereas students of Greek poetry have Aristotle's *Poetics* to thank, students of Hebrew poetry have received no such systematic theorization from the ancient Hebrews. Therefore, a student of Hebrew poetry faces a lack of information about how its poets versified reality and how their versification should be understood.

---

4. *Spring Dawn (Chun Xiao)*, quoted in Pine, *Poems of the Masters*, 9.
5. Unless otherwise stated, all biblical texts in this book are the writer's translation.

This difficulty is compounded by the fact that the poetic texts at hand, which are presented in the Masoretic Text (hereafter MT), are centuries after their composition. Having gone through layers of redaction and centuries of transmission, textual problems are therefore inevitable.[6] This being the case, what we have today does not look like exactly what the poets had composed originally.[7] As such scholars are uncertain about the original arrangement of the poetic lines, the overall structure which the poet had in mind, and the original pronunciation and rhythm.[8] While this does not undermine the inspirational nature of the text, it does hamper our understanding of its literary nature.

Given that so little information is accessible to us, James Kugel seems justified when he asks whether the term "biblical poetry" would in fact be foreign to the Old Testament poets.[9] The majority of scholars, however, do not share such pessimism. They are rather confident that the poetic texts themselves offer us many clues about their conventions. Robert Alter, for example, offers an optimistic note: "The difficulties, however, need not be overstated. There remains much that can be understood about biblical verse," and that Hebrew poetry "may exhibit perfectly perceptible formal patterns that tell us something about the operations of the underlying poetic system."[10]

This optimism is echoed by many biblical scholars, as testified by the many taxonomies of Hebrew poetry. The taxonomies are usually carried out mainly by looking within the Hebrew texts to understand the workings of Hebrew poetry, and by comparing them with poetic works contemporary to the Hebrew poets. The contemporary works, especially Ugaritic poems, have proved helpful in understanding Hebrew poetry.[11] Inevitably, modern theories of poetry are used in the process. Nonetheless, it is well acknowledged that many things in poetry cross time and culture. As we will see in the following chapters, poetry across the world shares common features

6. This fact is well recognized by scholars. See Alter, *Art of Biblical Poetry*, 3; Holladay, "Hebrew Verse Structure Revisited (I)," 20.

7. As we will show in chapter 3, the MT pronunciation and accentuation are based on a Hebrew dialect around the sixth century CE rather than those of the original poets.

8. Though, as Tov points out, at least 15 manuscripts of the Psalter found in Qumran are arranged in poetic lines (*Scribal Practices*, 168 and Table 8). Nevertheless, these texts are the products of long transmission and represent a small number of the Hebrew poetic texts.

9. Kugel, *Idea of Biblical Poetry*, 69, 302.

10. Alter, *Art of Biblical Poetry*, 3.

11. See for example, Young. *Ugarit in Retrospect*. As O'Connor notes, scholars' consensus is that the similarities between Hebrew and Ugaritic poetry have allowed better understanding of Hebrew poetry (*Hebrew Verse Structure*, 25).

such as parallelism, rhythm and metaphor. This being the case, modern theories may serve as a bridge between the present and the ancient Hebrew world. With this confidence, in this and the following chapters we will proceed to examine the conventions by which biblical poets versify reality.

HOW BIBLICAL POETS VERSIFY REALITY

As mentioned earlier, biblical authors have different means to represent reality, and versification is only one of them. This being the case, the task of studying the conventions of Hebrew poetry begins by asking two basic questions. The first is a question of genre: is this text a representation by versification? Put simply, is this poetry? E. D. Hirsch notes that *genre* is a system of conventions.[12] It follows that to have a grasp of how a text's conventions work to convey thought we must first identify its genre. In other words, there is a close correlation between our ability to recognize a text's genre and our ability to understand the text's conventions.[13] The second question is closely related to the first. "Is this poetry?" is in fact a question of "in what ways is versification different from other means of representation (such as narration)" or "what constitutes a poem"?

The Difficulties of Identifying Poetic Texts

To some readers the question "is this poetry" seems redundant. After all, it is commonly known that books such as Job, Psalms, Proverbs, Ecclesiastes, and Song of Songs have been classified as poetry. While this is true, prose and poetry are not defined by the books in which they appear. Often we have both prose and poetry in the same book, and their distinction is not always clear. Thus we have the Song of the Sea interwoven with the rest of the exodus narrative (Exodus 15), and the Song of Lamech almost tucked away in the middle of the story of the Cainites (Gen 4:23–24). In fact, even in some of the so-called poetic books we find both poetry and prose (e.g., Job 1–2; 42:7–17; Isaiah 36–39).[14]

This is by no means to suggest that the Hebrew Bible has never distinguished poetry from prose. Recently scholars have pointed out that many psalms found at Qumran have special spacing or layout, which betrays the

12. Hirsch, *Validity in Interpretation*, 92–93.

13. Barton defines literary competence primarily in terms of "*the ability to recognize genre*" (*Reading the Old Testament*, 16).

14. See Gillingham, *Poems and Psalms*, 28–36.

concept of poetic lineation.[15] Similarly, the medieval Masoretic manuscripts have special spacing for poetic passages, distinguishing them from prose texts.[16] Nonetheless, all this may not represent how the original authors viewed their works; consequently, categorizing a text as poetic remains a challenge.[17] The distinction in the Bible translations today is the format decision of modern scholars, which is evidently not free from conjecture, even subjectivity. Their subjectivity is reflected by their disagreements about whether or not a particular passage is poetic, which in turn lead to different formatting decisions. For instance, whereas KJV prints Gen 1:27 as prose, NIV prints the same text as poetry;[18] similarly, BHS and NIV print Isa 4:2 as prose; TANAKH and NAB print it as poetry.[19]

All these problems reveal that the poetry of the ancient Israelites and Judahites (or of any culture) may seem simple to recognize, but this is decidedly not so.[20] Wilfred G. E. Watson puts it well: "Everybody knows, or rather thinks he knows, the difference between prose and poetry . . . The problem for us is to establish criteria: *how* can we tell whether a particular passage is poetry or not?"[21]

Just in case we are said to trivialize this issue, history has shown that this seemingly simple issue has not only generated much debate and passionate agendas, but has also posed an occupational hazard. On one extreme, we have Paul Kraus, who argued in the 1930s that accent is the main indicator of poetry. He contended that once properly accented, he could prove that the whole Hebrew Bible has been written in poetry. But two-thirds of the way through his research he discovered that the texts would not support his thesis, so he committed suicide.[22] On the other extreme, we have James Kugel, who has devoted a whole book to prove that elements

---

15. See n8.

16. For further discussion, see Dobbs-Allsopp, *On Biblical Poetry*, 29–33

17. It is noteworthy that such a close association of prose and poetry at times poses a problem for classification to scholars. See Gillingham, *Poems and Psalms*, 28–36.

18. Ibid., 20–21.

19. As noted by Petersen and Richards, *Interpreting Hebrew Poetry*, 4–5; also Kugel, *Idea of Biblical Poetry*, 77–80.

20. Writing in 1947, Robinson notes, "Most of us know the difference between poetry and prose. When we hear or see a passage we have no difficulty in deciding to which class of literature it belongs" (*Poetry of the Old Testament*, 11). As we will soon see, later scholarship moved away from this simplistic conclusion.

21. Watson, *Classical Hebrew Poetry*, 44–45; emphasis his.

22. Cited in Alter, *Art of Biblical Poetry*, 2.

such as parallelism and terseness are just elevated style, and the term "biblical poetry" is a misnomer.[23]

The two cases above remind us that the issue is not as simple as it seems, and that we have to be cautious in our attempt to define poetry and avoid any extreme. As Peterson and Richards wisely suggest, in light of the problems, one can only hold a tentative notion of poetry.[24] Indeed, most scholars of Hebrew poetry today hold a tentative consensus of what Hebrew poetry is, and whether it can be easily distinguished from prose. This cautious approach is understandable especially in view of Kugel's vigorous argument against a sharp distinction between poetry and prose. For Kugel, the Hebrew Bible contains parts with different degrees of elevated style (or "heightening effects") such as parallelism and terseness. He contends that the sections with a high degree of elevated style are mistakenly called poetry, whereas the sections with a lower degree of elevated style are "erroneously" called prose.[25]

Most scholars agree with Kugel's concerns, but they do not think poetry and prose are completely indistinguishable. So though Alter admits that "it is rare to find anywhere a poetic style that does not bear some relation to the literary prose of the same culture,"[26] he is also confident that there are certain elements that would suggest the presence of poetry.[27] Alter's confidence perhaps represents the sentiment of other biblical scholars. This is evidenced by the fact that Kugel's argument has not prevented attempts to identify the elements or features associated with Hebrew poetry.

We share such an optimistic attitude. Given that people can generally recognize poetry suggests there are some general characteristics that make Hebrew poetry recognizable. Likewise, the fact that its criteria are difficult to set suggests that Hebrew poetry has certain things that would require a more technical examination. For this reason the *tentative* definition of Hebrew poetry proposed below will begin with what Watson calls "general indicators"[28] and be followed by more technical ones.

---

23. Kugel, *Idea of Biblical Poetry,* 7, 302.

24. Petersen and Richards, *Interpreting Hebrew Poetry,* 2.

25. Kugel, *Idea of Biblical Poetry,* 85, 94.

26. Alter, *Art of Biblical Poetry,* 5.

27. Ibid., 3–28.

28. Watson lists at least 19 general and structural indicators of poetry (*Classical Hebrew Poetry,* 46–57). Unfortunately, many of them are too technical for beginners, especially for those without a working knowledge of Hebrew. For this reason, we do not follow his categorization strictly.

General Indicators of Poetry

Though some aspects of the original poetry may have been lost in transmission, many others are still recognizable, even in modern translations. This is especially true of modern translations informed by recent scholarship of Hebrew poetry. Some of these elements may serve as indicators of its poetic nature. So identifying the following indicators does not require technical knowledge such as biblical Hebrew.

Parallelism

Simply put, parallelism refers to the relationship between poetic components (cola, strophes or stanzas).[29] In many cases, the relationship is described in terms of semantic correspondence. Such parallelism is often evident, even in translations, such as the one in Ps 114:1:

> When Israel went out from Egypt,
>
> the house of Jacob from a people of strange language.

For a long time since Robert Lowth (1710–1787) it had been asserted that parallelism is a key feature that distinguishes poetry from prose.[30] So, writing in the early twentieth century, Louis Israel Newman calls parallelism a universal "poetic motif."[31] This however, has changed, ever since scholars pointed out the presence of parallelism in Hebrew narratives, legal material, and genealogies.[32]

In fact, parallelism is not always present in Hebrew poetry. This was recognized as far back as the eighteenth century. For instance, Lowth treats some non-parallel lines as poetic; similarly, George Buchanan Gray also speaks of non-parallel lines in Lamentation 1–4.[33] In his study of the semantic parallelism in the Hebrew Bible, Kugel concludes that the relationship between lines ranges from "zero perceivable correspondence" to "near-zero perceivable differentiation."[34] The last statement confirms what the preced-

29. For a full discussion of parallelism, see chapter 2.

30. Lowth, *Lectures on Sacred Poetry*, 2:34; quotations in this book are taken from this English translation.

31. Newman and Popper, *Biblical Parallelism*, 3.

32. See the convincing argument by Kugel (*Idea of Biblical Poetry*, 3, 59–65). For an example of parallelism in biblical narrative, see Gen 21:1; see also the analysis of the creation story by Wenham (*Genesis 1–15*, 6–7).

33. Lowth, *Lectures on Sacred Poetry*, 2:48–49; see also Gray, *Forms of Hebrew Poetry*, 50–51.

34. Kugel, *Idea of Biblical Poetry*, 3, 7.

ing scholars have said all along: there are indeed poetic texts that are not parallel at all ("zero perceivable correspondence").

Nevertheless, it is quite true, as some scholars have observed, that high frequency of parallelism suggests the presence of Hebrew poetry.[35] We add, however, that this is usually corroborated by other indicators. So while parallelism figures prominently in poetry, it is only a corroborative characteristic instead of an absolute one.

Condensed Language

Before the invention of email or mobile phone text messages, people used the telegraph. For reasons of economy, telegraph messages were usually terse or condensed. The Hebrew poet, too, employs the terse "telegraph style,"[36] or to be more up-to-date, "text message" style. The purpose, however, is not for economy, but to make the expression more stylistic. It becomes evident when we compare the prose and poetic versions of the killing of Sisera in Judges. The narrator first tells the story in prose in Judg 4:19:[37]

> He [Sisera] said to her [Jael], "Please give me a little water to drink, for I am thirsty."
>
> So she opened a skin bottle of milk and gave him a drink and covered him.

The same story is also depicted in poetry in Judg 5:25, which keeps the essentials, only condensed and thus more stylistic:

> Water he asked,
>
> Milk she gave,
>
> In a princely bowl she brought curds.

Similar comparisons have also been identified elsewhere such as Exodus 14–15,[38] leading to the view that condensed language is another general indicator of poetry.[39]

---

35. Alonso-Schökel, *Manual of Hebrew Poetics*, 48.

36. So Kugel, *Idea of Biblical Poetry*, 87.

37. See Berlin, *Dynamics of Biblical Parallelism*, 12.

38. It is widely noted that the poetic version serves as the basis of the prose version. See Houston, "Misunderstanding (Part I)," 342–55 and Houston, "Misunderstanding (Part II)," 534–48.

39. E.g., Watson, *Classical Hebrew Poetry*, 49; Berlin, *Dynamics of Biblical Parallelism*, 5–6; Fokkelman, *Reading Biblical Poetry*, 15.

Those who do not read Hebrew have Bible translators to thank. In modern translations, poetic clauses (cola) are formatted concisely. Those who read the Hebrew would notice that a colon usually comprises no more than four or five Hebrew words.[40] But again, terseness is also a phenomenon in prosaic legal texts (e.g., the Ten Commandments)[41] and even some narrative texts such as Judg 4:19, 21.[42] For this reason, it is only a corroborative characteristic of Hebrew poetry; its usual corroborative counterpart is parallelism. As Berlin observes: "Where these two occur to a high degree we have what would be called (by everyone but Kugel) poetry."[43]

Ellipsis

Related to the concise nature of poetry, we often see a phenomenon called "ellipsis"[44] or otherwise called "gapping" in Hebrew poetry.[45] Ellipsis happens when one or two words are left out of a sentence but the meaning is still understood. Ellipsis is common even in daily conversation: "He is happy, but I'm not." Though the adjective "happy" is left out in the second clause, the remark is understood to say, "He is happy, but I'm not happy."

In Hebrew poetry, ellipsis occurs when one or two of the constituents in the second colon are left out, leaving the constituents in the first colon to govern both cola.[46] Interestingly, this phenomenon is not lost in translations, so Hebrew is not always necessary for its recognition. As Edward L. Greenstein illustrates below:

> Not for your sacrifices do I rebuke you,
> your burnt offerings ever before me. (Ps 50:8)[47]

---

40. Kugel, *Idea of Biblical Poetry*, 71; Gillingham, *Poems and Psalms*, 21.

41. Kugel notes the concision of legal text such as Lev 19:3 (*Idea of Biblical Poetry*, 92).

42. Berlin lists some terse and parallel narrative passages such as Gen 6:12, 17:17 and 1 Sam 1:28 (*Dynamics of Biblical Parallelism*, 37).

43. Berlin, *Dynamics of Biblical Parallelism*, 5. It is noteworthy that despite his denial, Kugel gives a rather detailed discussion of terseness (*Idea of Biblical Poetry*, 87–94).

44. Watson, *Classical Hebrew Poetry*, 48.

45. O'Connor, *Hebrew Verse Structure*, 122–29.

46. O'Connor (ibid., 124, 404) points out that in some languages (such as Japanese) gapping happens in the first colon, called "leftward gapping." There are only two such cases in Hebrew poetry: Judg 5:3c, 3d and Deut 33:4b,5a.

47. Translation is his; Greenstein, "How Does Paralelism Mean?" 47.

Note that the second colon leaves out the phrase "not for' and the verb "rebuke," yet the bicolon is understood to say: "Not for your sacrifices do I rebuke you; *nor for* your burnt offerings ever before me do I rebuke you."[48]

Figurative Language

Figures of speech normally feature prominently in modern poetry. Intriguingly, not many scholars list figurative language (such as simile and metaphor) among the indicators of Hebrew poetry,[49] though its importance as biblical poetic language is widely noted and has increasingly gained scholarly interest in recent studies of Hebrew poetry.[50] Perhaps one reason is that figurative speech is pervasive across genres: prose, poetry, monologues, and dialogues.[51] Meir Weiss and Luis Alonso-Schökel have gone too far as to assert that figurative language is "the essence of poetry,"[52] but it is true that its high concentration in a passage often suggests the presence of a poem.[53] This, however, is usually accompanied by the other two indicators: parallelism and terseness.[54] As such, figurative language as a poetic indicator is also corroborative rather than absolute. Thus when the three elements appear in Psalm 18:3 (ET 18:2), we assuredly have a poetic text:

> Yahweh is,
>
> my rock and my fortress and my deliverer,
>
> my God, my rock, I take refuge in him,
>
> my shield and the horn of my salvation, my stronghold.

48. As Greenstein suggests, without such an understanding, the bicolon would mean "Not for your sacrifices I rebuke you, and your burnt offers *are* ever before me" (ibid., italics mine). For more ellipsis cases, see our discussion of parallelism in the next chapter.

49. Gillingham is an exception (*Poems and Psalms*, 21–22).

50. Though they do not necessarily list metaphor among the poetic indicators, many introductions to Hebrew poetry devote most or all of an entire chapter to the topic. Among others are Alter, *Art of Biblical Poetry*, 231–54; Petersen and Richards, *Interpreting Hebrew Poetry*, 49–60; Watson, *Classical Hebrew Poetry*, 250–72; Watson, *Techniques in Classical Hebrew Verse*, 392–413. For recent discussions of metaphor in Hebrew poetry, see Oestreich, *Metaphors and Similes in Hosea 14:2–9 (1–8)*; and Jindo, *Biblical Metaphor Reconsidered*.

51. See Lakoff and Johnson, "Conceptual Metaphor," 454; cf. Knowles and Moon, *Introducing Metaphor*, 4.

52. Weiss, *Bible from Within*, 132; Alonso-Schökel, *Manual of Hebrew Poetics*, 95.

53. Petersen and Richards, *Interpreting Hebrew Poetry*, 49–50.

54. Jindo rightly argues that merely the high concentration of imagery "does not make a text a poem—it only makes it more *poetic*" (*Biblical Metaphor Reconsidered*, 22).

In sum, we concur with David L. Petersen and Kent Harold Richards that none of the features mentioned above can in and of itself be called the hallmark of poetry; rather, when all of them occur prominently in a more intense and denser way than they do in prose, we have poetry.[55] The following elements may further help identify poetry.

Technical Indicators

Many of the following indicators are technical, as they require a good working knowledge of biblical Hebrew to detect.

The Low Frequency of Some Hebrew Words

The fact that the language of Hebrew poetry is more elevated in style than prose usually results in the low frequency of some Hebrew words or particles normally associated with prose. So, perhaps due to the tendency of terseness,[56] the following Hebrew particles normally associated with prose occur less frequently in poetry: the definite article *ha*, the relative pronoun *ăšer* and the object marker *ʾet*.[57] Also, it is widely accepted that the *wayyiqtol* form (*waw* consecutive + Imperfect), which is ubiquitous in prose,[58] is conspicuously less frequent in Hebrew poetry.[59]

Irregular Word Order

While the regular word order of biblical Hebrew is verb-subject-object,[60] irregular word order (any order which deviates from the regular order) is

---

55. Petersen and Richards, *Interpreting Hebrew Poetry*, 14.

56. So Kugel, *Idea of Biblical Poetry*, 90.

57. See Andersen and Forbes, "'Prose Particle' Counts," 165–69. For example, comparing the use of *šāmayim* (heaven) in Ps 8:9 (without the definite article) and in Gen 1:1 (with the article). Freedman shows that the distribution of these particles is one determinant factor which distinguishes prose from poetry (*Pottery, Poetry and Prophecy*, 2–3).

58. The close association of the *wayyiqtol* verb-form with narratives is not only found in biblical Hebrew, but also Ugaritic. See Joüon § 117c; for detailed discussion, see Smith, *Origins and Development of the Waw-Consecutive*.

59. Though not as frequent as in prose, the *wayyigtol* does occur in poetic passages. See Finley, "*Waw*-Consecutive," 251; Gosling, "Waw Consecutive," 403–10; Bloch, "The Prefixed Perfective," 34–70.

60. Waltke and O'Connor, *Biblical Hebrew Syntax*, 635; Longacre, "Left Shifts," 332.

also frequently found in the Hebrew Bible, such as the subject-verb-object order.[61] Some scholars have observed that the word order of narrative texts tends to be more regular than that of poetic texts.[62] In a recent study of selected narrative and poetic texts of the Old Testament, Nicholas P. Lunn discovers that the occurrences of irregular word order in poetry are more than twice as frequent as in narrative.[63] One may draw two conclusions from this ratio. First, the fact that irregular word order also appears in prose (though at a lower frequency) suggests that it is not an absolute indicator. This notion is reinforced by Lunn's discovery that certain kinds of irregular word order appear in poetry just as in prose,[64] making them ineffective as a poetic indicator in those texts. Second, the significantly higher frequency of irregular word order in poetry suggests that density could well be a differentiating factor. Only when coupled with high density of parallelism and terseness does a high density of irregular word order indicate the presence of a poem.

Rhythm or Meter?

For centuries, many biblical scholars have viewed rhythm or meter as one key feature of Hebrew poetry. For instance, in his seminal *Lectures on the Sacred Poetry of the Hebrews*, Lowth argues that two features characterize Hebrew poetry: one is parallelism (as mentioned earlier), the other is meter.[65] Since Lowth many prominent scholars have held similar views. For example, David Noel Freedman and his student Douglas Stuart believe that the syllabic-count metric system is one defining factor of Hebrew poetry.[66] However, since around the second half of the last century, this position has been disputed. In fact, as we will soon see, the very existence of meter in Hebrew poetry has been questioned by many scholars. While the debate on

61. Regular word order is called "unmarked" order, and irregular word order is called "marked" order (so Groom, *Linguistic Analysis*, 149). The regular word order is also called "canonical order" (so Lambrecht, *Information Structure*, 16).

62. Watson, *Classical Hebrew Poetry*, 49; Gillingham, *Poems and Psalms*, 24.

63. Out of 1,190 verbal clauses from narrative texts and 1,243 verbal clauses from poetic texts, Lunn (*Word-Order Variation*, 8) finds the irregular word-order in the narrative texts occur 173 times, whereas the same word-order occurs 422 times in the poetic texts.

64. Ibid., 94.

65. Lowth, *Lectures on Sacred Poetry*, 2:24–25, 54.

66. Freedman, "Biblical Hebrew Poetry," 18–27. Stuart argues that at its oral stage, Hebrew poetry was recited according to rhythmic patterns and thus syllable metrical counting offers an objective basis for defining poetry (*Early Hebrew Meter*, 10, 17–18).

Hebrew metrics has resulted in an evolutionary development of its theories, it has also led to its decline in importance. In recent scholarship, while rhythm in Hebrew poetry is widely recognized, Hebrew metrics has become the view of a minority of scholars.[67]

Linguistic Characteristics

Our discussion of word-order in Hebrew poetry earlier should have alerted us to the possibility of describing Hebrew poetry in linguistic terms. Indeed, some scholars who are not satisfied with the traditional definitions of poetry (by its features such as semantic parallelism and terseness) have argued for a linguistic definition. Standing out among them is Roman Jakobson. Jakobson sees poetic lines as combinations of selected equivalent words or constituents that are arranged in a contiguous chain. The combination results in what he calls "parallelism." Clearly, Jakobson's idea of parallelism is not exactly the same as the traditional one. For him, parallelism is a poetic function that "projects the principle of equivalence from the axis of selection into the axis of combination."[68] For Jakobson, being a poetic function, parallelism is then "the indispensable feature inherent in poetry."[69]

This characteristic poetic feature becomes more evident when a poem comes with a prose counterpart. At this junction, Alviero Niccacci's example may prove helpful. We noted earlier that the killing of Sisera is narrated in prose in Judg 4:19:

> He said to her, "Please give me a little water to drink, for I am thirsty."
>
> So she opened a skin bottle of milk and gave him a drink and covered him.

Niccacci points out that the poet transforms the prose into poetry by matching the nouns in prose (water and milk) with the same or equivalent nouns (water, milk and curd). He also matches the verb of requesting (to ask) with two verbs of granting (to give and to bring); hence we have the following:[70]

---

67. Some older works still list meter as a characteristic of Hebrew poetry. See for example, Watson includes meter in the list of Hebrew poetic indicators (*Classical Hebrew Poetry*, 46, 50). See chapter 3 for a fuller discussion of meter.

68. Jakobson, "Linguistics and Poetics," 358; italics his.

69. Ibid.

70. Niccacci, "Analysing Biblical Hebrew Poetry," 78–79. Berlin uses the same passage to illustrate grammatical parallelism (*Dynamics of Biblical Parallelism*, 12).

> Water he asked,
>
> Milk she gave,
>
> In a princely bowl she brought curds.

Niccacci adds that in this case the difference between prose and poetry can also be described in terms of linear versus segmented presentations.[71] In the poetic version, the straight (linear) sequence of request and granting the request in the prose (Judg 4:19) is transformed into a group of parallel lines which are contiguous and segmented (Judg 5:25).[72] Following Jakobson's principle, such a deliberate selection and combination of matching constituents characterizes the poetic nature of Judg 5:21.[73]

Section Conclusion

Having gone through the survey above, one would come away realizing that the question "what constitutes a poem?" is similar to the question "how would you describe what you see?" The answer to such a question depends very much on the lens through which one looks at the object in question. Different lenses result in different descriptions. A chemist would describe a bronze artifact from the ancient Near East in terms of its chemical elements; a historian would describe it in terms of its date, origin, historical context and significance; while an art dealer would describe it in terms of its market value. Their descriptions may vary, but none of them is wrong. The artifact does fit every one of those descriptions: it is made of chemical elements; it does have a date, origin, historical context and significance; and it does command certain market value. The reason for the different descriptions lies in the lenses through which the artifact is viewed. This may serve as a helpful analogy for answering the question "What constitutes a Hebrew poem?"

The survey above suggests that in general scholars offer us two lenses through which we can view Hebrew poetry. The first one is a literary lens. This results in seeing Hebrew poetry in terms of writing style. Scholars like Kugel, Alter, and to some extent, Berlin, speak of the Hebrew Bible as composed in language of elevated style. The elevated style is represented by a continuum on which various features (parallelism, terseness, figurative language, specific vocabulary, and rhythm) stand. The degree of the elevated style (the frequency or concentration of parallelism, terseness, figurative language and so on) is not homogeneous throughout the Hebrew Bible;

---

71. Niccacci, "Analysing Biblical Hebrew Poetry," 77.

72. Ibid., 78–79.

73. For a detailed discussion, see 31–35.

some parts more concentrated than others. The scholarly consensus is that high degree of style often serves as a good indicator of poetry.

Another lens through which one can view Hebrew poetry is a linguistic one. Scholars with a linguistic prism such as Jakobson, Greenstein, and Berlin view poetry as composed of selected grammatically corresponding constituents which are syntactically arranged in a contiguous way.

Given that poetry is multi-faceted, we need both lenses. It is inadequate to describe Hebrew poetry in terms of its literary features alone; for being expressed through language, it is also a linguistic phenomenon. Likewise, it is equally inadequate to describe Hebrew poetry in linguistic terms alone; for being a literary product, it does involve literary features. Therefore, in keeping with Petersen and Richards's suggestion cited earlier, we should see both lenses as tentative and useful. So instead of pitting one against the other, the wise student of Hebrew poetry would learn how to integrate them for the best benefit. With this tentative notion of what poetry is, we can now move on to look at the components that form Hebrew poetry.

COMPONENTS OF HEBREW POETRY AND TERMINOLOGY

Hebrew poems are constructed by components (or units). But scholars have never agreed upon a common terminology for identifying poetic components. To avoid confusion, we will suggest the following nomenclature and definitions.[74] What we suggest are by no means the best, but we hope they may serve as a common understanding between this writer and the reader by which our discussion is to be understood.

Colon

Normally, the basic component or unit of a Hebrew poem is called "colon" (plural: cola; otherwise called "line"[75]). A colon can be a full sentence or a

---

74. As Watson's work is the current standard introduction to Hebrew poetry, principally we follow his terminology and definitions (*Classical Hebrew Poetry*, especially 11–15). Cf. Lunn, *Word-Order Variation*, 11–12.

75. Scholars use different terms for the poetic unit (colon), such as stich (thus half colon = hemistich; bicolon = distich (e.g., Anderson, "Song of Miriam," 288); verset (Hrushovski, "Note on the Systems," 58; following him is Alter [*Art of Biblical Poetry*, 3]); line (Berlin, *Dynamics of Biblical Parallelism*, 22; O'Connor, *Hebrew Verse Structure*, 85; Clines, "Parallelism of Greater Precision," 78); whereas Kugel uses "line" to refer to bicolon or tricolon (*Idea of Biblical Poetry*, 2–3).

clause. The clause may contain constituents such as finite or infinite verbs, vocatives, participles, nouns and pronominal suffixes.[76] Proverbs 10:1a is an example:

> A wise son makes a father glad.

In the Hebrew (as well as the English translation), the preceding colon consists of nouns (son and father), an adjective (wise) and a verb (makes someone glad).

Hebrew poetry is generally constructed in the format of either a monocolon, or bicolon, tricolon and at times tetra or even pentacolon. The monocolon refers to a colon that "does not cohere with another colon in the same sub-section of a poem."[77] It is not very common, but does occur in Hebrew poetry, such as the last colon of Jer 12:4:[78]

> because they said, "He will not see our latter end."

This is considered a monocolon as it is not connected directly or closely with the following cola, though one way or another it is associated with them.

The most common poetic construction in Hebrew poetry is the bicolon (otherwise called couplet[79]), such as the case of Prov 10:1:

> A wise son makes a father glad,
>
> but a foolish son is a grief to his mother.

But the tricolon (sometimes called triplet[80]) format is also fairly common, as in Prov 30:15:

> The leech has two daughters, "Give," "Give."
>
> There are three things that will not be satisfied,
>
> four that will not say, "Enough."

Some scholars have also presented poetic units in the format of tetracolon (four cola) or pentacolon (five cola).[81] Ps 1:3 is an example of a tetracolon:

---

76. Cf. O'Connor, *Hebrew Verse Structure*, 68–78.

77. Watson, *Classical Hebrew Poetry*, 168.

78. Allen (*Jeremiah*, 144 nf) notes that this is a closing monocolon.

79. E.g., Berlin, *Dynamics of Biblical Parallelism*, 25.

80. Watson, *Classical Hebrew Poetry*, 13.

81. Ibid., 185–90.

He is like a tree transplanted by the streams of water,

which yields its fruit in its season,

and its foliage does not wither.

Whatever he does, prospers.

Strophe and Stanza

While many biblical scholars deal with biblical poetry on the colon (line) level, others believe one should deal with the poetry in terms of larger building blocks such as strophes and stanzas.[82] According to Watson, a strophe is a poetic unit which consists of "one or more cola." A strophe then can be a monocolon, bicolon or tricolon. As for a stanza, it may consist of one or more strophes.[83] Normally, a poem may comprise one or more stanzas.[84]

Dividing a biblical poetic text into cola, strophes, and stanzas (at times called lineation), however, is not a straightforward affair. The reason is that the poetic texts as available to us today—in the MT or the earliest biblical manuscripts such as the Qumran Isaiah—do not come with cola and stanzas.[85] Thus we have no idea as to how they were originally structured. This has resulted in a long history of debate on how to divide them into strophes and stanzas.

Over the past few centuries several approaches have been proposed.[86] Some scholars argue that Hebrew poems are to be divided according to their metrical system. As will be shown in our discussion of Hebrew meter, this approach has its theoretical as well as practical problems.[87] Other scholars theorize that strophic division can be guided by criteria such as coherence of the thought-content, thematic flow, transition markers, and repetition.[88]

82. The question of whether biblical poems have been composed in terms of strophes or stanzas is a subject of debate. For instance, Habel advises against dividing a poem into strophes and stanzas (*Job*, 47). For more on the debate see the discussion below.

83. Some scholars use the term strophe when they refer to stanza. See Watson, *Techniques in Classical Hebrew Verse*, 334–35.

84. Based on the literal meaning of stanza (Italian for "room"), Watson offers an analogy from a house: a poem = house; stanzas = rooms; strophes = furniture (*Classical Hebrew Poetry*, 161–62).

85. Except for some Psalms fragments found in Qumran; see n. 8 above.

86. For a history of the debate, see the survey and comprehensive discussion of van der Lugt, *Cantos and Strophes*, esp. 1–68. This is a revised and expanded edition of his earlier monograph, *Rhetorical Criticism*.

87. See our discussion of meter in chapter 3.

88. Watson, *Classical Hebrew Poetry*, 13, 163–64, 168; Muilenburg, "Form Criticism," esp. 11–18; and van der Lugt, *Cantos and Strophes*, 76–84. Recent scholarship has

The following strophic division is an example of lineation based on coherent thought-content:

> Yahweh is my shepherd,
> I lack nothing. (Ps 23:1)

Notice that both cola share a common thought: the role of the shepherd as a provider; hence they belong to a strophe. The subsequent strophe of the same psalm may be demarcated by its repetition (parallelism):

> In green pastures he makes me lie down,
> beside still waters he leads me. (Ps 23:2)

In this case, the two cola are bound into a strophe by the seemingly repetitive thought, that is, what the divine provider does as a shepherd. Both cola speak of Yahweh as the provider of food and drink. These two strophes may be grouped into a stanza on the basis of their thematic flow: both strophes focus on Yahweh as the faithful provider:

> Yahweh is my shepherd,
> I lack nothing.
> In green pastures he makes me lie down,
> beside still waters he leads me.

In some other cases, strophic division may be based on what scholars call transition markers, such as particles (e.g., 'al-kēn, kî, and hinnēh), the imperative, interrogative pronouns (e.g., mah), and personal pronouns. Below is an example of strophic division based on a transition marker, coherent thought-content and parallelism:

> Listen, and I will speak.
> I will ask you, and you will tell me. (Job 42:4)

The beginning of the strophe is marked by the imperative "Listen" (the imperative of šmʿ); the two cola are grouped into a strophe by their common thought (i.e., communication between two speakers), and repeated use of corresponding verbs (listen and speak—ask and tell). Likewise, the strophe below is formed by transition marker and parallelism:

> So I recant and I repent
> on dust and ashes (Job 42:6).

---

drawn attention to closure markers at the endings of biblical poems, especially those in the book of Job. Seow, "Poetic Closure," 433–46; Seow, Job 1–14, 77–78.

The transition marker "So" (*al-kēn*) marks the start of the strophe; the two cola are bound together as a strophe by their common thought-content and semantic repetition.

In longer poems, more strophes and stanzas occur, such as the following example from Psalm 114 based on Watson's lineation:[89]

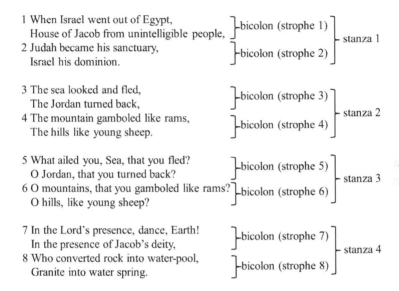

1 When Israel went out of Egypt,
House of Jacob from unintelligible people,
 —bicolon (strophe 1)
2 Judah became his sanctuary,
Israel his dominion.
 —bicolon (strophe 2)
 stanza 1

3 The sea looked and fled,
The Jordan turned back,
 —bicolon (strophe 3)
4 The mountain gamboled like rams,
The hills like young sheep.
 —bicolon (strophe 4)
 stanza 2

5 What ailed you, Sea, that you fled?
O Jordan, that you turned back?
 —bicolon (strophe 5)
6 O mountains, that you gamboled like rams?
O hills, like young sheep?
 —bicolon (strophe 6)
 stanza 3

7 In the Lord's presence, dance, Earth!
In the presence of Jacob's deity,
 —bicolon (strophe 7)
8 Who converted rock into water-pool,
Granite into water spring.
 —bicolon (strophe 8)
 stanza 4

The Difficulties of Poetic Lineation

Generally, the criteria mentioned above are helpful, and we will follow them as far as we can. However, as will be shown in our poetic analyses (chapters 5–7), difficulties abound. Difficulties aside, subjectivity is another issue. The missing information about the original poems leaves the length of individual cola, strophes and stanzas to the judgments of commentators and Bible translators. Inevitably, matters such as where a colon ends, or how many stanzas in a poem, are open to debate. This has resulted in what we mentioned in the early discussion: different translators have proposed different structures for the same text. This problem occurs even in critical editions of the Hebrew Bible such as Biblia Hebraica Württembergensia (BHK, 1937) and Biblia Hebraica Stuttgartensia (BHS, 1983). For example, BHS prints the first line of Isa 5:7 as one whole long colon:[90]

> For the vineyard of Yahweh of hosts is the house of Israel.

89. Watson, *Classical Hebrew Poetry*, 189–90; translation is his.

90. Petersen and Richards, *Interpreting Hebrew Poetry*, 4–5.

BHK, however, prints the same line as if they were a parallel bicolon:

> For the vineyard of Yahweh of hosts
> is the house of Israel.

As we will soon find in the following chapter, in such cases a poetic text may be taken either as a single colon, two cola (bicolon), or even one and a half cola, depending on whom we consult.

Inter-Component Relationship: Parallelism

The various poetic components are not put together at random, but according to their relationship with each other in terms of parallelism. Usually, most scholars would begin with the parallelistic relationship between two cola (inter-colon relationship). However, parallelism goes beyond the bicolon. Therefore, many scholars would also look at the parallelistic relationship between two larger poetic components (inter-component relationship), such as the parallelism between two strophes or stanzas.

Depending on the lens, readers may see the relationship in different ways. Those who use the literary lens view the inter-component connection in terms of semantic correspondence (called semantic parallelism); whereas those who use the linguistic lens view it in terms of syntactical dynamics (some scholars call it grammatical parallelism). The inter-component relationship creates crucial dynamics within a poem and is crucial to the meaning of the poetic text.

CONCLUSION

In this chapter we have basically discussed what Hebrew poetry is. We have pointed out that biblical Hebrew poetry is a kind of versification of reality. Scholars have used two lenses to view what and how biblical Hebrew versification is done. Through the literary lens, we can see the versification as being made of a high concentration of literary elements such as parallelism, terseness, figurative language, and of line arrangements which result in strophes and stanzas. Through the linguistic lens we can view poetry as composed of selected grammatically corresponding constituents that are syntactically arranged in a contiguous and segmented way. As all these things represent the elements that make a poem, they serve as a good map for our journey through biblical Hebrew poetry. Therefore, understanding

Hebrew poetry would require a closer examination of them. This is what we will do in the following chapters.

2

Parallelism

WHILE REPETITION IS ALSO found in Old Testament prose, it is more frequent in Old Testament poetry. This fact does not come as a surprise, for the relationship between repetition and poetic texts is universally known. Popular songs are made catchy by their refrains (which are sung repeatedly[1]), such as that of "Jingle Bells." In poetry, this phenomenon is traditionally called parallelism, such as John Denham's *Cooper's Hill* (1655):

> a Though deep, yet clear;
> b though gentle, yet not dull[2]

The second colon repeats some of the words of the first (though, yet) and its antithetical pattern (gentle yet not dull//deep yet clear), forming an a//b relationship.

Such a repetitive phenomenon is not only universal, but also ancient. It was not only known to biblical writers but also their contemporaries such as ancient Egyptian, Sumerian, Babylonian, Assyrian, and Ugaritic poets.[3] Outside the ancient Near East, parallelism is also known in many other

---

1. Derived from Latin *refringere*, "to repeat."

2. Denham, *Cooper's Hill*, 11.

3. See Newman and Popper, *Biblical Parallelism*, 20–39; Ceresko, "Chiastic," 303–11; Pardee, "Ugaritic," 128–30; Watson, *Techniques in Classical Hebrew Verse*, 31; Parker ("Ugaritic Literature," 229) points out that the three longest and poetic Ugaritic texts found in Ras Shamra (Syria) in 1929 are written in poetic form and parallelism is pervasive.

cultures such as the Finnish[4] and Chinese.[5] However, as will be noted in our discussion, parallelism is much more than just repetition. Therefore, at the outset, we need to clarify what parallelism is.

DEFINITION

Put simply, parallelism refers to the relationship of poetic components that are related to each other in some specific ways. Over the centuries, scholars have offered different descriptions of the inter-component relationship,[6] depending on what aspect of the component they focus on, and how thorough they attempt to be. Some describe the relationship in terms of semantic aspect; others go beyond the semantics to other aspects such as grammar, syntax, morphology and phonetics. All this has resulted in a whole range of taxonomies (theories), from more general ones to more sophisticated ones, and from describing parallelism in terms of correspondence to viewing it as development. To begin with, we will trace the treatment of biblical parallelism all the way back to its pre-modern history.

PARALLELISM IN POST-BIBLICAL LITERATURE: A HIDDEN GEM

Though parallelism has been in the Hebrew Bible since it was written, according to Kugel, Jewish commentators in post-biblical times showed very little interest in it.[7] In fact, parallel lines were commonly treated as two distinct statements in rabbinic literature. The poetic passage in Deut 33:10 is a good example:

> Let them teach your statutes to Jacob,
>
> your teaching to Israel

To a modern biblical scholar, the semantic correspondence between "your statutes to Jacob" and "your teaching to Israel" is obvious, and they would recognize them as parallel lines. But as Kugel points out, in the *Sifre* to

---

4. Gray mentions parallelism in the Finnish epic *The Kalevala* (*Forms of Hebrew Poetry*, 38); also Newman and Popper (*Biblical Parallelism*, 5–12).

5. Newman and Popper, *Biblical Parallelism*, 12–19; Liu, "Parallel Structures," 639–53.

6. At times Lunn uses the term *intercolon* relationship (*Word Order Variation*, 21). While this is useful for describing the relationship between cola, it should be noted that parallelism goes beyond bicolon.

7. Kugel, *Idea of Biblical Poetry*, 96–134.

Deuteronomy (a rabbinic collection on Deuteronomy), they are viewed as two distinct referents to two kinds of laws: "statute" refers to the written Torah, "teaching" refers to the oral Torah.[8] Interpretations such as these indicate that biblical parallelism remained a hidden gem for a long time, until it was "discovered" in the eighteenth century.

ROBERT LOWTH AND PARALLELISM

The first person who conceptualized and popularized biblical parallelism was Robert Lowth, a professor at Oxford University in the eighteenth century. His permanent association with biblical parallelism began after his lectures from the 1740s, which were published as *De Sacra Poesi Hebraeorum Praelectiones Academicae* in 1753,[9] a work noted to be the first systematic treatment of Hebrew poetry.

Gray opines that the impact of this work on Hebrew poetry studies is as seminal as Jean Astruc's *Conjectures sur les memoires originaux dont il paroit que Moyse s'est servi pour composer le livre de la Genese* on Pentateuchal studies (published in the same year).[10] Recently, he has even been called the "father of parallelism."[11] Even if this accolade is justifiable, it has come to him accidentally for the following reasons. First of all, he was a professor of poetry, not a professor of Hebrew.[12] Secondly, parallelism is not the major concern of his *De Sacra Poesi Hebraeorum*. Out of his thirty-four lectures on poetry, only the nineteenth lecture gives an elaborate discussion of biblical parallelism. Even then parallelism was not the original intention of the lecture; rather Lowth attempted to prove that the presence of parallelism makes the Prophets as poetic as the Psalms.[13]

Little did Lowth realize that this lecture would propel him to international fame and lead to so much discussion and debate in the subsequent centuries. It should suffice to highlight two major issues in the debate. First is the relationship between parallelism with prose and poetry. Although

---

8. Cited in Kugel, ibid., 98.

9. ET: *Lectures on Sacred Poetry.*

10. Gray, *Forms of Hebrew Poetry*, 5. Gray's view may be seconded by Oxford's "Sacred Conjectures" conference in 2003, in which international scholars discussed the seminal contributions of Lowth and Astruc to biblical scholarship. See Jarick, *Sacred Conjecture.*

11. So Cullhed, "Robert Lowth," 25.

12. Ibid.

13. Lowth, *Lectures on Sacred Poetry*, 2:33–34.

his third lecture already points out that parallelism is also found in prose,[14] somehow his nineteenth lecture has led to the perception that parallelism characterizes Hebrew poetry.[15] This perception has been a subject of criticism, because later scholarship would doubt whether parallelism is the key feature that distinguishes prose from poetry.

The second issue comes as the consequence of Lowth's definition of parallelism. Though Lowth offered a definition of parallelism in his *De Sacra Poesi Hebraeorum,* a more clearly articulated definition is found in the introduction to his translation of Isaiah. There Lowth defines parallelism as "propositions" that are "equivalent" or "contrasted" in *sense* or similar "in the form of *grammatical* construction."[16] This definition implies that Lowth recognized parallelism on two levels: on the *sense* (meaning) level and *grammatical* level. In the eighteenth century, however, Lowth and his contemporaries did not have the advantage of the linguistic knowledge available today.[17] Perhaps for this reason, Lowth could only develop what Alter thinks is the "most obvious thing": parallelism on the sense level (semantic parallelism).[18] For centuries, subsequent discussions of biblical parallelism after Lowth stayed on the semantic level; parallelism on the grammatical level remained undeveloped until the middle of the twentieth century. Working on the semantic level, Lowth classified Hebrew parallelism into three categories: synonymous, antithetical, and synthetic parallelisms.[19]

Synonymous Parallelism

For Lowth, synonymous parallelism refers to a repetition of an idea "in different, but equivalent terms."[20] We can find such parallelism in many biblical poems. Lowth cites quite a number of examples. One of them is taken from Judg 15:16:

> With the jawbone of a donkey, heaps upon heaps,
>
> with the jawbone of a donkey have I struck down a thousand men.[21]

14. Lowth pointed out that though parallelism is prevalent in Hebrew poetry, it "seldom fails to produce even in prose" (*Lectures on Sacred Poetry,* 1:69).

15. Lowth, *Lectures on Sacred Poetry,* 2:34.

16. Lowth, *Isaiah,* ix; italics are the author's for emphasis.

17. Cf. Cullhed, "Robert Lowth," 25–47.

18. Alter, *Art of Biblical Poetry,* 6.

19. Lowth, *Lectures on Sacred Poetry,* 2:34–59. For a refined articulation, see his introduction to *Isaiah,* ix–xxii.

20. Lowth, *Lectures on Sacred Poetry,* 2:35.

21. Ibid., 2:39.

It is obvious that the meaning of the second colon is equivalent to that of the first. In fact, the prepositional phrase of the first colon ("with the jawbone of a donkey") is repeated verbatim, forming a mirror image effect.[22] Another example is taken from Ps 114:1–2:

> a When Israel went out from Egypt,
>
> a' the house of Jacob from a people of strange language;
>
> b Judah became his sanctuary,
>
> b' Israel his dominion.[23]

The meaning of a' is equivalent to that of a; and b' equivalent to b; so it is an aa'//bb' parallelistic relationship.

Antithetic Parallelism

Lowth describes antithetic parallelism as "a thing illustrated by its contrary" on thought and word levels. The first example he cites is Prov 27:6:

> Sincere are the wounds of a friend,
>
> false are the kisses of an enemy[24]

Here, the word "wounds" is the opposite of "kisses," and "friend" the opposite of "enemy." Consequently, the second colon is opposite to the second colon. Here is another example taken from Isa 54:7–8:[25]

> a For a brief moment I deserted you,
>
> b but with great compassion I will gather you.
>
> a' In overflowing anger for a moment I hid my face from you,
>
> b' but with everlasting love I will have compassion on you.

Here, semantically, a is the opposite of b and a' the opposite of b'. In fact, Lowth failed to point out that there are both synonymous and antithetic parallelisms in the passage: a is equivalent to a', so is b to b'.

---

22. Watson illustrates this well by his analogy of the mirror image of cats (*Classical Hebrew Poetry*, 115–17).

23. Ibid., 2:35.

24. Ibid., 2:45.

25. Ibid., 2:48.

Synthetic Parallelism

Lowth also pointed out other intercolon-relationships that neither fall under any of the first two categories nor bear any apparent semantic resemblance. He coined a catch-all term for them: *synthetic parallelism*. Lowth offered a vague elaboration on this term; for him, it means cola that relate to each other "by the form of construction" (hence also called "constructive" parallelism).[26] Lowth observed that such parallelism usually involves a tricolon (triplets) or multicolon. As an example of a tricolon, he cited Ps 77:18–19 (ET: 77:17–18):

> The clouds poured out water,
>
> the skies gave forth thunder,
>
> your arrows flashed on every side.
>
> The crash of your thunder was in the whirlwind,
>
> your lightnings lighted up the world;
>
> the earth trembled and shook.

Notice that each colon of the two tricola above is neither synonymous nor antithetic to one another, but *structurally* (constructively) they are connected to one another.

A similar observation is made by Lowth on the multicolon Ps 19:8–11 (ET: 19:7–10):[27]

> The law of Yahweh is perfect, reviving the soul.
>
> The testimony of Yahweh is sure, making wise the simple.
>
> The precepts of Yahweh are right, rejoicing the heart.
>
> The commandment of Yahweh is pure, enlightening the eyes.
>
> The fear of Yahweh is clean, enduring forever.
>
> The rules of Yahweh are true, and righteous altogether,
>
> more to be desired are they than gold, even much fine gold,
>
> sweeter also than honey and drippings of the honeycomb.
>
> Moreover, by them is your servant warned;
>
> in keeping them there is great reward.

Lowth commented that such parallelism comes in "very great" variety and "the degrees of resemblance almost infinite."[28] This comment and the use of the catch-all term betrays Lowth's struggle at the time. First, he rec-

---

26. Ibid., 2:48–49.

27. Ibid., 2:49–50.

28. Ibid., 2:52.

ognized that parallelism comes in various manifestations and goes beyond the semantic level. As mentioned earlier, for Lowth, parallelism occurs also on the grammatical level; elsewhere he suspected a relationship between parallelism and meter.[29] Yet, at the same time, Lowth also felt uncertain about how to proceed from there; perhaps he realized that it was beyond his scope then.[30] As Petersen and Richards observe correctly, such recognition presaged the developments that emerged centuries later.[31]

REFINEMENT OF LOWTH'S BASIC CATEGORIES

In the twentieth century, two developments are particularly of interest. First, the basic categorization of Lowth continued to be accepted, though not without attempts at refinement. Second, beginning from the second half of twentieth century, in light of linguistics studies, many have moved beyond Lowth's theory in fundamental ways. All this has brought about three outcomes. Firstly, scholars no longer equate parallelism to Hebrew poetry; secondly, dissatisfaction with Lowth's synthetic parallelism has led to its demise; thirdly, discussion of biblical parallelism has moved beyond the semantic level.

Writing in the early twentieth century, Gray points out that parallelism was no more to be equated with Hebrew poetry as it also occurs in prose.[32] While he affirms the "soundness of Lowth's exposition of parallelism," he also argues that Lowth's descriptions of inter-component relationship need a "restatement."[33] The restatement is necessitated by the fact that inter-component relationships come in more variety than what had been identified by Lowth. So while he recognizes synonymous and antithetic parallelisms, he prefers the terms *complete* and *incomplete parallelism*. Gray recognizes cases which display exact resemblance (complete parallelism), such as the case of Songs 2:9 below:[34]

> He looks in at the windows;
>
> He glances through the lattice

---

29. Though Lowth noted that parallelism may also be formed on the metrical level, he expressed doubts about the metrical theories then and was unsure about how meter was exactly related to parallelism (ibid., 2:53–56). See the discussion of meter in 62–63.

30. As Lowth admitted: "sometimes the scheme of the parallelism is very subtle and obscure" (ibid., 2:52).

31. Petersen and Richards, *Interpreting Hebrew Poetry*, 26.

32. Gray, *Forms of Hebrew Poetry*, 38.

33. Ibid., 49–52.

34. For Gray, complete parallelism refers to cola which are exactly parallel in terms of meaning, word order and so on (ibid., 60–61).

He also points out that some of Lowth's examples are in fact subdivisions of synonymous or antithetic parallelism, because the cola are only corresponding (synonymously or antithetically) partially. As such, they are better called incomplete parallelism.[35] Here is an example from Deut 33:28 cited by Gray:[36]

	a	b	c
	And so	dwelt Israel	securely,
	c'		b'
	by itself	the fountain of Jacob	

Gray also takes issue with Lowth's treatment of non-parallel cola. Since they bear zero resemblance, he questions whether the term "parallelism" is appropriate. For Gray, the term "synthetic parallelism" obscures rather than helps solve the problem.[37]

Similar to Gray, though Theodore H. Robinson affirms Lowth's first two categories, he questions whether his third category is true parallelism.[38] Likewise, he finds there is much more variety of parallelism than what Lowth has mentioned. Thus following Gray's complete and incomplete descriptions, Robinson attempts to further define and name the various inter-colon relationships.[39] Among other parallel patterns, he notes what has come to be known as "staircase" parallelism, a parallel pattern which involves more than two cola, as he illustrates by Ps 29:1–2:[40]

Ascribe to Yahweh,
  sons of God.
Ascribe to Yahweh
  glory and strength.
Ascribe to Yahweh
  the glory of his name.
Bow before Yahweh,
  in the splendor of holiness.

35. Gray notes that in Hebrew poetry, incomplete parallelism is more frequent than complete parallelism (ibid., 49–50, 59, 72–82).

36. Ibid., 77; translation is his. By incomplete parallelism Gray means the pattern is:

a	b	c
	b'	c'

37. Ibid., 50–51.

38. Robinson, *The Poetry of Old Testament*, 23–24.

39. Ibid., 23–37.

40. Ibid., 23.

Here, the colon "Ascribe to Yahweh" is repeated three times, and each time serves as a starting-point for a new step, forming a "stair-like" effect.[41]

Alonso-Schökel is another biblical scholar who furthers the discussion of semantic parallelism. Like Robinson, while he recognizes the first two categories of Lowth's parallelism, he expresses doubt about the third.[42] Alonso-Schökel reminds us to look beyond the usual bicolon parallelism (what he calls "binary parallelism"). He notes that while bicolon parallelism is the predominant pattern in Hebrew poetry, tricolon or tetracolon parallelism, or a combination of bicolon and tricolon parallelism are also frequent.[43] The parallelistic relationship in such structures is different from that of bicolon parallelism. One example is Ps 28:3:[44]

> Take me not off with the wicked and evil-doers
>
> who speak peace with their neighbor,
>
> while mischief is in their hearts

The first sentence ends with two synonyms, "wicked" and "evil-doers," but they are not presented in a parallelistic manner. Then, the first sentence is further qualified by two clauses, which are not presented as parallels either; instead each of them is parallel to "the wicked and evil-doers." What Alonso-Schökel fails to mention is that grammatically, the verb of the first colon governs also the two clauses of the subsequent cola. Intriguingly, while Alonso-Schökel insists that the semantics of a poem should take precedence over its grammatical aspects,[45] the preceding example suggests he has unknowingly ventured into the grammatical realm of parallelism,[46] a subject we will soon discuss below.

PARALLELISM BEYOND THE SEMANTICS

Indeed, parallelism is more than just semantic correspondence between two cola. In fact, what is called semantic parallelism often comes with

41. For more discussion of staircase parallelism, see Watson, *Classical Hebrew Poetry*, 150–56.

42. Alonso-Schökel, *Manual of Hebrew Poetics*, 52.

43. Ibid., 51.

44. Ibid., 54.

45. Alonso-Schökel, "Hermeneutical Problems," 10–11.

46. For similar examples, see ibid., 55–60. In the section on biblical parallelism, Alonso-Schökel's mentions nothing of grammatical parallelism, this is because he subsumes it under the rubric of poetic style (*Manual of Hebrew Poetics*, 48–63).

correspondence in other aspects. As Alter points out, in Gen 4:23–24 parallelism can be detected both on semantic (meaning) and syntactic levels (word order):[47]

| Adah and Zillah, hear my voice | personal names + imperative + noun + suffix[48] |
| wives of Lamech, listen to my speech | plural proper noun + imperative + noun + suffix |

Nevertheless, discussions of biblical parallelism in the past century have led to descriptions of more than just the syntactic correspondence noted above.

Roman Jakobson and Linguistic Approaches to Parallelism

At this juncture, the impact of Jakobson's linguistic approach to parallelism on biblical studies merits a mention. Departing from the traditional notion of parallelism, Jakobson contends for a broader sense of the term. As cited in chapter 1, parallelism, he argues, is "the indispensable feature inherent in poetry."[49] He defines parallelism as "the principle of equivalence from the axis of *selection* into axis of *combination*."[50] By "selection" Jakobson means the selection of a group of similar (otherwise called "paradigmatic") elements. These may be a group of semantically equivalent nouns ("child" has other paradigmatic words such as "kid," "the youngster," "tot," "little one"); or verbs ("to sleep" is cognately related with "to doze," "to nod," "to nap"). By "combination" Jakobson refers to putting together the selected words into a contiguous (or "syntagmatic") chain.[51] Berlin illustrates how Jakobson's principle works by taking the sentence:[52]

The child sleeps.

A parallel sentence would require the selection of a noun from a similar semantic group (such as "youngster," or "little tot") as well as a verb from a

---

47. Alter, *Art of Biblical Poetry*, 6.

48 In Hebrew grammar, a suffix refers to Hebrew letters appended to a word. In this case, the appended letters indicate the possessive pronoun "my."

49. Jakobson, "Linguistics and Poetics," 358.

50. Ibid.; italics mine for emphasis; cited frequently in discussions, such as Berlin, *Dynamics of Biblical Parallelism*, 7; Niccacci, "Analysing Biblical Hebrew Poetry," 77 n3; Tsumura, "Vertical Grammar of Parallelism," 174.

51. Jakobson, "Linguistics and Poetics," 358.

52. Berlin, *Dynamics of Biblical Parallelism*, 8.

similar semantic group (such as "doze"). Thus the parallel sentences could be arranged as follows:

> The child sleeps, the youngster dozes

The selected words ("youngster" and "dozes") are connected with the first sentence, forming a contiguous chain. Another variation of parallelism could be:

> The child, the little tot, gently dozes and sleeps

In this case, while the selected words ("little tot" and "dozes") are arranged differently from the previous one (i.e., are placed between "child" and "sleeps"), they are nevertheless still part of the contiguous chain.

While the foregoing description of parallelism involves semantic parallelism, nevertheless it is more sophisticated than Lowth's theory in that it speaks of parallelism in terms of linguistic classes. In other words, the parallelisms involve *semantic classes* (words in the same classes as "child" and "sleep") and grammatical classes (matching the noun "child" with another noun of the same class "little tot," and the verb "sleep" with "dozes"). For this reason, for those who practice Jakobson's theory, "semantic equivalent" does not always mean *semantic synonymity*. It also refers to nouns or words which are perceived to belong to the same class, even if they are in fact semantically in contrast to each other, such as "father" and "mother," "orphan" and "widow," "strong" and "weak," and "to love" and "to hate."[53] In a nutshell, the term "parallel" refers to the juxtaposition of two same-class expressions rather than their semantic similarity.

Notice that for Jakobson, parallel relationship is not limited to these two linguistic classes; rather it may be extended to lexical and phonological classes. In his article published in 1966, after surveying the pervasiveness of parallelism in the poetry of many cultures (Finnish, Chinese, and especially Russian poetry), Jakobson writes:[54]

> Pervasive parallelism inevitably activates all the levels of language—distinctive features, inherent and prosodic, the morphologic and syntactic categories and forms, the lexical units and their semantic classes in both their convergences and divergences acquire an autonomous poetic value.

---

53. Ibid., 11–12; cf. Alter, *Art of Biblical Poetry*, 42.
54. Jakobson, "Grammatical Parallelism," 423.

Influenced by Jakobson's principle, some scholars began to look at biblical parallelism in a new way,[55] leading to descriptions such as "pairing" or "matching" of various linguistic classes.

Parallelism as Constituent Pairing

Scholars such as M. O'Connor and Terence Collins look into the pairing of grammatical constituents that form Hebrew parallelism. O'Connor's grammatical analysis gives much attention to *parallel pairs*. The first kind of parallel pairs is called *word pairs*. One example is taken from Ps 106:10:

wayyôšî'ēm miyyad śônē'	He saved them from the hand of the foe
wayyigʾālēm miyyad 'ōyēb	redeemed them from the hand of the enemy[56]

Each of the parts (constituents) of the two cola is corresponding and paired with the other: the verb *ys'* (to save) is paired with *g'l* (to redeem); so is the phrase *miyyad* (from the hand) in each cola, and *śônē'* (foe) with *'ōyēb* (enemy).

O'Connor's next level of pairing involves the whole syntactical structure of cola, called "line match," which refers to cola which contain syntactically corresponding or identical units.[57] "Line match" may co-occur with word pairing. The example from Ps 106:10 shows not only word pairs, but also line match:

verb + prepositional phrase // verb + prepositional phrase[58]

Also approaching parallelism in terms of linguistics, Collins attempts a more detailed description of inter-component relationship by "an analysis of lines based on grammatical structures."[59] By this he means to look at inter-component relationship "thoroughly and systematically so as to bring out all the relevant similarities and differences in line structures."[60] For Collins, lines (i.e., cola) are sentences, and structurally, sentences comprise constitu-

---

55. Berlin, *Dynamics of Biblical Parallelism*, 18; Tsumura, "Vertical Grammar of Parallelism," 167–81.

56. O'Connor, *Hebrew Verse Structure*, 110.

57. Ibid., 118–19.

58. In Chinese poetry, word pair and line match are often demanded, especially evident in couplets (*dui lian*). For more discussion of word pairs in Hebrew poetry, see Watson, *Classical Hebrew Poetry*, 128–42.

59. Collins. *Line-forms in Hebrew Poetry*, 7.

60. Ibid.

ents such as subject, object, verb and verb-modifier. By subject or object he includes pronouns, nouns, noun phrases and noun clauses (coded NP1 and NP2 respectively); by verb he includes a finite verb, participle or infinitive (coded V); and by modifier he includes adverbs, prepositional phrases and so on (coded M).[61] This way, Collins's analysis yields four basic sentences:

> a NP1 V
>
> b NP1 V M
>
> c NP1 V NP2
>
> d NP1 V NP2 M

Collins explains further that structurally there are four general types of poetic line. Type I contains only one of the basic lines above; Type II contains two basic lines of the same kind (all the words of the first line are repeated in the second, though not necessarily in the same order); Type III contains two basic sentences of the same kind, but only some of the words are repeated in the second colon; Type IV contains two different basic sentences.[62]

In fact, Collins's grammatical analysis is much more complex than what has been shown above; the basic sentences are open to numerous permutations called *Line-Forms*.[63] Of interest, however, are Types II and III, as they are directly relevant to parallelism.[64] For Type II, Collins cites Isa 9:5a (ET 9:6a) as an example:[65]

kî-yeled yullad-lānû	NP1 V M	For a child is born to us
bēn nittan- lānû	NP1 V M	A son is given to us

The two cola are not only semantically parallel but also grammatically (syntactically); it is evident that syntactically the second colon (NP1 V M) is parallel to the first colon (NP1 V M).

As an example for Type III, Collins cites Isa 19:1:[66]

---

61. Ibid., 22–23.

62. Ibid., 23–24.

63. Ibid., 24–29.

64. Though Berlin points out that Collins' Type IV may at times show certain correspondence, such as Hos 5:3; so may Type I (*Dynamics of Biblical Parallelism*, 19–20).

65. Collins. *Line-forms in Hebrew Poetry*, 28.

66. Ibid.

hinnēh YHWH rōkēb 'al-'āb qal	NP^1 V M	Behold Yahweh is riding on a swift cloud
ûba'miṣrayim	V M	he came to Egypt

As we can see, the two cola both semantically and syntactically show partial parallelism. Syntactically, the second colon (V M) repeats the first line (NP1 V M) only.

Examples like these successfully demonstrate the connection between grammatical (structural) and semantic parallelisms, achieving one of the key objectives of Collins's method.[67] In some respects his treatment strikes a resemblance with Gray's in that his Type II is equivalent to Gray's complete parallelism and Type III to incomplete parallelism. Nonetheless, it is evident that Collins's approach is more sophisticated and refined than that of Gray.

Deep Structure Parallelism

Some biblical scholars, however, are not satisfied with such "surface" syntactical/structural correspondence. Encouraged by Jakobson's argument that parallelism is not only pervasive, but that the structure of parallelism "requires a rigorous linguistic analysis,"[68] scholars such as Greenstein, Stephen A. Geller and Berlin take a step further. They go under the surface and look at the "deeper structure," a term referring to how two cola relate to each other through some *underlying* connection. Greenstein argues that once we go down to the deeper structure, what is perceived as "incomplete" will be "all present and accounted for in the underlying representation."[69] This is particularly evident in cola where one or two of the words are "deleted" in the second colon (hence Greenstein calls it "deletion").[70] He points out the deep structure of Ps 50:8:[71]

> Not for your sacrifices do I rebuke you,
> your burnt offerings ever before me

Notice that the two cola are semantically parallel, but only partially. The partial nature is obvious: the second colon does not have the negation phrase

---

67. For an example how Collins see the various connections between grammatical and semantic parallelism, see ibid., 227–249.

68. Jakobson, "Grammatical Parallelism," 400–401.

69. Greenstein, "How Does Parallelism Mean?" 53.

70. Greenstein, "Two Variations," 89–90.

71. Greenstein, "How Does Parallelism Mean?" 46–47. For more discussion and illustrations by Greenstein, see Greenstein, "Two Variations," 87–96.

"not for" and a verb to match the first colon. Gray would call this incomplete parallelism. In spite of this, however, a reader can still make sense of the two cola. This is because it is understood that the phrase "not for' and the verb "rebuke" govern both the first and the second cola (a case of ellipsis). In sum, in the second colon the two constituents are "deleted" from the surface representation, yet their presence is implied, or deep down, hence the "deep structure."[72] Thus on the deep structure level, what was "incomplete" is now complete.[73]

Another biblical scholar who does deep structure analysis of parallelism is Geller. At the outset it should be pointed out that Geller's contribution is more than grammatical parallelism, for he also makes an attempt to refine semantic parallelism. As he states, he intends to address the major aspects of parallelism "with emphasis on grammatical and semantic parallelism."[74]

By Geller's admission, his analysis of biblical parallelism was inspired by Jakobson,[75] though he also notes the limitations of Jakobson's linguistic approach.[76] Interestingly, while Geller's work on parallelism was done around Collins's time, he goes beyond surface structural correspondence, and "is able to move to a deeper grammatical level than Collins."[77] However, what Greenstein calls deep structure, Geller calls "reconstruction." The following example from a line of David's song in 2 Sam 22:14 may illustrate it well:[78]

yarʿēm min-šāmayim YHWH	Yahweh thundered from heaven
wĕ ʿelyôn yittēn qôlô	Elyon sent forth his voice

In Collins' framework, this verse would belong to Line-Type IV, because grammatically the two cola are two different basic sentences; in Geller's words, they are incongruent. The first colon (the intransitive verb *yrʿm* [to thunder] + adverb + subject) is incongruent with the second (subject + intransitive verb *ytn* [to send forth] + object). However, by *reconstructing* it,

72. Greenstein, "How Does Parallelism Mean?" 47.

73. Greenstein also extends his grammatical analysis is to staircase parallelism ("Two Variations," 98).

74. Geller, *Parallelism in Early Biblical Poetry*, 4.

75. Ibid., 1.

76. Geller (ibid., 2) expresses the concern that while Jakobson's linguistic approach may work well with languages well known to us, it would encounter problems when applied to an ancient literature such as Hebrew poetry, in view especially of the uncertainties in Hebrew grammar and phonetics.

77. So Berlin, *Dynamics of Biblical Parallelism*, 21.

78. Geller, *Parallelism in Early Biblical Poetry*, 17.

the two are actually grammatically compatible, because they serve the same function:

> Yahweh   thundered
>
>   from heaven[79]
>
> Elyon   sent forth his voice

On a deeper grammatical level, Geller notes that the transitive "sent forth his voice" forms "an indivisible idiomatic unit and occupies the same position as the intransitive "thundered."[80] The two "different" basic sentences, then, are actually different realizations of the same underlying sentence, so much so they are interchangeable.[81]

Geller shows that this approach can even treat non-parallel texts (what Lowth classified "synthetic" parallelism) where "enjambment" is present. Grammatically, enjambment is similar to the ellipsis cases above, only that the second colon is shorter than the first, and is actually *syntactically an integral part* of the first colon. In other words, the syntax and the sense of the first colon run over to the second (shorter) part. Job 42:6b is a case of enjambment:

> So I recant and I repent
> on dust and ashes

Likewise Deut 32:6a:[82]

> Do you thus repay Yahweh,
> [you] foolish and unwise people?

Strictly speaking the second "colon" is not really a colon, but a syntactically integral part of the first. As such they may be called parts instead of cola. Semantically it is evident that the two parts are not parallel. However, by going deeper we may see the grammatical parallelistic relationship. In the Hebrew text, the second person ("you") is represented by the verb "repay" in the first part. This verb is "deleted" in the second part, but understood to be there. This being the case, the verb "repay" governs both parts, hence it is said the line is enjambed. Geller's keen eye for such grammatical phenomena shows that his treatment not only goes beyond the superficial grammatical

79. It is understood that "from heaven" also serves as the prepositional phrase of the second colon, thus it is a gapping.

80. Geller, *Parallelism in Early Biblical Poetry*, 17.

81. Ibid., 18.

82. As cited by Geller, ibid., 295–96.

differences and deeper into the underlying grammatical relationship, but also alerts us to "the numerous categories of grammatical parallelism."[83]

While Geller pays special attention to grammatical parallelism, he does not neglect the importance of semantic parallelism. In the reconstructed sentence, the two cola in 2 Sam 22:14 cited above are not only parallel grammatically, but also semantically: the expression "sent forth his voice" is semantically parallel to "thundered." Geller further refines semantic parallelism by the theory of semantic paradigms (groups of words which share semantic affinities). This in turn leads to more detailed descriptions, showing parallelism of different grades,[84] a further refinement of Gray's complete-incomplete parallelism.

Compared to the two foregoing scholars, Berlin seems to take Jakobson's principle most seriously. She argues that there is more to parallelism than what has been explored. Berlin likens parallelism to a forest: "Parallelism, like a forest, has many aspects. Some are well known, others little studied."[85] She covers some little known aspects, particularly aspects that demonstrate *multilevel* parallelism.

In keeping with Jakobson's principle, Berlin defines grammatical parallelism as "the pairing of two different grammatical structures."[86] For this reason, Berlin focuses on how cola pair at multiple levels: syntactically, morphologically, lexical-semantically, and phonologically. However, drawing upon Jakobson's view that parallelism is pervasive,[87] she seeks to go beyond the surface structure.[88] So for Berlin, syntactical parallelism is not the same as syntactical repetition. A case of syntactical parallelism is found in Ps 103:10:[89]

lōʾkaḥṭāĕnû ʿāśāh lānû	Not according to our sins has he dealt with us
wĕlōʾkaʿônōtênû gāmal ʿālênû	not according to our iniquities has he repaid us

Each constituent of the cola is paired in such a way that the second colon is a neat syntactical repetition of the first:

83. Ibid., 366.

84. Ibid., 31–42.

85. Berlin, *Dynamics of Biblical Parallelism*, 2.

86. Berlin, "Grammatical Aspects," 20.

87. Ibid., 19.

88. Berlin, *Dynamics of Biblical Parallelism*, ix, 19.

89. Ibid., 31–32; Berlin, "Grammatical Aspects," 20.

Negation particle + prepositional phrase + verb + indirect object

Negation particle + prepositional phrase + verb + indirect object

Unlike syntactical repetition, Berlin argues, syntactical parallelism involves cola with different syntax; that is, the second colon "substitutes something grammatically *different*, but *equivalent*" for a grammatical feature in the first colon.[90] For Berlin, Ps 33:2 is a case of syntactical parallelism:[91]

hôdû laYHWH běkinnôr	Give thanks to Yahweh on the lyre
běnēbel 'aśôr zammrû-lô	on a harp of ten strings make music to him

Morphologically, the proper name *YHWH* (Yahweh) in the first colon is of a different word class from the third personal suffix *lô* (to him). This way, the second colon substitutes something grammatically different for a grammatical feature in the first colon, yet remains equivalent in its syntactical function (i.e., serving to refer to the same subject, Yahweh). Thus syntactically they are considered parallel.

By no means does Berlin suggest that the line between the surface and the deeper level cannot be crossed. On the contrary, her multilevel approach encompasses parallelism which involves the intertwining of grammatical aspects and structural levels. As she writes: "it is the intertwining of aspects and levels that contributes to the feeling of pervasiveness in biblical poetic parallelism."[92] A case in point is her illustration from Lam 5:2:[93]

naḥlātēnû nehepkāh lězārîm	Our inheritance was turned over to strangers
bātênû lěnakěrim	our houses to foreigners

On the surface structure, the semantic parallelism is evident (what Lowth would call synonymous parallelism),[94] and so is their syntactical equivalence:

subject + verb + prepositional phrase

subject + prepositional phrase

90. Berlin, *Dynamics of Biblical Parallelism*, 32.

91. Ibid., 33; also Berlin, "Grammatical Aspects," 21.

92. Berlin, *Dynamics of Biblical Parallelism*, 27. Particularly helpful is her diagram on p. 29; for elaboration of this, see pp. 31–126; also Berlin, "Grammatical Aspects," 17–43.

93. Ibid., 27–28.

94. As a matter of fact, the parallelism is partial: The subjects *naḥlātēnû* (our inheritance) and *bātênû* (our houses), the prepositional phrases *lězārîm* (to strangers) and *lěnakěrim* (to foreigners) are not exactly equivalent to each other semantically.

Intertwined with these are the grammatical equivalences and contrasts. The subjects *naḥlātēnû* ("our inheritance") and *bātênû* ("our houses") are grammatically equivalent as they are of the same word class (i.e., nouns with suffixes) and both serve the same syntactic function (subject). Likewise, grammatically *lĕzārîm* ("to strangers") corresponds to *lĕnakĕrim* ("to foreigners"). In terms of gender, however, *naḥlātēnû* and *bātênû* form a contrast, since the former is a feminine plural noun whereas the latter is a masculine plural.

Berlin's multilevel approach is also extended to phonological parallelism that exists either between the consonant sounds or vowel sounds of two cola. As for Lam 5:2, she demonstrates that there are three phonological equivalences, involving both consonant and vowel equivalents:[95]

naḥlātēnû nehepkāh lĕzārîm // bātênû lĕnakĕrim

naḥlātēnû // bātênû

lĕzārîm // lĕnakĕrim

Grammatical parallelism continues to attract scholars, and there is no lack of effort in offering new insights or even attempts to break new ground.[96] This is by no means to say that there is lack of interest in semantic parallelism. As a matter of fact, even as grammatical parallelism began to gain traction, fresh approaches to semantic parallelism were taking place in the 1980s. Eventually, the development would take the studies of Hebrew poetry beyond the idea of the "parallel."

BEYOND "PARALLELISM": PARALLELISM AS MOVEMENT

Our earlier discussion of deep structure parallelism highlights for us the fact that two cola which are parallel may well be two parts of a single statement. Let us return to Greenstein's example taken from Ps 50:8:

> Not for your sacrifices do I rebuke you,
> your burnt offerings ever before me

We pointed out earlier that the two cola share a common phrase ("not for") and a common verb ("rebuke"), a phenomenon generally called ellipsis

---

95. The underlined syllables represent the correspondence between the consonant and vowel sounds of the two cola.

96. See 45–47.

or "gapping"[97] (at times "incomplete parallelism"[98]). The fact that the two sentences are qualified by a common phrase and a common verb suggests that instead of two *parallel* sentences, they are actually two parts of a *single statement*. The second part clarifies the first: "burnt offerings" clarifies (or specifies) "sacrifices" (i.e., telling the reader what kind of sacrifices). Such a phenomenon forces us to rethink parallelism: should we take out the parallel sign (//), and replace it with a comma? Two scholars who did just that in the 1980s were Kugel and Alter.

Kugel: Parallelism as Progression

Typically, Kugel is critical of much of the terminology used in discussions of Hebrew poetry.[99] So instead of using terms such as "colon" or "bicolon" Kugel prefers to call them parts, or "A and B."[100] Kugel recognizes that the relationship of "A and B" involves grammatical issues; nevertheless his discussion stays mostly on the semantic level.[101] Kugel is the first scholar who argues that the parallel sign between A and B should be removed. Though frequently he uses the expression "parallelistic" for corresponding "lines,"[102] he contends that the term "parallelism" is misleading. The reason is that the relationship between A and B comes in a great variety, ranging from "zero perceivable correspondence" to "near-zero perceivable differentiation," and the majority of the cases fall between the extremes.[103] This being the case, the traditional "correspondence" or "equivalence" concept is too general to account for the variety. More pointedly, Kugel contends that what are putatively viewed as two parallel cola are in fact two parts of a *single statement*. B usually particularizes, defines, expands, or extends the meaning of A. hence the well cited paradigm "A is so, and what's more, B is so."[104] In other words,

97. So O'Connor, *Hebrew Verse Structure*, 122–29.

98. So Holladay, "Hebrew Verse Structure Revisited (I)," 23.

99. Kugel even argues that the term "poetry" is foreign to the Hebrew Bible; what is called "poetry" is simply "high style" writing (*The Idea of Biblical Poetry*, 69, 302).

100. This is despite Kugel's opinion that the Latin word "membrorum" in Lowth's "parallelismus membrorum" actually refers to colon, instead of "member" as it is often (wrongly) translated (ibid., 2 n. 4).

101. Kugel views "parallelistic line" as a biblical style which establishes correspondence of two parts through "syntax, morphology and meaning" (*The Idea of Biblical Poetry*, 2).

102. E.g., ibid., 2, 3.

103. Ibid., 3, 7.

104. Ibid., 7–8. Intriguingly, for Kugel, B not only looks beyond A (prospective), but at the same also looks back to A (retrospective).

the relationship between A and B is not one of parallelism, but of continuation: B continues or completes the idea of A. In doing so, Kugel removes the parallel sign between A and B, and replaces it with a comma, citation markers or even subordinating conjunctions.[105] Kugel illustrates this by Job 3:3:

> A May the day I was born perish,
>
> B and the night it was said, "Let a boy be conceived"

Kugel writes that instead of being a repetition, B is something more emphatic than A: "My whole life is a waste! Blot out the day of my birth, *in fact*, go back to the very night I was conceived and destroy it."[106] Kugel argues that this understanding can solve parts which are not exactly equivalent, such as Isaiah 1:3. For Lowth, the two parts in the verse are synonymous parallelism; namely, the poet says the same thing twice:[107]

> The ox knows its owner,
>
> and the ass its masters' trough

Kugel, however, contends that such a description fails to see two things. First, the ass is less obedient than the ox, and "owner" is different from "masters' trough." Second, the verb "knows" (which suggests obedience[108]) qualifies both A and B (a case of ellipsis[109]). This in turn creates an accumulative effect of differences which serves as a climactic descent: "An ox knows its owner, and *even* an ass (which is less attentive), at least knows where to stand to be fed."[110] For this reason, treating it as a synonymous parallelism also fails to see B as the completion of what A has begun, and misses the semantic progress ("A is so, and what's more, B is so").[111]

This understanding of parallelistic relationship can even account for parts which do not show evident correspondence at all, as Kugel illustrates by Eccl 7:1:[112]

---

105. Ibid., 4–5.

106. Ibid., 9; italics are Kugel's, alerting the reader to the fact that the traditional parallel sign is now replaced by a subordinating conjunction "even."

107. See Lowth, *Isaiah*, xiii.

108. See Kugel, *The Idea of Biblical Poetry*, 9 n18; cf. Huffmon, "The Treaty Background," 31–37.

109. Unknowingly, here Kugel is applying something similar to Geller's "reconstruction" (*The Idea of Biblical Poetry*, 9).

110. Ibid.

111. Ibid., 9, 13.

112. Ibid., 10.

> Better a name than good oil,
>
> and the day of death than the day of birth.

A Lowthian would probably call this synthetic parallelism, for evidently there is no correspondence between a "better name" and "the day of death" in terms of meaning. However, Kugel argues that this will change when we see B as the continuation of A. Part A says a name is better than oil because oil will succumb to decay; a name will not. Part B picks up and carries the idea forward: a newborn has no name (fame), but as he grows and builds his name (the idea of A), on the day of his death, he is better than on the day of his birth.

Likewise, for Kugel, Lowth's antithetic parallelism should also be viewed as two independent sentences which present a kind of progression. Consequently, he has a different take on Lowth's example from Prov 27:6:

> Sincere are the wounds of a friend,
>
> false are the kisses of an enemy[113]

For Kugel, instead of being antithetical, it is "another way for B to pick up and complete A": just as a friend's criticisms are sincere, so are an enemy's kisses false.[114]

Alter: Parallelism as Movement

Not long after the publication of Kugel's *The Idea of Biblical Poetry*, Alter published *The Art of Biblical Poetry*. Like Kugel, Alter's discussion of biblical parallelism also mostly revolves around the semantics, though he also notes how syntax and rhythm are integrated with semantic parallelism.[115] To understand Alter, allow us to cite an example from Jer 48:11c, in which the prophet speaks of Moab:[116]

> Moab has been undisturbed from youth,
>
> settled in his dregs.

For those who follow Jakobson's principle, one may see a gapping here: "Moab" serves as the subject of both clauses. Also, the poet seems to have put words of the same classes ("undisturbed" and "settled in his dregs") in

---

113. Ibid., 13. "False" is Kugel's translation of *na'tărôt*, (Niphal Participle fp of *'tr*) a word variously translated by "profuse" (ESV) or "deceitful" (NAB).

114. Ibid.

115. Alter, *Art of Biblical Poetry*, 6–7.

116. Ibid., 17.

contiguous relationship so as to form a single statement: Moab has remained undisturbed like settled dregs. Alter, however, contends that such a Jakobsonian description is not only "incomplete," but also "misleading,"[117] because it fails to point out a "movement" from the first clause to the second. In fact, so he argues, the first clause moves from the literal statement (Moab's state of unruffled security) to a metaphorical elaboration (the settled dregs) in the second clause.[118]

It does not take long for one to notice the similarities between Alter and Kugel. More to the point is that both scholars draw attention to the semantic progress/movement in what is traditionally called parallelism. The similarities led to Kugel's accusation of Alter's book being "*Kugel Slightly Altered*" and the ensuing intense dispute between the two scholars.[119] As a matter of fact, Alter is at once in agreement and disagreement with Kugel.[120] While both speak of parallelism as semantic progress, one should not miss their differences. If Kugel speaks of *progression* from A to B, Alter speaks of a "dynamic *movement* from one verset to the next."[121] The difference between Kugel's progress and Alter's movement is made clear when Alter speaks of two kinds of movement. The first kind of movement is similar to Kugel's observation, that is, semantic progression, which is "one of heightening or intensifications. . . of focusing, specification, concretization, even what could be called dramatization."[122] The second kind, however, is distinct from Kugel's: it is a movement from ordinary words to literary words. One example is taken from Isa 59:9b–10a:[123]

> We hope for light and behold, darkness! for brightness, but we walk in gloom.
>
> We grope for the wall like the blind; we grope like those who have no eyes.

According to Alter, the first kind of semantic movement refers to the second colon ("We grope for a wall like the blind; we grope like those who have no eyes") intensifying the meaning of the first colon (the idea of walking in

---

117. Alter, *Art of Biblical Poetry*, 42.

118. Ibid. 17.

119. See Gammie, "Alter vs Kugel," 26–29.

120. Alter agrees with but criticizes Kugel at the same time (*Art of Biblical Poetry*, 5, 19).

121. Alter, ibid., 9.

122. Ibid., 14, 20. It is worth noting, however, that Alter does not think that some of Kugel's examples belong to semantic parallelism; for him, they are instances of free rhythm in which the semantic component of parallelism is dropped.

123. Ibid., 15.

darkness). In other words, the general image of walking in the dark in the first colon is transformed into a more concrete picture of a blind man in the second. Besides this kind of movement, there is also a movement from the ordinary words such as "light" (*ŏr*) and "darkness" (*ḥŏšek*) to the more literary "brightness" (*nĕgōhôt*) and "gloom" (*ăpēlôt*).[124] Alter also illustrates his point from Job 15:14:[125]

> What is man, that he should be pure?
> Or he who is born of a woman, that he should be righteous?

For Alter, the phrase "born of a woman" (*yĕlûd 'iššāh*) in the second colon not only reinforces "man" (*ĕnôš*) in the first colon, but also a literary (metaphorical) expression which replaces the more general term "man" (*ĕnôš*).

The idea that parallelism displays semantic progress continued to be a topic of discussion after Kugel and Alter. Biblical scholars have used a range of descriptions to describe the phenomenon, from general ones such as "better precision"[126] or "process of amplification"[127] to more detailed ones such as "generic-specific," "action–consequence," "reason–result," and temporal movement "event-sequence."[128] Suffice it to say that by then many had moved beyond Lowth's idea of "parallelism." In other words, the inter-colon relationship was no more seen as mere parallels, but also as a progress or movement.

RECENT DEVELOPMENT: BICOLON AS A SINGLE STATEMENT

While semantic parallelism continues to be mentioned and applied (especially along the lines of Kugel and Alter), it is grammatical parallelism that sees further development in biblical scholarship today. For instance, in the modified version of his PhD thesis on the variations of word order in Hebrew poetry, one of the issues Lunn explores is the relationship between word-order and parallelism. While his discussion of parallelism is simply a reference to the many categories and analyses of parallelism in current

---

124. Ibid.

125. Ibid., 16.

126. So Clines, who uses the expression "the parallelism of greater precision," noting that in many cases the second colon is more precise or specific than the first ("Parallelism of Greater Precision," 77–100).

127. Fokkelman, *Reading Biblical Poetry*, 74–75.

128. Zogbo and Wendland, *Hebrew Poetry in the Bible*, 24–25.

scholarship (semantic, syntax, lexical, phonological, and so on),[129] Lunn also shows how word-order "figures prominently within the context of parallelism."[130]

More interesting are recent discussions that tend to assert a much closer relationship between two cola—so close that they are in fact seen as syntactically one linguistic unit (sentence). For example, in keeping with deep structure parallelism, David T. Tsumura views a bicolon as a single linguistic unit that expresses a single thought, or in his words, "one thought through two lines."[131] He cites an example from Ps 24:3:

> Who shall ascend the hill of the Lord?
> Who shall stand in his holy place?[132]

The surface structure of each colon is synonymously parallel to each other, as both consist of identical grammatical constituents and in the same word order: interrogative pronoun + verb + prepositional phrase. But below this surface structure is actually a deeper syntactical superimposition of two cola which expresses the single meaning "Who will ascend the hill of Yahweh and stand in his holy place?" Apparently picking up from studies by scholars such as Greenstein and Geller, Tsumura also contends that such superimposition applies also to cases of ellipsis, such as the case of Prov 5:15:

> Drink waters from your own cistern
> flowing from your own well

As the verb "drink" governs both the first and the second cola, Tsumura argues that "waters" and "flowing" are to be read as a whole as a composite object of "drink" (thus "Drink flowing waters from your cistern."). As such, the two cola are in fact two cola which express a single thought.[133]

While Tsumura focuses frequently on the relationship of two full cola, more recently F. W. Dobbs-Allsopp turns our attention to the relationship of one and a half cola, where the two are "enjambed," a phenomenon already noted by Geller.[134] Previously, Lowth broke such texts into a bicolon and

---

129. Lunn, *Word-Order Variation*, 14–21.

130. Ibid., 95–120.

131. Tsumura "Vertical Grammar of Parallelism," 169. Elsewhere Tsumura also demonstrates similarities between Hebrew parallelism and parallelism in Tang Poems such as Du Fu's Deng Gao ("Parallelism in Hebrew and Chinese Poetry").

132. Tsumura "Vertical Grammar of Parallelism," 170.

133. Ibid., 171–72.

134. Dobbs-Allsopp, "Enjambing Line (I)," 219–39; see our discussion of Geller in 37–38.

made them conform to synthetic parallelism. Dobbs-Allsopp cites Ps 2:6 as an example:

> I have installed my king upon Zion
> my holy mountain

Though Lowth admitted that the two cola actually represent a single line, he broke them into two cola in order to meet "the general norm and nature of the Psalm."[135] However, following the theory of enjambment, the shorter part (noun phrase) should be treated as an enjambment rather than an individual colon.

Dobbs-Allsopp focuses particularly on such cases in the *non-parallel* cola in Lamentations 1–4. He writes that the shorter part comes in many forms: as as vocative, an adverbial phrase, a prepositional phrase, a subject, a object, or a verbal phrase. Lamentations 2:13b is a case of vocative enjambment:[136]

> To what shall I compare you so to comfort you,
> O maiden, daughter of Zion?

The vocative phrase "O maiden, daughter of Zion" is not a separate colon, but part of the preceding remark and its syntactical function is to clarify the second person "you." It should be noted that in some cases, what Dobbs-Allsopp calls enjambment may in fact be called "ellipsis" or "gapping" in grammatical parallelism. This is especially true for cases of "apposition enjambment," such as Lam 2:20b:[137]

> Should women eat their own fruit
> the children they have raised?

Grammatically, the subject (women) and the verb (eat) govern both the first and the second parts. It follows that the two cola are in fact two parts of a single statement. This being the case, one may say that enjambment analysis is a kind of deep structure analysis.

Summary and Implications

Overwhelming to beginners as it may seem, the preceding survey of parallelism theories is by no means exhaustive. If anything, the survey indicates

---

135. Lowth, *Lectures on the Sacred Poetry*, 2:53.
136. Dobbs-Allsopp, "Enjambing Line (I)," 224.
137. As Dobbs-Allsopp admits (ibid., 228–29).

that inter-component relationship is so complex that no one theory has been able to capture all of its essence; as a result, there may be no end to its taxonomy. Berlin's introductory remarks sum it up well:

> Parallelism has both delighted us, for its effect is unmistakable, and frustrated us, for the way that it works is elusive. We have sought it by collecting and classifying its types, as Lowth began, and when the three original types could not capture its essence we added more types and subtypes . . . Given the powers of discrimination that the human mind possesses, the longer we examine parallelism the more discrete types we are likely to find."[138]

Ironically, however, the various attempts to describe biblical parallelism have resulted in a blurring of the line between two cola and diminishing the parallel idea. The taxonomies of parallelism over the centuries have evolved from seeing inter-colon relationship as two corresponding statements (Lowth's semantic parallelism), to a single statement constructed by two corresponding parts (grammatical parallelism and the semantic parallelism of Kugel and Alter), to a single statement formed by two (or one and a half) non-corresponding parts (enjambment). So as these scholars discuss and conceptualize parallelism, they also blur the line between two parallel cola and diminish the prominence of their parallelism, a phenomenon which may be fittingly called a disappearing act of parallelism!

Lest we get distracted or discouraged by the downside of the various theories, the plethora of parallelism theories has actually sharpened our understanding of the subject. The cumulative effect of the attempts is unmistakably clear: now we have a better idea about biblical parallelism than Lowth did. Consequently, while we cannot capture the *full essence* of parallelism, we can now have a better grasp on the *essentials*. This notion is important, as it will help us avoid mistaking the trees for the forest. With this optimistic note, we will now highlight the following essentials.

Parallelism Is More than Semantic Correspondence

The first thing to note here is that parallelism is more than just repetition (contra J. P. Fokkelman[139]). It is not even just about two sentences (cola) that are "parallel" to each other for reason of semantic correspondence. To be

138. Berlin, *Dynamics of Biblical Parallelism*, 2.

139. Fokkelman's statement, "The first thing a parallel construction does is to introduce a form of repetition" (*Reading Biblical Poetry*, 78), not only over-generalizes, but also misleads.

more precise, parallelism is primarily about a kind of connection between two cola on multiple aspects and levels (semantics, grammar, syntax, morphology, even phonology).

Secondly, the connection between two cola is not monolithic but comes in great variety, allowing various permutations. On the semantic level, Kugel rightly points out that the connection ranges from "zero perceivable correspondence" to "near-zero perceivable differentiation." In other words, at times, the semantic correspondence is partial, or in contrast to each other, or even nil; at other times we do encounter semantic correspondence between two cola, despite Kugel's skepticism. When the correspondence comes as near-zero differentiation, they may be justifiably called "thought rhyme."[140]

On the grammatical level, Geller and Berlin have been helpful in pointing out both the surface structure and the deeper structure of parallelism. We do have cola which are syntactically repetitive (Berlin's syntactical repetition) or syntactically equivalent (syntactical parallelism). We also encounter words of the same class (morphological parallelism), or words of the same group of sounds (phonological parallelism).

Parallelism Is More than Correspondence

Nevertheless, taken as a whole, parallelism *is not just about correspondence*. Rather, the corresponding relationship between two cola creates the effect of *continuation, completion*, or *sequence*. As the subsequent colon corresponds to the preceding colon, frequently it is also a "going beyond" of the latter's thought. As a matter of fact, correspondence is not always the best term for the phenomenon. Kugel has shown us that that even sentences with no apparent correspondence (such as Eccl 7:1) can have some sort of "parallelistic" connection (i.e., the second sentence continues the thought of the first). Granted that making this sort of connection often depends on one's interpretation,[141] it does suggest that to make sense of such poetic texts, one should pay attention to the developmental phenomenon.

Outside biblical poetry, the developmental phenomenon can also be observed in Chinese poetry, as shown in the following Tang poem by Liu Zongyuan (c. 773–819), *River Snow*:

---

140. So Kidner, *Psalms 1–72*, 2.

141. Kugel's way of connecting "name" and "day of birth" in Eccl 7:1 reflects his interpretation of the text rather than explicit information from the text. Such an argument from silence is debatable, as it is open to more interpretations than one. For further critique of Kugel's argument, see 43, n113.

Over a thousand mountains, gone are the birds,

on a thousand paths, vanished are human footprints.

In a lone boat an old man in rain hat and raincoat

drops his fishing line down the cold river.[142]

On the semantic level, we may detect a narrowing down development in the poem. The first colon shows us a broad picture (ranges of mountains), the second colon directs attention to a relatively narrower area (trails), the third colon shifts to a much narrower scope (a lone boat where an old man is), and the last colon narrows down to an even smaller object (the fishing line).[143]

To sum up, the major theories of parallelism discussed in this chapter may be presented as follows:

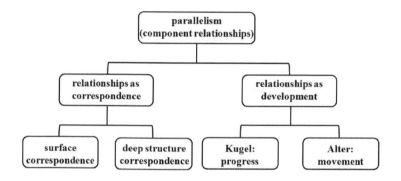

Hebrew Poetry Is More than Parallelism

Upon a close examination, the existing theories of parallelism have their limitations for at least two reasons. Firstly, given the pervasiveness of parallelism it is impossible for any one theory to account for all the phenomena in all the biblical poetic texts. We should take into account of the fact that the theories are built not on all but selective poetic texts. Consequently, the sample data which is used to construct the theories are limited, as are the theories developed from it. Therefore it should not come as a surprise if we encounter data which cannot be accounted for satisfactorily by any of the theories.

142. My translation.

143. In the Chinese original, one can also detect the phonological parallelism in the last characters of the first, second and fourth cola (respectively mie, jue, and xue).

It is true that there are cola that are not completely parallel semantically, and Kugel's model "A is so, and what's more, B is so" works better for such cases.[144] However, despite his robust argumentation, Kugel does not suggest that all parallelism is a case of "A is so, and what's more, B is so."[145] This in turn leaves room for other explanations. In fact, there are some poetic texts which fall outside of his and Alter's paradigms. For example, while Alter may be right in criticizing a shortcoming of Jakobson's theory of parallelism,[146] he fails to recognize that at times Jakobson's grammatical parallelism can fulfill a task his "theory of movement" cannot. Job 28:1 is a case in point:

kî yēš lakkesep môṣā'	Surely there is a mine for silver,
ûmāqôm lazzāhāb yazōqqû	and a place for gold that they refine

Following Alter, one may say that the second colon is a "going beyond" of the first (semantic movement from "mine" [*môṣā'*] to "refine" [*zqq*]), indicating a progress from mining to refining. However, the mining and the refining involve two different materials: one is silver and the other is gold. Also, grammatically the two words serve different functions. The Hebrew word for "mine" (*môṣā'*) is a noun referring to the source of silver; whereas the Hebrew word for "refine" (*zqq*) is a verb referring to the act of refining gold. The two cola describe two different processes involving two different materials, and they are hardly a single idea shaped by movement. This being the case, this text may be at best called incomplete parallelism or better still explained by Jakobson's axes of selection and combination.[147]

Secondly, the diversity of inter-component relationship is so great that not every poetic text can be treated as a case of parallelism. As Kugel observes, the variety ranges from "zero perceivable correspondence" to "near-zero perceivable differentiation." At issue are then poetic texts which bear zero resemblance. This is not a new issue, as it was discussed as early as the time of Lowth in the eighteenth century, and mentioned by Gray in the early twentieth century. As noted earlier, Lowth spoke of cola which are not parallel; unfortunately, he made these texts conform to the

144. As convincingly advocated by Gruber ("The Meaning of Biblical Parallelism," 289–93).

145. Kugel admits that there are indeed lines which are exact repetition, not progression (*Idea of Biblical Poetry*, 3).

146. Alter, *Art of Biblical Poetry*, 42.

147. Following Jakobson's axes, we may see the nouns "mine" (*môṣā'*) and "place" (*māqôm*) as words belonging to the same category, and "silver" (*kesep*) and "gold" (*zāhāb*) as words paired according to their word class.

norms of parallelism by assigning them to a catch-all category "synthetic parallelism."[148] Though Gray highlighted the presence of non-parallel cola, he did not propose anything which would advance the discussion.[149] If Alter is correct, even Kugel is guilty of a similar problem. One of Alter's criticisms of Kugel is that the latter extends the formula "A is so, and what's more, B is so" to include cola with no semantic parallelism.[150] To make his point, Alter uses his own example from Ps 137:2:

> On the willows there
> We hung our lyres

Alter argues that not only are the two cola not semantically parallel, the second colon does not serve as "going beyond" the first either. The reason is, the relationship between the two is one between an adverbial phrase (first colon) and main clause (second colon).[151]

The example above not only reinforces the notion that some biblical poetic texts cannot be explained by just one theory, but also that some poetic texts should not be treated by parallelism but in different terms. Indeed, such poetic texts exist in the form of non-parallel lines in Lamentations 1–4, as Gray and Dobbs-Allsopp point out.[152] In short, poetic cola are related to each other in several ways, and parallelism is just one of them. When parallelism is nowhere to be found, we should look at an inter-component relationship in other terms such as syntactical (grammatical) connections.

Parallelism Is beyond Bicolon

Having given many examples of bicolon relationship, we should note that parallelism is not always about the relationship of *two* cola. As scholars point out, while the most common parallelism is bicolon parallelism (an estimate of 75% of total number of poetic lines,[153] particularly the wise sayings in Proverbs), threefold or fourfold parallelism is also frequent, or

---

148. See 27–28.

149. Though Gray notes there are cola in at least 242 sections in Lamentation 1–4 which cannot be explained by parallelism, he is more interested in how such peculiarity relates to poetic rhythm (*Form of Hebrew Poetry*, 50–51, 112).

150. Alter, *Art of Biblical Poetry*, 20.

151. Ibid.

152. Gray, *Form of Hebrew Poetry*, 50–51, 112; Dobbs-Allsopp, "The Enjambing Line (I)," 219, 238–39; and Dobbs-Allsopp, "The Effects of Enjambment (II)," 370–85.

153. See Wendland, *Discourse Perspective*, 11.

even combinations of binary and threefold parallelism.[154] Consequently, the student of Hebrew poetry has to view parallelism beyond two adjacent cola. Moreover, Berlin raises the importance of a "global view" of parallelism. She points out that parallelism not only involves the relationship between one sentence and the adjacent sentence, but also with sentences anywhere within a text.[155]

This alerts us to the presence of parallelism involving multi-cola, strophes, or even stanzas. Frequently, such multi-cola parallelism exhibits a chiastic structure, about which Watson offers us numerous illustrations.[156] The following analysis of Isa 28:15–18 is one such illustration:[157]

a Because you have said, "We have made a covenant with death,

　and with Sheol we have made a pact,

　the overwhelming scourge will not reach us when it passes by;

b for we have made falsehood our refuge,

　and we have concealed ourselves with deception."

c Therefore thus says my Lord Yahweh,

　"Behold, I am laying in Zion a stone, a tested stone,

　a precious cornerstone for the foundation, firmly founded.

　He who believes in it will not be disturbed.

c' I will establish justice the measuring line,

　and righteousness the level.

b' Then hail will sweep away the refuge of lies,

　and the waters will overflow the secret place.

a' Your covenant with death will be canceled,

　and you pact with Sheol will not stand.

---

154. E.g., Alonso-Schökel, *Manual of Hebrew Poetics,* 51. Alter's translation of the wisdom books (*Job, Proverbs, and Ecclesiastes*) may reflect such a notion: the "lines" are presented in bicolon generally, but at times in tricolon.

155. Berlin, *Dynamics of Biblical Parallelism,* 3.

156. Watson, *Classical Hebrew Poetry,* 206–7; Watson, *Techniques in Classical Hebrew Verse,* 342–48, 354–73.

157. Watson makes reference to the chiastic parallelism of this poetic text without demonstrating it (*Classical Hebrew Poetry,* 206). The illustration provided here is based on his view that the chiastic pattern is abcc'b'a'.

When the overwhelming scourge passes through, you become its trampling."

Scholarly interest in chiasm in Hebrew poetry as well as narrative was evident in the second half of the twentieth century, as reflected in a slew of articles published in the period.[158] While chiasm may be widely found in the Bible, one should avoid the assumption that it is everywhere. Given the complexity and diversity of parallelism demonstrated in this chapter, it is presumptuous to assert that chiastic parallelism is the main style of biblical writers.

THE FUNCTIONS AND EFFECTS OF PARALLELISM

The Hebrew poets employed parallelism not simply because it was part of the ancient literary conventions, but because the conventions themselves serve specific poetic functions and effects. With regard to the functions and effects of parallelism, Greenstein raises two pertinent questions. First, how does parallelism shape the reader's perception of the message? Second, how, through parallelism, does a poem "attract, appeal to and move its audience?"[159]

The Semantic Functions of Parallelism

The key function of parallelism is to shape the reader's perception of the message of a poem. In other words, parallelism is integral to communicating the poet's message. If parallelism is a phenomenon of semantic progression (following Kugel), it helps the reader understand a poem. When one colon reinforces, specifies, or continues the thought of the preceding colon, the reader gets a better idea about what the poet has to say.

At times two corresponding cola function to associate thoughts which are otherwise perceived as unrelated. Berlin writes how parallelism in Ps 114:3 associates two thoughts to form a message:[160]

The sea saw and fled,

the Jordan turned backward.

158. Such as Ceresko, "The Function of Chiasmus," 1–10; Lichtenstein, "Chiasm and Symmetry," 202–211; Fredericks, "Chiasm and Parallel Structure," 17–35. For a recent example, see van Leeuwen, "Meaning and Structure," 377.

159. Greenstein, "How Does Parallelism Mean?" 42–43.

160. Berlin, *Dynamics of Biblical Parallelism*, 136.

The first colon refers to the parting of the Red Sea (Exod 14:21), the second to the parting of the Jordan River (Jos 3:16). In the Pentateuchal narrative, these are two separate biblical incidents whose relationship is not obvious. The poet now puts the two seemingly independent incidents together through the parallel cola, suggesting their theological association. The first incident marks the leaving of Egypt for the promised land, the second the entering of the promised land; this way the two cola frame the whole Exodus narrative by way of *inclusio*.

At times two contrastively parallel cola serve to heighten an idea. A case in point is God's judgment over the women in Jerusalem in Isa 3:24:

> Instead of perfume,
> there will be rottenness.
> Instead of a belt,[161]
> a rope.
> Instead of well-set hair,
> baldness.
> Instead of a rich robe,
> a girding of sackcloth.
> Scar
> instead of beauty.

Here is a series of five contrasting pairs: perfume is contrasted with rottenness; belt with rope; well-set hair with baldness; rich robe with sackcloth; beauty with scar. Alonso-Schökel observes that they serve to describe a changing situation by "expressing nostalgia for former better times and presenting a contrast with the present."[162] But we may add that by contrasting the terrible conditions to the former better times, the sense of loss and pain is heightened, thus stressing the severity of God's judgment.

As biblical poetry is a theological text, such effects are important, for by studying the parallelism, a reader can receive the message of the biblical poet. Therefore, given the numerous theories of parallelism, the student may want to be guided by a practical question: how effectively would these theories help us understand the theological message? This question would have two implications. Firstly, though precise taxonomy or classification of parallelism is important, it should not distract us from the meaning of the text. So, while churning out "more discrete types" (to borrow Berlin's words)

---

161. This is another case of ellipsis. Starting from this colon, the Hebrew verb for "there will be" (which occurs in the first pair) is deleted.

162. Alonso-Schökel, *Manual of Hebrew Poetics*, 89.

may help further refine our understanding of parallelism, we should ask how effective a given theory is in helping us interpret the text. This leads to the second implication.

The second implication is that grammatical parallelism should eventually contribute to the understanding of a poem. We make the assertion on a few grounds. First, our earlier discussion of grammatical parallelism shows that grammatical parallelism is often closely associated with semantic parallelism. Literary critics remind us that formal features (including grammatical parallelism) help structure a poetic text, so they have an impact on its meaning. So Kugel writes: "rarely is semantic parallelism found without some accompanying parallelism of grammatical forms, syntax, and line length."[163] Likewise, Nigel Fabb argues that semantic parallelism is frequently accompanied by formal (grammatical) parallelism.[164]

Lest we are lost in the woods of linguistics, linguistic considerations alone would not help us understand the theology of a text. Berlin is correct when she quotes Jonathan Culler: "Linguistics is not hermeneutics. It does not discover what a sequence means or produces a new interpretation of it."[165] Therefore, grammar considerations should not be pursued at the expense of meaning. Rather, our study of grammatical parallelism should ultimately help us understand the theology of the text. The case of ellipsis (or gapping) may serve as an example of how grammatical parallelism plays a role in the reader's understanding of a poem. An analysis of the grammatical parallelism helps the reader connect the two seemingly un-parallel (or partially parallel) cola; and by doing so, the reader also learns what the poet means.

The Rhetorical Functions of Parallelism

The biblical poet, however, is not just interested in communicating his message. As Greenstein correctly notes, they are also concerned about the effectiveness of their deliverance.[166] Therefore they seek to engage or involve the reader's mind and heart. For this reason, other than conveying a message, biblical parallelism seeks to produce certain rhetorical effects as well.

---

163. Kugel, *Idea of Biblical Poetry*, 49; also Berlin, *Dynamics of Biblical Parallelism*, 135. There are indeed rare occasions, as Bratcher and Reyburn point out, on which syntactically parallel lines have not much parallelism of meaning (*Handbook to the Psalms*, 5).

164. Fabb, *Linguistics and Literature*, 138.

165. Culler, *Structural Poetics*, 31, cited in Berlin, *Dynamics of Biblical Parallelism*, 135.

166. Greenstein, "How Does Parallelism Mean?" 42–43.

Alter speaks of the effects in terms of the semantics. In keeping with his description that parallelism is a semantic movement, Alter sees the effects as "heightening or intensification," and "focusing, specification, concretization."[167] This holds true either for the Kugelian understanding of parallelism and the old school's understanding of antithetic parallelism. For the old school (Lowthian) practitioner, an antithetic bicolon sets two thoughts in contrast, the contrast in turn heightens the thought the poet seeks to convey. The same bicolon may be seen by Kugel or Alter as a strengthening or heightening movement from the first colon to the second.

Greenstein is concerned himself with effects that involves the reader. He avers that parallelism which demands much of the reader's involvement is "staircase" ("climactic") parallelism. As he writes, "Nowhere does parallelism demand more audience involvement than in certain forms of the 'staircase' or 'climactic' variation."[168] As mentioned, staircase parallelism refers to an arrangement in which the initial words of the first colon are repeated in the subsequent colon,[169] such as the case of Ps 77:17 (ET 77:16):[170]

rā'ûk mmayim ĕlōhîm	The waters saw you, O God!
rā'ûk mmayim yāḥîlû	The waters saw you, they whirled!
'ap yirggĕzû tĕhōmôt	Also the depths trembled!

Each of the cola releases a little information about God's awesome power: the first colon tells us that the waters saw God, but does not tell us what happened to the waters; the second colon releases more information by revealing that when the waters saw God, they whirled; then the third colon reveals more: the waters trembled. Greenstein observes that such an arrangement acts to slow the pace of the poem and at the same time heighten our perception of it.[171] It follows that as it heightens our perception, it intensifies our emotions.

Likewise, phonological parallelism plays a significant rhetorical role in Hebrew poetry. In fact, the parallel sounds are at times closely associated with meaning. As Jakobson writes, "Words similar in sound are drawn

---

167. Alter, *Art of Biblical Poetry*, 20.

168. Greenstein, "How Does Parallelism Mean?" 54.

169. See 29–30.

170. Greenstein, "How Does Parallelism Mean?" 56; Greenstein, "Two Variations of Grammatical Parallelism," 98.

171. Greenstein, "How Does Parallelism Mean?" 54. Gitay notes a similar rhetorical effect of the tricolon in Amos 3:9 ("Rhetorical Analysis," 307).

together in meaning."[172] To this statement Berlin adds "phonologic similarity or equivalence promotes the perception of semantic equivalence."[173] In other words, the poet's choice of words is important. When the chosen words bear phonological correspondence, the sounds help reinforce the message. Berlin illustrates this by Ps 104:19:[174]

'āśâ yāreaḥ lemō 'ēdim	He made the moon for time-markers
šemeš yāda' mĕbōō	the sun knows its setting

The semantic correspondence between the two cola is not apparent. But the phonological equivalence between *yāreaḥ lemō 'ēdim* and *yāda'mĕbōō* connects them and suggests some equivalence of sense.[175] This in turn gives the idea that just as the moon is made to mark the coming of the night, so does the setting of the sun. The phonological aspect of parallelism raises the question about the significance of other aspects of sound in Hebrew poetry: rhythm and meter, two subjects to which we will turn in the following chapter.

172. Jakobson, "Linguistics and Poetics," 371.

173. Berlin, *Dynamics of Biblical Parallelism*, 112.

174. Ibid., 111.

175. Berlin sees phonological equivalence only between *lemō 'ēdim* and *yāda'mĕbōō* (ibid., 112), but we argue that the phonological equivalence would be more evident if we include *yāreaḥ* whose last syllable phonologically corresponds to the last syllable of *yāda'* (so *yāreaḥ lemō 'ēdim* and *yāda' mĕbōō*).

3

Meter and Hebrew Poetry

MUSIC AND HEBREW POETRY

The close association between Hebrew poetry and music is attested by the fact that many biblical poems are often regarded as songs (*šîrāh*). For example, Psalm 18 begins with the superscription: "the servant of Yahweh, David who spoke to Yahweh the words of this song" (Ps 18:1).[1] Similarly, Song of Songs begins with "Song of songs which is Solomon's" (Song 1:1). The poem in Exodus 15 is referred to as a song that "Moses and the Israelites sung" (Exod 15:1). Besides, even psalms not explicitly called "songs" used to be sung to a tune or accompanied by musical instruments. Psalm 4 begins with the musical superscription "For the director of music on *Neginoth*" (Ps 4:1);[2] likewise Psalm 5 has the musical heading "For the director of music, for flutes."[3] All this suggests that at one point of time, the psalms were sung.[4]

Naturally, such a close association has given rise to several questions: Is there a musical aspect to Hebrew poetry? Does Hebrew poetry, like music in general, involve rhythm and meter? This is all the more intriguing as we learned the close association between sound and parallelism in chapter 2.

1. Though superscriptions are later additions, this one at least suggests that at one point of during its transmission, this psalm was regarded as a song.

2. The term *Neginoth* is a musical term that means stringed music/instruments. See Weiser, *Psalms*, 22, 119 n1; Kraus, *Psalms 1–59*, 26–27.

3. The Hebrew term *hannehîlôt* may refer to flutes by which the song would be accompanied.

4. So Mowinckel, *Psalms in Israel's Worship*, 159.

Before we go any further, it would be helpful to know the relationship between rhythm and meter.

Rhythm

Human language involves rhythm and patterns of rhythm. Put simply, rhythm is a recurring pattern of sounds.[5] Rhythm is observable in an ordinary statement like "I'll have a sandwich and a cup of tea." Each underlined syllable represents a stressed syllable, and the ones without are unstressed syllables; the alternation between stressed and unstressed syllables creates syllable-timed rhythm. Rhythm is obvious in nursery rhymes such as "Twinkle Twinkle Little Star":

> "<u>Twink</u>le <u>twink</u>le <u>lit</u>tle <u>star</u>,
>
> <u>how</u> I <u>won</u>der <u>what</u> you <u>are</u>."

Here we have another example of syllable-timed rhythm. The rhythm in the first line is repeated in the second line, thus forming a pattern of rhythm.

Like other languages, biblical Hebrew as presented in the MT is rhythmic, and the rhythm is marked by the presence of accent on one or another syllable in a word. Often where the accent rests makes a difference. For instance, it sets *banû* ("they built," the accent falls on the last syllable) apart from *banû* ("in us," the accent falls on the first syllable). The MT offers different accent markers; generally they serve as a chanting (cantillation) guide as well as syntactical markers.[6]

With the presence of these markers, when read or chanted, a biblical poem sounds rhythmic. For instance, the MT Ps 2:1 can be divided into two cola, and each has 3 accented syllables, forming a rhythmic pattern of 3+3:

לָמָּה רָגְשׁוּ גוֹיִם	*lāmmāh rāgĕšû gôyīm*	Why do the nations rage?
וּלְאֻמִּים יֶהְגּוּ־רִיק	*ûlĕʾummîm yehgû-rîq*	And the peoples plot in vain?

---

5. Watson, *Classical Hebrew Poetry*, 87.

6. Generally, the accents are divided into two categories: conjunctive and disjunctive. For a quick reference of these accent markers, see the *Tabula Accentuum* insert of BHS. For an explanation of how they work, see Dresher, "Prosodic Basis," 3–4.

Meter

Basically, there are two patterns of rhythm in songs or poetry: one is regular, the other is irregular.[7] For example, whereas the nursery rhyme "Twinkle Twinkle Little Star" demonstrates a regular pattern of rhythm (four stresses on each colon, thus the rhythmic pattern is 4+4), the Christmas carol "The First Noel" does not. According to the classical definition, regular pattern of rhythm is called meter; as R. Winslow notes, meter is the "measure of sound patterning in verse, occurring when a rhythm is repeated throughout a passage of language with such regularity that the base unit. . .becomes a norm and governs poetic composition."[8] By *regularity* poetic analysts usually mean an equal number of stresses (thus symmetrical) in each colon of a bicola. Following this conventional definition, one may say while meter is present in the nursery rhyme (4 stresses on each colon, thus 4+4), it is not in the Christmas carol.

In view of the above, two questions arise. Is Hebrew poetry, like poetry in many cultures, metrical? If so, what does the metrical system look like? Unfortunately, these questions cannot be answered in a straightforward fashion. In English literature, meter is a much debated topic;[9] the topic of meter in Hebrew poetry is no exception.

VARIOUS THEORIES OF HEBREW METER

The subject of Hebrew meter has generated centuries of search, debate and various theories. The discussion focuses on studying the metrical patterns of biblical poems (called "scansion").[10] Over the centuries, Hebrew metricists have analyzed the poems by either the *length* of syllables (quantitative), or the *accents* on syllables (accentual) or the *number* of syllables (syllabic). The history of such studies is well covered in many introductions and discussions,[11] so a brief survey will suffice here.

---

7. Some poetic analysts offer more detailed categories. See Brogan, "Rhythm," 1067–68.

8. Winslow, "Meter," 872.

9. See, for example, Winsatt and Beardsley, "Concept of Meter," 585–98.

10. Such analysis indicates metrical patterns such as 2+2 or 3+3 or 3+2 and so on.

11. For a brief survey, see Stuart, *Early Hebrew Meter*, 1–10; Petersen and Richards, *Interpreting Hebrew Poetry*, 39; for a more recent and detailed survey, see Vance, *Question of Meter*, 47–222.

Quantitative Approaches: Scansion by Syllable Length

The studies of Hebrew meter can be traced back to Philo (15 BCE—45 CE) and Josephus (37–100 CE). Philo mentioned that Moses was taught rhythm and meter in Egypt, but did not actually say that he wrote any metrical texts in the Pentateuch.[12] Josephus is the historian who made reference to Hebrew metrics when he spoke of the poetic passages such as Exodus 15[13] and Deuteronomy 32[14] in terms of hexameters.[15] By hexameter, Josephus may have referred to Greco-Roman meter, which is a kind of regular syllable-timed rhythm classified as "quantitative meter" (a meter based on the length of the syllable, distinguishing between long and short syllables by how long it takes to pronounce them).[16] A bicolon is called a hexameter when it has 3 feet (each foot being one or two syllables) in each colon, forming the 3+3 metrical pattern.

As the Hebrew texts of these ancient historians were closer to the original form of the Hebrew Bible then, some scholars aver that their references attest the presence of Hebrew meter.[17] However, other scholars argue that the two Jewish historians could have applied their understanding of Greco-Roman meter to the Hebrew texts.[18] As we have no access to the texts Philo and Josephus were referring to, the debate remains open.

The metrical thesis along the line of Greco-Roman metrics continued after Philo and Josephus, through the Early Church and the medieval period, perpetuated by prominent Church Fathers such as Origen, Eusebius, Jerome, and Augustine.[19] The Greco-Roman thesis was followed until Lowth's systematic study of Hebrew poetry, and it has been abandoned ever since.[20]

---

12. Philo, 6.1.23.

13. Josephus, *Ant.* 2.346.

14. Josephus, *Ant.* 4.303.

15. Hexameter refers to a verse with 6 feet (each foot being one or two syllables); the metrical pattern is 3+3.

16. See Hrushovski, "Prosody, Hebrew," 1212. Some literary critics think such a metrical system is found in English poetry, but others challenge this view; see Winsatt and Beardsley, "Concept of Meter," 588–90.

17. E.g., Gray, *Forms of Hebrew Poetry*, 11.

18. Among others are ibid., 16; and Eissfeldt, *Old Testament*, 59.

19. For a survey, see Kugel, *Idea of Biblical Poetry*, 147–170; Eissfeldt, *Old Testament*, 60; Vance, *Question of Meter*, 97–222.

20. Freedman, "Archaic Forms," 167; Vance, *Question of Meter*, 94–95; Petersen and Richards, *Interpreting Hebrew Poetry*, 39.

As noted in chapter 1, for Lowth, besides parallelism, meter is an essential characteristic of Hebrew poetry.[21] Lowth's contribution to the discussion is significant for two reasons. First, he distinguishes Hebrew poetry from Greek poetry, thus departing from the Greco-Roman metrics thesis.[22] Second, he recognizes that the MT poems do not represent the original pronunciation of the original poets. So while Lowth believes that Hebrew poetry is metrical,[23] due to the absence of original pronunciation, he admits a precise scansion would not be possible.[24] Given this reality, Lowth suggests that meter is best understood as part of parallelism, though he expresses uncertainty as to how parallelism can be observed at the metrical level.[25]

Accentual and Syllabic Approaches: Scansion by Accents and Syllable Count

The subject of Hebrew meter continued to fascinate biblical scholars into the modern period. In the course of their studies these biblical scholars have turned to definitions and "systems" of Hebrew metrics other than the Greco-Roman one. For our purposes, it will suffice to mention two major strands of arguments: those which define Hebrew metrics by the accentuation of the Hebrew text (called the accentual system), and those by the number of syllables (called the syllabic system).

Accentual System

The accentual system is advocated by German scholars such as Julius Ley,[26] Karl Budde,[27] and Eduard Sievers[28] (hence is called the Ley–Sievers–Budde method).[29] The system was once accepted by most scholars, as testified by

---

21. See 12.

22. Lowth, *Lectures on Sacred Poetry*, 1:70–71

23. Ibid., 1:55.

24. Ibid., 1:66–67.

25. Ibid., 1:68, 2:53–56. Gray observes that since parallelism comes with patterns (such as repetition or abc//a'b'c'), it may create rhythm (*Forms of Hebrew Poetry*, 112). We will revisit the relationship between parallelism and rhythm in 3.4.3.

26. Ley, "hebräische Metrik," 212–17.

27. Budde, "hebräische Klagelied," 1–52; also Budde, "Poetry (Hebrew)," 5.

28. Sievers, *Metrische Studien* (Eerster Teil) and Sievers, *Metrische Studien* (Zweiter Teil).

29. Though these three German theorists hold individually nuanced positions, in fact they share many things in common. See Eissfeldt, *Old Testament*, 60; Stuart, *Early*

prominent names representative of this approach such as Gray,[30] Sigmund Mowinckel,[31] Stanislav Segert,[32] W. F. Albright,[33] and Jerzy Kurylowicz.[34]

Instead of defining meter by long and short syllables (as in the Greco-Roman metrical system), the accentual system defines meter by the accents of poetic lines. While the general view is that the accents are for cantillation and syntactic purposes,[35] Hebrew metricists argue they also serve a metrical purpose. In the case of Ps 117:1, the MT text can be divided into two cola:

| הַלְלוּ אֶת־יְהוָה כָּל־גּוֹיִם | halĕlû 'et-YHWH kol-gôyīm | Praise Yahweh, all nations! |
| שַׁבְּחוּהוּ כָּל־הָאֻמִּים | šabbĕhûhû kol-hā'ummîm | Extol him, all peoples |

Alonso-Schökel counts three accents in each colon, and on this basis he notes that the verse displays a regular (or symmetric) 3+3 rhythmic pattern, thus may be called meter.[36]

However, things are not as simple as they seem. For one thing, there has been a debate over whether or not to consider certain monosyllabic words (such as independent personal pronouns, the negation particle lō', and the polysemic particle kî) accented.[37] The confusion not only opens to different meter counts of a poetic passage, but also betrays the method's arbitrariness.[38] Another difficulty is that for various reasons the practitioners do not always follow the accentuation of the MT. For illustration, let us return to Isa 1:10:

Hebrew Meter, 1–4.

30. As reflected in Gray's discussion of Lamentations (*Forms of Hebrew Poetry*, 85–120, 147–54).

31. Mowinckel, *Psalms in Israel's Worship*, 159–75.

32. Segert, "Hebrew Prosody," 283–91.

33. Albright, "Catalogue," 7; Abright, *Gods of Canaan*, 9.

34. Kurylowicz, *Semitic Grammar and Metrics*.

35. GKC (§15.1) observes that while their original musical function is now largely lost in transmission, the accents still serve grammatical and syntactical purposes, i.e., "as marking the tone" and "as marks of punctuation to indicate the logical (syntactical) relation of single words to their immediate surroundings, and thus to the whole sentence." For this general consensus, see Dresher, "Prosodic Basis," 5–6.

36. Alonso-Schökel, *Manual of Hebrew Poetics*, 37.

37. Especially so when these particles are not accented in the MT.

38. The confusion is seen in inconsistencies in treatment of monosyllabic words, a problem that Vance observes in Sievers' metrical analysis (*Question of Meter*, 144). One detects arbitrariness when Alonso-Schökel avers that whether these words are accented or not depend on "the demands" of meter of the poem (*Manual of Hebrew Poetics*, 40).

שִׁמְעוּ דְבַר־יְהוָה קְצִינֵי סְדֹם   Listen to the word of Yahweh, rulers of Sodom

הַאֲזִינוּ תּוֹרַת אֱלֹהֵינוּ עַם עֲמֹרָה   Give ear to the teaching of our God, people of Gomorrah

Following the MT, the first colon has four accents, the second five accents (thus forming a 4+5 pattern). Disagreeing with the MT and Siever, Gray opines that the noun דבר ("word," maqqephed in the MT, thus unaccented) in the first colon should be accented, because it is parallel to the word תּוֹרַת ("teaching," accented in the MT) in the second colon. So, for Gray the scancion of the bicolon is 5+5 instead of 4+5.[39]

The preceding analysis reveals two issues. Firstly, it shows that practitioners of the accentual system are at liberty to emend the MT for reasons they consider valid. As we will see below, such freedom has led to different conclusions about the meter of a text, and thus presents confusion for the student of Hebrew poetry. Secondly, the 4+5 pattern does not fit the standard (conventional) definition of meter, which requires regularity or symmetry (i.e., there must be the same number of accents on both cola, forming patterns such as 2+2 or 3+3 or 4+4). Frequently, even without emending the MT accents, such an "unbalanced" pattern appears in the middle of an otherwise regular rhythmic pattern. While Budde still considers such pattern to be meter (such as the 3+2 pattern, called the *qinah* meter),[40] one has yet to square it with the standard definition of meter.

Such problems appear in the early metrical analyses of Frank Moore Cross and Freedman. Under the influence of their teacher, W. F. Albright, the two scholars developed the Ley–Budde–Sievers method further by making a connection with Ugaritic poetry, a topic of great interest in biblical studies in the 1970s. To address the problem that the MT does not reflect the original vocalization,[41] they turned to what they believed to be the surviving early passages of the ancient Hebrews (such as the Song of Deborah in Judges 5 and Exodus 15) and made a connection with their contemporary, namely, Ugaritic poetry. They argued that the early Hebrew poets adopted the poetic conventions of their neighbors, including their metrical system.[42] This being the case, Ugaritic metrics can serve as "a background and a control in the analysis of prosodic forms and formulae in

---

39. Gray, *Forms of Hebrew Poetry*, 151–52.

40. Budde, "Poetry [Hebrew]," 5; see also Gray, *Forms of Hebrew Poetry*, 89–92.

41. See Cross and Freedman, *Ancient Yahwistic Poetry*, 127.

42. For example, Cross and Freedman (ibid., 5–6) believe both Hebrew poetry and Ugaritic poetry are characterized by a 2+2 meter or 3+3 meter. This is in keeping with their teacher's views; see Albright, *Gods of Canaan*, 8–9.

earliest Hebrew poetry."[43] On this basis, here is how Cross and Freedman treat of Exod 15:1b:[44]

אָשִׁירָה לַיהוָה	'āšîrāh laYHWH	Let me sing to Yahweh
כִּי־גָאֹה גָּאָה	kî-gāōh gāāh	for he is highly exalted

Cross and Friedman take the accentuation in the Hebrew text as to indicate two accents in each colon, forming a 2+2 pattern.[45] However, the two scholars' scansion of Exod 15:5a shows that the poem departs from such regular rhythm:[46]

תְּהֹמֹת יְכַסְיֻמוּ	tĕhōmōt yĕkasyumû	The deeps covered them
יֵרְדוּ בִמְצוֹלֹת כְּמוֹ־אָבֶן	yārdû bimṣōlōt kĕmô-'āben	they sank in the depths like a stone

According to Cross and Freedman's scansion the verse shows a pattern of 3+3. Two issues arise from the analysis. First, while the MT text shows only two accents in the first colon, Cross and Freedman emend it to three. They opine that based on their metrical analysis, a third accent must have been there originally, but due a scribal error, it dropped out of the text.[47] This leads to another issue: whereas their scansion of the preceding verses are consistently 2+2,[48] it is now disrupted by a different rhythmic pattern (3+3). This being the case, their scansion of Exodus 15 displays an irregular rhythm, that is, a mixture of 2+2 and 3+3 patterns. Indeed, though Cross and Freedman state repeatedly that symmetric patterns (two stressed syllables on each of the cola, forming 2+2 or 3+3 meter) characterize Hebrew and Ugaritic poetry, they also note the presence of "unbalanced meter," that is 3+2.[49] The problem is that such irregularity does not fit the standard definition of meter.

---

43. Cross and Freedman, *Ancient Yahwistic Poetry,* 128.

44. Ibid., 35.

45. This suggests they do not seem to regard the conjunction כִּ in the second colon as accented.

46. Ibid.

47. Ibid., 35, 41 n11.

48. Ibid., 35.

49. Ibid., 5–6; cf. Budde's *qinah.*

Syllabic System

As Longman points out, problems with the accentual system led to dissatisfaction, and for this reason some scholars turned to a system that defined meter by the number of syllables in a colon.[50] Intriguingly, representatives of this approach include Cross and Freedman, scholars who at first followed the accentual system.[51] As early as 1960, Freedman had begun to explore a different method, one that shifted from focussing on accented syllables to syllable counting.[52] In the *postscriptum* to their dissertation reissued in 1975, this methodological shift was made explicit. There Freedman expressed his doubt about the accentual system:

> Instead of isolating stressed syllables to the exclusion of others, or employing a more complicated system for measuring quantity ... the provisional conclusion is that these factors either tend to cancel out, especially in lengthy pieces, or cannot be sufficiently discriminated on the basis of present or foreseeable knowledge to justify the efforts required or the results achieved.[53]

Probably in view of this, Cross "finds syllable counting useful in analyzing Canaanite and Hebrew verse."[54] They categorize a poetic line into long colon (called longum, abbreviated "l," equivalent to 3 in the accentual system) and short colon (called breve, abbreviated "b," equivalent to 2 in the accentual system), and argue the common metrical patterns are: l:l, l:l:l, and b:b//b:b.[55]

Freedman's syllable counting system is laid out more fully in his later article on Psalm 137. As in the *postcriptum* of the dissertation, Freedman contends that the accentual system is ineffective and subjective, whereas syllable counting is objective and simpler.[56] Though he intends to follow the MT vocalization as much as possible, he also concedes that he makes changes when necessary.[57] Applying his syllable counting scheme, Freedman finds

---

50. Longman, "Two Recent Metrical System," 230.

51. And certainly they are not alone. Culley also attempts to solve the problem of Hebrew meter by syllable counting ("Metrical Analysis," 12–28).

52. Freedman, "Archaic Forms," 101–7.

53. Cross and Freedman, *Ancient Yahwistic Poetry,* 129. Freedman's methodological discussion also appears in Cross and Freedman, "Pottery, Poetry and Prophecy," 6–11.

54. Cross and Freedman, *Ancient Yahwistic Poetry,* 129.

55. Ibid.

56. Freedman, "Structure of Psalm 137," 188–89.

57. Ibid., 189.

a chiastic structure in Psalm 137, with the segment in 137:5–6 as its center.[58] His scansion of the segment in 137:5a–6b reflects such chiasm:

v. 5a	*'im 'ĕškĕḥēkī yĕrûšālēm*	9 syllables	If I forget you Jerusalem
v. 5b	*tiškaḥ yĕmînî*	5 syllables	let my right hand forget
v. 6a	*tidbaq lĕšônî*	5 syllables	may my tongue cling
v. 6b	*lĕḥīkkî 'im lō'ezkĕrēkî*	9 syllables	to the roof of my mouth if I do not remember you

As shown above, the scansion presents a symmetric abb'a' chiastic pattern. Such scansion, however, requires a certain way of treating the text. Notice that the MT reading of 137:5a has 8 syllables (*'im 'eškāḥ ēk yĕrûšālēm*). But Freedman adopts a different reading, which has 9 syllables (*'im 'ĕškĕḥēkī yĕrûšālēm*). Moreover, in order to have five syllables in 137:6a, Freedman breaks the prepositional phrase *lĕḥīkkî* ("to the roof of my mouth") away from the colon and places it at the following colon (137:6b). In doing so, Freedman presents a neatly balanced pattern: 9+5+5+9. Though this may be justified by the pause marker (*pasēq*), which precedes the phrase *lĕḥīkkî*, it breaks up the otherwise syntactically intact clause.[59] Syntactically the phrase is the integral part of 137:6a and functions to qualify *tidbaq lĕšônî* ("May my tongue cling"). Given that the *pasēq* is a later addition of the Masoretic scribes, one can choose to follow the syntax, as most scholars do,[60] and offer a different scansion: a 9+6+4+9 pattern. All this shows how subjectivity can come to play in the accentual metrical analysis and bring out diverse scansions.[61]

After Freedman there have been variant theories that attempt to improve the syllable counting system. Among others is Freedman's student, Stuart.[62] Building on Freedman's model, Stuart proposes the syllable counting as "a newer method," which "describes the meter of Hebrew poetry more precisely than the scansions of other schools."[63] Like his predecessors, Stuart is not satisfied with the MT vocalization; thus he argues that the MT

---

58. Ibid., 195–96.

59. As pointed out by Halle and McCarthy, "Metrical Structure of Psalm 137," 162.

60. E.g., ibid.; also Dahood, *Psalms III*, 268; Kraus, *Psalms 60–150*, 500; Allen, *Psalms 101–50*, 301.

61. Cf. Vance's critique of Freedman in Vance, *Question of Meter*, 189–93.

62. The influence of syllable counting method is also seen in discussions which seek to improve the system. E.g., Coogan, "Song of Deborah," esp. 157–58; Halle and McCarthy, "Metrical Structure of Psalm 137," 161–67.

63. Stuart, *Early Hebrew Meter*, 28–29.

vocalization should be reconstructed. Like Cross and Freedman, Stuart sees Ugaritic poetry as a good model after which the vocalization of early Hebrew poetry can be reconstructed.[64] However, the outcome of his theory differs from that of Cross and Freedman. In the case of Exod 15:1, Stuart's reconstruction leads to a 5+5 meter, in contrast to his teacher's 3+3.[65] All this reinforces the impression of lack of consensus we spoke of above.

Recent scholarship shows there is no lack of interest in syllable counting. Two Dutch biblical scholars, J. P. Fokkelman and Pieter van der Lugt, have made fresh attempts to offer a better system of syllable/word counting.[66] Yet, like the theories of their predecessors, their theories do not lack criticism. One of the main concerns is, as expressed by some scholars, that in their arguments for syllable/word counting, they fail to engage and address either the previous discussions or criticisms of syllable counting we mentioned above.[67] In addition, for reason of different strophic division, the two scholars' word counts of each colon of the same text are at times in disagreement with each other. For example, van der Lugt breaks Job 42:3a into two cola:[68]

> Who is this that obscures design
> without knowledge?

Fokkelman, however, regards it a single colon:[69]

> Who is this that obscures design without knowledge?

Such a treatment results in different word counts for the same colon: for Fokkelman, Job 42:3a has six words; for van der Lugt, four words. These problems reflect not only their subjectivity in strophic division, but the fluidity of their word counting methods.

---

64. Ibid., 24, 28; see his comparative study of Ugaritic poetry in pp. 51–76.

65. Ignoring the accents, Stuart counts 5 syllables in each colon (*Early Hebrew Meter*, 79–81).

66. Fokkelman, *Major Poems IV*. It should be noted that for van der Lugt word counting is only one of the several ways of strophic division (*Cantos and Strophes*, 75–87).

67. Vogels, Review of *Major Poems IV*, 516–17; Gilingham, Review of *Major Poems I*, 154. Like Fokkelman, van der Lugt discusses and advocates syllable counting theories without pointing out the complications noted by other scholars (*Cantos and Strophes*, 42–46; 56–59; 84–87).

68. Van der Lugt, *Rhetorical Criticism*, 407.

69. Fokkelman, *Major Poems IV*, 318 n40, 318–20.

EVALUATION

If anything, the foregoing survey shows that the prospect of finding ancient Hebrew metrics is not very promising. It becomes clear that the search has been faced with a number of hurdles.

The Absence of Original Vocalization and Accents

Accentuation and pronunciation are crucial both to the accentual and syllabic methods. This poses the first obstacle to establishing Hebrew metrics: we have no access to the original accentuation and vocalization of the biblical poems. As we pointed out, the vocalization and accentuation accessible to us today are added by the Masoretes to what was originally written in consonantal script. The vocalization and accentuation were based on the Tiberian dialect in the medieval period, thus do not represent the vocalization and accentuation of the original poets who lived almost one millennium earlier than the Masoretes.[70] This problem is compounded by the fact, as some scholars note, that between the time the biblical poems were written and the Masoretes' accentuation, various rhythmical systems were developed.[71] Understandably, the general concern is that the MT vocalization and accentuation do not represent the originals, a problem discussed as early as Lowth's time.[72] This problem is further complicated by the possibility that the consonantal texts were already corrupted before they reached the Masoretes, as testified by the text-critical issues we encounter in exegesis.

We mentioned earlier that scholars such as Cross and Freedman have addressed this concern by their comparative studies of Ugaritic poetry. Assuming that biblical poets followed the conventions of Ugaritic poetry, they use the latter as a basis to reconstruct Hebrew poetry. Unfortunately, even Ugaritic scholars themselves recognize the limitations of Ugaritic poetry. Like ancient Hebrew, except a few vowel letters, ancient Ugaritic too is written mainly in consonantal script.[73] As such, the vocalization of Ugaritic texts themselves needs a reconstruction. Interestingly, as Cross and Freedman use Ugaritic poetry as the model for Hebrew meter, in the same breath they

70. For a discussion on the MT accentuation and its purposes, see Dresher, "Prosodic Basis," 1–52.

71. Cf. Hrushovski, "Systems of Hebrew Versification," 60–61.

72. Despite his belief that Hebrew poetry is metrical, Lowth admitted such a problem (*Lectures on Sacred Poetry*, 1:65); also Eissfeldt, *Old Testament*, 59; Gray, *Forms of Hebrew Poetry*, 125; Alonso-Schökel, *Manual of Hebrew Poetics*, 39; Stuart, *Early Hebrew Meter*, 28.

73. Healey and Craigie, "Ugaritic," 227.

admit uncertainty about establishing the original vocalization of Ugaritic texts.[74] This being the case, one wonders if Ugaritic poetry is a good model for studying Hebrew meter. Furthermore, even if one could ascertain the actual Ugaritic vocalization, by no means is the way to Ugaritic meter open. In fact, even scholars of Ugaritic such as J. C. de Moor and Dennis Pardee question the presence of what is classically called meter in Ugaritic poetry.[75]

The Lack of Consensus on the Original Vocalization and Accents

In order to get back to the presumed original form, most scholars deem it necessary to do what Kugel calls "text-rewriting."[76] As Vance points out, in his effort to demonstrate the accentual meter of Lamentations, Budde makes a 22 percent emendation.[77] Similarly, as discussed earlier, in their works on syllabic meter of biblical poems, scholars such as Cross, Freedman, and Stuart have to reconstruct the texts. Given the absence of the original pronunciation and accents, such a reconstruction is at best conjectural.

The problem is further complicated by the lack of consensus as to what the original form looked like. As shown above, Cross and Freedman suggest that the three accents in MT Exod 5:1 be emended to two accents so as to make a regular 2+2 meter. Stuart emends the vocalization of Exod 15:1 but concludes that it is in a 5+5 meter. Thus while all these scholars agree that the text is to be emended, they differ on how to do it. Their methodological differences are not just in terms of metrical systems (accentual versus syllable counting), but also in terms of emendation: the former takes away an accent, the latter reconstructs the vocalization. Their differences show that emendation is open to more possible reconstructions than one, and thus runs the danger of subjecting the text to one's presumed original form.[78] In view of this, Hauser's caution is aptly: "The student of the text must be careful not to resort too readily to emendations, lest he find himself interpreting his own interpretations."[79]

---

74. Cross and Freedman, *Ancient Yahwistic Poetry*, 7, 21–25.

75. De Moor, "Versification in Ugarit and Israel I," 120–21; Pardee, "Ugaritic," 115.

76. Kugel, *Idea of Biblical Poetry*, 296.

77. Vance, *Question of Meter*, 127–28.

78. While Culley takes the syllable counting approach, he expresses reservations about Stuart's reconstruction (Review of *Early Hebrew Meter*, 255–56). For more critique of Stuart's views, see O'Connor, *Hebrew Verse Structure*, 35–37.

79. Hauser, "Judges 5," 25.

The Lack of Consensus on Hebrew Metrics

The discussion above shows clearly that even those who advocate the existence of Hebrew meter are divided on the Hebrew metrical system. The student of Hebrew poetry is offered at least three major "systems" (quantitative, accentual, or syllabic), not to mention their respective variants. One's choice is important, as it would lead to a different conclusion about the meter of a text. As Petersen and Richards have demonstrated, the scansion of Isa 5:1–7 may vary from one scholar to another, depending on whether it is based on accents or syllables.[80] Furthermore, either basis may still result in different scansions. We observed above that accent-based scholars disagree over whether or not prepositions and monosyllabic words are to be treated as independent words having one accent.[81] Likewise, disagreements among syllable-counting practitioners have also been noted, and ultimately the number of syllables depends on what one thinks might be the length of a line or colon.[82]

The Lack of Consensus on the Definition of Meter

While many scholars observe that the common metrical pattern is 3+3, they also recognize the presence of other patterns in the same poem such as 2+2, 4+4, even 5+5. Also, one would frequently encounter the irregular *qinah* meter (3+2 pattern).[83] The variety of metrical patterns (frequently within a poem) raises the pertinent question about definition. As the standard definition of meter is regular rhythm, how does one account for the irregularity? Some scholars expect meter to be true to the classical sense of meter. For instance, Kugel sees the main flaw of Hebrew metrical argument is in the lack of regularity. More pointedly, he questions the term "non-regular meter": "what does this concept of 'irregular' or (still more diplomatically) 'non-regular' meter mean when it cannot be distinguished from no meter at all?"[84] For Kugel, the so-called biblical meter "will always prove rather half-hearted, suddenly dropping an established pattern of regularity without apparent purpose, as well as cultivating a semi-regular form which is

---

80. See Petersen and Richards, *Interpreting Hebrew Poetry*, 40–41.

81. See 64–65.

82. See Petersen and Richards, *Interpreting Hebrew Poetry*, 40; Halle and McCarthy, "Metrical Structure of Psalm 127," 161.

83. Cross and Freedman, *Ancient Yahwistic Poetry*, 7; Alonso-Schökel, *Manual of Hebrew Poetics*, 37; Zogbo and Wendland, *Hebrew Poetry in the Bible*, 35.

84. Kugel, *Idea of Biblical Poetry*, 297.

neither quite 'prose' nor yet of the same uniformity achieved in very regular sections."[85] Besides the issue of regularity, scholars also question whether, strictly speaking, syllable counting can be called meter. As Culley contests: "Since a meter in which both syllables and stress are relevant would not be called syllabic, it might be better in the meantime to speak of syllable counting rather than syllabic meter.[86]

Nonetheless, some scholars allow flexibility and redefinition to accommodate their scansions, using different terms such as "non-regular meter" or "mixed meter" for irregular rhythm. Watson, for instance, observes that meter "is not monolithic and inflexible" and ascribes the rejection of Hebrew meter to the fact that "scholars fail to distinguish between meter as actually present in verse, and *regular* meter. There is meter, yes, but not regular meter."[87] All this betrays the fact that there are diverse views even on what meter means.

CONCLUSION

The discussion above leads us back to the initial questions. Is Hebrew poetry metrical? If so, what does the metrical system exactly look like? Unfortunately, these seemingly simple questions have led to a protracted, complicated process of searching and inconclusive arguments. In sum, after centuries of searching, the Hebrew metrical system remains elusive.

The State of the Discussion of Hebrew Meter

The failure highlighted above has led to two kinds of responses. On the one hand are scholars who think that the whole affair is like the search for the Holy Grail. As Miller sums it up, "There is no *clear* system of meter in biblical poetry of the precision of classical meter."[88] Kugel puts it in stronger words: "Surely an objective look at the origins and fruits of metrical speculation should long ago have resulted in a rejection of the whole idea . . . no meter has been found because none exists."[89] In the same vein, O'Connor writes: "we have proposed that no consensus had ever been reached in the matter of

85. Ibid., 298; for the same view see Petersen and Richards (*Interpreting Hebrew Poetry*, 41).

86. Culley, Review of *Early Hebrew Meter*, 255–256.

87. Watson, *Classical Hebrew Poetry*, 92 (italics his); so does Gillingham (*Poems and Psalms*, 57). Cf. Alonso-Schökel, *Manual of Hebrew Poetics*, 41.

88. Miller, "Meter, Parallelism," 102; emphasis his.

89. Kugel, *Idea of Biblical Poetry*, 301.

Hebrew meter because there is none."[90] In a short statement, Alter brushes it aside: "the term meter should probably be abandoned for biblical verse."[91]

On the other hand, some scholars remain hopeful. Watson believes that the system is out there: "Surely the original Hebrew had some additional 'native' component (meter?) which is filtered out in a rendering."[92] Collins does not agree that the search should be given up; instead, he contends, "the fact that no system has emerged from all the laborious studies of stress patterns and syllable counts does not mean that there is no system. However, it does suggest that we probably ought to be looking for it somewhere else."[93]

In recent years, however, such a voice has become the minority, as more and more scholars express misgivings about the existence of Hebrew meter.[94] Dobbs-Allsopp may represent the majority sentiments in his most recent study on Hebrew poetry. He contends that regular rhythmic patterns do not get repeated for long stretches in biblical poetry, thus "Biblical poetry is not metrical."[95] For him, to fully appreciate the nature and dynamics of biblical poetry, one should stop looking to "the metrical varieties of poetry from classical antiquity or their imitators in the vernacular national traditions of the West so favored by the nineteenth and the twentieth century biblical critics."[96]

Distinguishing Rhythm from Meter

In the final analysis, the studies of Hebrew meter have come to an end similar to that of the Documentary Hypothesis: just as nobody has found the *Urtext*, so nobody has found the *Urmetrics*. For this reason, we can only work with the poetic texts in their present form. Before the original Hebrew metrics can be found with certainty, we can only conclude that Hebrew poetry in its present form defies any metrical theory. What is more certain, however, is that there is rhythm in Hebrew poetry; only that the rhythm occurs in more patterns than one (thus there is no consistently

90. O'Connors, *Hebrew Verse Structure*, 138.

91. Alter, *Art of Biblical Poetry*, 8.

92. Watson, *Classical Hebrew Poetry*, 109.

93. Collins, *Line-forms in Hebrew Poetry*, 7; and he proposes a grammatical approach to Hebrew meter as the new approach.

94. In recent scholarship, discussions on Hebrew meter are still found occasionally, such as deCaen, "Variation in Psalm 111," 81–109. Nonetheless, more and more scholars express doubts about Hebrew metrics.

95. Dobbs-Allsopp, *On Biblical Poetry*, 99–100.

96. Ibid., 98–99.

regular rhythm).[97] The various experiments we surveyed above can testify to this fact; it is also in keeping with observations of poetry in non-biblical literature. The nursery rhyme "Twinkle Twinkle Little Star" demonstrates a regular 4+4 rhythmic pattern (thus metrical), whereas the Christmas carol "The First Noel" does not (thus not metrical). Indeed, literary critics have recognized that poetry in general has more patterns of rhythm than one.[98]

Watson's assertion that Hebrew meter "is not monolithic and inflexible"[99] not only reinforces this fact, but also betrays the very nature of Hebrew poetry. Being an art, it does not conform to a mechanical rhythmic pattern. Imposition of meter not only ignores the creativity of Hebrew poetry, but also reduces it to a predictable run-of-the-mill product. Such reductionism misses much of the richness biblical poetry has to offer.

Rhythm and Parallelism

Biblical scholars who pursue Hebrew metrics are at times motivated by the importance of meter.[100] But a more interesting reason is what some perceive as the close connection between meter and parallelism. To them parallelism is not only formed by grammatical and semantic parallels, but also sound patterns.[101] Alonso-Schökel cites Ps 92:2 as an example of metrical parallelism:[102]

> *tôb lĕhōdôt laYHWH // ûlĕzammēr lĕšimkā ʿelyôn*
>
> Good to praise the Lord // to play to your name Elyon

The MT verse has three accents in each colon (forming a 3+3 meter), so metrically the first colon is parallel to the second colon. However, throughout this discussion we have shown a persistent problem: the regular rhythm

---

97. Now this represents the majority view. See Hrushovski, "Systems of Hebrew Versification," 58–60; O'Connor, *Hebrew Verse Structure*, 33–34; Gillingham, *Poems and Psalms*, 68; Petersen and Richards, *Interpreting Hebrew Poetry*, 42; While Gray is uncertain about Hebrew meter, he is certain about the existence of rhythm (*Forms of Hebrew Poetry*, 124).

98. Brogan mentions 4 patterns of rhythm: regular, variation, grouping and hierarchy ("Rhythm," 1067–68).

99. See 73.

100. For instance, Watson thinks that meter is important for the appreciation of the sound and artistic quality of Hebrew poetry (*Classical Hebrew Poetry*, 111–12).

101. Lowth, *Lectures on Sacred Poetry of the Hebrews*, 2:53–56; Gray, *Forms of Hebrew Poetry*, 112–13; cf. Longman, "Two Recent Metrical Systems," 230.

102. Alonso-Schökel, *Manual of Hebrew Poetics*, 34.

is represented by some cola only. Frequently, we encounter irregular rhythm such as unbalanced/asymmetrical 3+2 rhythmic patterns. If parallelism counts on equivalence in metrical patterns, the irregularity then does not always allow us to build parallelism on Hebrew metrics.

Nonetheless, given the presence of phonological parallelism, we should not discount the contribution of *rhythm* to biblical parallelism. Indeed, recently, more and more scholars recognize what B. Hrushovski calls "free rhythm," that is, an effect created not by accent only but by a combination of a variety of parallelisms.[103] If this is correct, it is more likely to find parallelistic connections in terms of rhythm than in terms of meter.

Nevertheless, the uncertainties pertinent to the Hebrew metrics are more an advantage than a disadvantage. In some cultures poems are not easy to translate because their essence is often inextricable from their rhyme and meter.[104] But it is not so with Hebrew poetry. As we can approach it on the semantic and grammatical level, we can reproduce the poetry without losing much of its essence.[105]

---

103. Hrushovski notes how various types of parallelism (semantic, syntax and accent) relate freely to each other in a variety of ways in different bicola (lines) so as to create free rhythm ("Prosody, Hebrew," 1201). See also Hrushovski, "Free Rhythm," 1960), 173–190; esp p. 189. Agreeing with Hrushovski is Alter (*Art of Biblical Poetry*, 7–8). Kugel views semantic parallelism as a kind of "meter": "to speak of meter apart from parallelism is to misunderstand parallelism" (*Idea of Biblical Poetry*, 298).

104. Among others are some of the *Tang Poems*, Chinese couplets and Malay pantun.

105. This was noted as early as Lowth (*Lectures on Sacred Poetry*, 1:70–71). See also Gillingham, *Poems and Psalms*, 73.

4

Figurative Language

As discussed in chapter 1, though not unique to poetic language, figurative language is prominent and pervasive in Hebrew poetry. Therefore, to understand Hebrew poetry, it is necessary to be familiar with this feature.

THE RELATIONSHIP BETWEEN IMAGES AND FIGURATIVE LANGUAGE

Figurative language is complex and modern studies of biblical figurative language have gone through a century-long development. In the course of the development, discussions have moved from the surface phenomena of figurative language to its deeper structure, from its physical, concrete images to its conceptual phenomenon. We will begin with the surface phenomena.

Images and Words

Frequently, pictures represent something better than words do. For example, no words can represent the grandeur of the Grand Canyon or the picturesque Swiss Alps more than images shot by a camera. This is a universal notion, as testified by adages across different cultures, such as the English well-known adage: "A picture is worth a thousand words." These adages suggest that thoughts are often better visualized than spoken. In other words, thoughts are more effectively expressed through images than words. This is especially so to artists. The great paintings such as Da Vinci's *Mona Lisa* or Monet's *Water Lilies* still "speak" today, even after their creators are long gone. In fact, recent biblical scholarship has explored the impact of the visual exegesis displayed in paintings such as Rembrandt's *Bathsheba*, Matthias Stom's *Isaac Blessing Jacob*, and even the watercolor works on Job by William Blake.[1] Apparently, many ideas, especially intangible ones, are made vivid and better understood when concretized with images. Of course, to today's young generation, the power of images is self-explanatory. As the media can testify, meanings are more often visualized than spoken.

From Words to Images: Figurative Language

Ironically, though images frequently work better than words, frequently it takes words to evoke images. This is especially true for poetry. So C. Day Lewis defines poetic image this way: "In its simplest terms, it is a picture made out of words."[2] Norman Friedman offers a better definition: "in literary usage, imagery refers to images produced in the mind by language."[3] In literature, pictures made out of language are called *imagery* or *figurative language*.[4] This being the case, images are a kind of figurative language. As Lewis writes, "Every image . . . is to some degree metaphorical."[5] In the same vein, Watson notes that imagery is a device for "evoking pictures with figurative language."[6]

Figurative Language with No Images

It should be pointed out that whereas imagery is most of the time metaphorical, not every metaphor is imagery (namely, figurative meaning grounded on a physical image).[7] Figurative language is not always derived from

---

1. For example, The Blackwell Bible Commentaries pays attention to the influence of biblical text on art, literature and films. See also Bal, *Reading "Rembrandt"*; Drury, *Painting the Word*; O'Kane, "Bible through the Visual Arts," 388–409.

2. Day Lewis, *Poetic Image*, 18.

3. Friedman, "Imagery," 363. It is a better definition because as we will soon see, imagery is not confined to the word level, but also sentence, even cognitive (deep) level.

4. Friedman classifies imagery into three categories: mental imagery, imagery generated by words (figurative language), and imagery involving symbolism (ibid.). The first two categories will overlap each other in our discussion of biblical figurative language.

5. Day Lewis, *Poetic Image*, 18.

6. Watson, *Classical Hebrew Poetry*, 251.

7. Ibid.

visualized images, but also from "things" that cannot be visualized, such as smell and feeling. G. B. Caird cites Robert Burns's poem to illustrate this:

> O my Love is like the melodie,
> That's sweetly play'd in tune.[8]

As Caird points out, the remark that likens the lover to sweet melody is figurative, but not derived from any image (melody is sound rather than image; sweetness is about taste rather than figure).[9] Critics have also argued that many metaphors are based on conceptual correspondences rather than on images, such as "he is in the *pink* of health," "my income *fell* last year," or "the prices keep *going up*."[10]

Nevertheless, the close association between imagery and figurative language is not to be ignored. Though images are not the basis of all figurative language, in many cases figurative language is indeed derived from images. This is especially true of Hebrew poetry. Intangible ideas such as God's protection is expressed by "shield" (as in "But you, Yahweh, are a shield about me," Ps 3:3), and his provision by "shepherd" (as in "Yahweh is my shepherd, I lack nothing," Ps 23:1).

For this reason, it is not surprising that the terms *imagery, figurative language*, and *metaphor* are interconnected and often used interchangeably by scholars.[11] For our purposes, we will primarily use the term *figurative language*, while at times *metaphor* will also be used as and when contextually appropriate.

---

8. From Burns, "My Love Is Like a Red Red Rose," cited in Caird, *Language and Imagery*, 150.

9. Ibid., 149–50.

10. Note that "health," "income" and "prices" are not physical images. See Lakoff and Johnson, "Conceptual Metaphor," 454. This article is reprinted in *Philosophical Perspectives on Metaphor*, 296–300; and parts of it are used in Lakoff and Johnson, *Metaphors We Live By*.

11. Some scholars (e.g., Friedman, "Imagery," 363–70; Watson, *Classical Hebrew Poetry*, 251) see imagery as distinct from metaphor, but covers both metaphor and simile. But others (e.g., Johnson, "Introduction," 3–47, esp. p. 5) use "figurative language" and "metaphor" interchangeably. Intriguingly, for Alonso-Schökel figurative language means imagery, and "figures of speech" refers to literary devices such as irony, sarcasm, and hyperbole (*Manual of Hebrew Poetics*, 95–169).

FIGURATIVE LANGUAGE: LANGUAGE OF THE POET OR THE MAN ON THE STREET?

Given the close association between figurative language and poetry, people in general assume figurative language is the language of poets or those gifted in the art of literature. This assumption is only half true. As a matter of fact, figurative language is everybody's language.

Everyday Figurative Language

George Lakoff (a linguist) and Mark Johnson (a philosopher) point out: "metaphor is pervasive in everyday life, not just in language but in thought and action."[12] In other words, figurative language permeates all aspects of life. One may be surprised by the amount of figurative expressions we use in our ordinary life. These everyday figurative expressions are generally called "lexicalized" figurative language (also called dead or frozen metaphor).[13] They are so common that we use them without realizing that they are figurative. Think of "the leg of a table," "the arm of the chair," "the head of the country," "the foot of the hill," and "a hot-tempered person." In English, the color pink is used to describe good health: "he is in the pink of health." In Chinese, one of the four seasons is used to describe youthfulness: "spring." Among young people, a common metaphor today is "cool," as in "the new cellphone is cool."

The everyday nature of figurative language is also evidenced by the fact that it is universal. Frequently, equivalent figurative expressions for a particular sense are found across cultures. Think of the following metaphorical expressions which refer to an incorrigible personality: "A leopard never changes its spots" (English, cf. Jer 13:23); "It is like trying to straighten the monkey's tail" (Malay); "It is easier to move rivers and mountains than changing one's personality" (Chinese). These idioms are widely used daily in their respective cultures, by poets as well as the person on the street.

Stock Figurative Language

Being everyday language, lexicalized figurative expressions belong to everybody, poets and non-poets. Some of these everyday figurative expressions

12. Lakoff and Johnson, "Conceptual Metaphor in Everyday Language," 454.

13. In terms of originality, Watson classifies biblical metaphor into lexicalized, conventionalized and creative metaphors (*Classical Hebrew Poetry*, 264); whereas Alter categorizes it into conventional, intensive and innovative (*Art of Biblical Poetry*, 237).

may have found their way into the stock metaphors of the biblical poets, and are variously called "conventionalized metaphors," or "conventional imagery."[14] Thus the Genesis author uses the metaphor "seed" to refer to offspring (e.g., Gen 3:15; 12:7; 13:16); various biblical authors frequently use the "grass" simile to describe the transience of life (Ps 37:2; 90:5; 103:15; Isa 40:6–8), or the wing metaphor to describe God's protection (Ps 17:8; Ruth 2:12). The fact that these are stock figurative expressions is evidenced by their being used repeatedly and widely by different biblical authors of different eras.

Creative Figurative Language

There are, however, figurative expressions which are not commonly used by the man on the street, but by those who are more imaginative and creative, such as poets. Poets exercise their creative mind in one of the following ways. Firstly, they use a stock metaphor in a fresh way, usually by building something on the old.[15] Biblical poets demonstrate such creativity in figurative expressions which Watson calls "a worn-out expression given a new twist."[16] Alter argues that such expressions are "the most figurative mode par excellence of prophetic poetry." He calls them "intensive" imagery, as they are usually used to intensify the sense of the everyday metaphorical expressions.[17] For example, Isaiah intensifies the grass metaphor in Isa 40:6–8:[18]

> All flesh is grass,
>> and all its loveliness is like the flower of the field.
> Grass withers, flower fades,
>> when the breath of Yahweh blows upon it.
> Surely the people are grass.
> Grass withers, flower fades,
>> but the word of our God stands forever.

In the first colon we have the typical grass metaphor (40:6a). The conventional metaphor is intensified first by the flower metaphor, then by the repetition of "grass withers, flower fades" (twice). This is further intensified by

---

14. So Watson, *Classical Hebrew Poetry*, 264; Alter, *Art of Biblical Poetry*, 237.

15. Hrushovski, "Poetic Metaphor," 34.

16. Watson, *Classical Hebrew Poetry*, 264.

17. Alter, *Art of Biblical Poetry*, 237.

18. Ibid., 237, 239. Watson cites the stock metaphor depicting God as lion in Amos 1:2 (*Classical Hebrew Poetry*, 24–65).

the reference to the power of God's breath on grass and flowers and finally by the permanence of God's word. In Jer 17:8 we find an intensification of a stock simile also found in Ps 1:3:[19]

> He is like a tree transplanted by the water,
> which extends its roots by a stream.
> It does not fear when heat comes,
> for its leaves remain green;
> In the year of drought it is not anxious,
> for it does not cease to bear fruit.

Note that the tree-by-the-water simile is intensified by adding the following cola: "which extends its roots by a stream," "does not fear when heat comes," "in the year of drought it is not anxious," and so on.

The second kind of creative figurative language is a new invention. Alter notes that such language reflects the poet's extraordinary imagination, the rarest among the two categories, but found in high concentration in Job.[20] In Job 10:10 the poet portrays the forming of Job in his mother's womb through some creative images:

> Did you pour me out like milk,
> like cheese did you curdle me?

Also in Job 19:22, where Job uses such creativity to satirize his friends' criticism:

> Why do you, like God, pursue me?
> Why are you not satisfied with my flesh?

Here the poet transforms the otherwise ordinary verb *śābaʾ* (to be satisfied) into a horrific image of cannibalism, intimating the perverted nature of Job's friends' criticism.

---

19. As Creach has demonstrated, the question of whether Ps 1:3 borrows from Jer 17:7–8 or vice versa is debatable ("Like a Tree Planted," 36–39). In our opinion, the debate is inconclusive. But it is reasonable to suggest, as Carroll does, that the language similarity between the two texts may be more likely due to the conventional nature of the tree simile rather than literary dependency (*Jeremiah*, 351).

20. So Alter, *Art of Biblical Poetry*, 237.

FIGURATIVE LANGUAGE: MERE RHETORIC OR EXTENSION OF TRUTH?

Besides the assumption that figurative language is the language of the literary arts, many people also think that figurative expressions are only a rhetorical or stylistic device to make one's proposition persuasive. As such, they play only a decorative role, as Weiss disapprovingly describes it: "like cherries tastefully arranged on a cake."[21] This implies that even if the figurative expressions are removed from a poem, the proposition will remain intact. This, however, has been challenged in modern scholarship. The debate can be traced back to the ancient Greeks.

The Debate among the Ancient Greeks

The ancient Greeks utilized figurative language mainly as a rhetorical device in mythology and poetry.[22] The Greek poet Plato (428–348 BCE) is known for his skill of metaphor, so much so he is called "the master of metaphor."[23] But Plato was also a philosopher; and ironically, his philosophical side views poetry and metaphor as inferior vehicles of truth. In his opinion, poetry (and metaphor) imitates things without knowing reality and they cater to irrational emotions rather than the mind.[24]

His student Aristotle (384–322 BCE), however, disagrees with him. In defense of poetry, Aristotle gives an extended philosophical treatment of poetry and metaphor in his lectures which are now known as *Poetics*.[25] While Aristotle asserts the significant role of metaphor both in poetry and rhetoric, of interest is his discussion of poetic metaphor. For him, metaphor is an artistic representation (mimesis) of reality. Contrary to his teacher, Aristotle argues that when the poet imitates, he is imitating something very real, in fact, mimicking real life experience.[26]

---

21. Weiss, *Bible from Within*, 130; for him, metaphor is much more than just literary decoration.

22. Johnson, "Introduction," 4.

23. Ibid.

24. Plato equates the effect of poetry to sex, anger and other emotions, making people out of control (*Republic*, X, 597e, 606d). Johnson avers that Plato is concerned about the misuse of metaphor that leads people away from truth ("Introduction," 4–5).

25. So Else, "Introduction," 4. In our discussion, citations are primarily based on Aristotle, *Poetics I* (1987).

26. Aristotle (*Poetics*, 1447a, 1447b, 1448b) notes that representation (imitating) of reality is natural to human beings from birth; and that humans learn through images. Representation of real life experience can be in terms of colors and shapes (such as in

The Debate from Medieval through Modern Eras

While ancient Greco-Roman rhetoricians and medieval theologians continued to speak of metaphor, there had not been significant theoretical development after Aristotle.[27] Medieval theologians spoke of it because they had to offer an explanation for the use of figurative language in Scripture. The well-known thirteenth-century theologian Thomas Aquinas (1224–1274) affirmed that the use of figurative language is both "necessary and useful" for doctrinal teaching. He wrote that it is appropriate for Scripture to "convey divine and spiritual things through bodily likeness," because "it is natural for human beings to arrive at what is intelligible through what is sensible, since our knowledge originates in sensation";[28] only that one should not misuse it.[29] Interestingly, despite such an affirmation, there were no studies done on biblical figurative language during the long medieval period.

In the post-medieval period, the positivism of the Enlightenment led to the diminished significance of figurative language in philosophy. As they viewed figurative language as mere rhetorical device, thinkers such as Thomas Hobbes and John Locke looked at rhetoric and metaphor with deep suspicion. They contended that being rhetoric, metaphor distorts rather than promotes truth and knowledge.[30] Though other thinkers such as Kant and Nietzsche affirmed the importance of figurative language, there was no significant development, not until the mid-twentieth century.

Beginning from the twentieth century, scholars such as I. A. Richards and Max Black challenged the Enlightenment excesses and argued that metaphor is part of human cognition.[31] Their effort has not gone in vain. Today, figurative language is no more the pariah of scholarship, but "the real stuff of philosophy, the domain where issues of meaning and truth arise and can be dealt with."[32] Figurative language is not viewed as a rhetorical device to work up people's emotions (though it can be used this way), but as an integral part of human cognition. Recent scholarship speaks of figurative language not only as the language of the literary art, but also the language of linguistics, philosophy and science.[33] Thus figurative language is not just

---

painting), sound (such as in music and speech).

27. Johnson, "Introduction," 8–9.

28. Thomas Aquinas, *ST* I, 1, 9.

29. Ibid., I, 13, 6.

30. See Johnson, "Introduction," 11–13.

31. Richards, *Philosophy of Rhetoric*, 90–93; Black, "Metaphor," 64; see also, Martin, "Metaphor," 762–66.

32. Lakoff and Johnson, "Conceptual Metaphor in Everyday Language," 453.

33. Quine gives some examples of metaphors in science: scientific terms such as

the language of the man on the street and the poet, but also the scientist. As will be discussed, this development will have significant implications for biblical studies.

Figurative Language and Modern Biblical Studies

Prior to the mid-twentieth century, the excesses of the Enlightenment found in philosophy were also evident in modern biblical scholarship. Old Testament scholars were primarily interested in issues related to the composition history of biblical books (historical criticism); as a result, biblical metaphor was a neglected topic. Nevertheless, compared to the field of philosophy, metaphor faced less resistance in biblical studies. As early as the eighteenth century, Lowth addressed the subject in his *Lectures on the Sacred Poetry of the Hebrews*. Unfortunately, in his extensive treatment of the subject (in four lectures, lectures 6–9)[34] no significant contribution was made. For Lowth, "poetic imagery" is more or less a rhetorical tool, playing only a decorative role in Hebrew poetry.[35]

The importance of biblical figurative language began to get the attention of biblical scholars upon the rise of literary approaches to the Bible in the mid-twentieth century. James Muilenburg is one of the pioneers of literary approaches. In his SBL presidential address published in 1969, Muilenburg drew attention to the importance of rhetorical devices employed by biblical poets.[36] As a new generation of biblicists were drawn to biblical rhetorical devices, metaphor began to be more widely noticed and intensively studied.[37] As will be shown below, soon studies of biblical figurative

---

"bodies of gas," and "light waves" ("A Postscript on Metaphor," 161). Figurative language is evident in computer science and information technology, such as "memory," "disk," "virus," "bug," "command," "menu," "download" and so on. For more discussion of metaphor in science, see Kuhn, "Metaphor in Science," 409–19.

34. Lowth, *Lectures on Sacred Poetry*, 1:120–213.

35. Lowth views the purpose of Hebrew figurative language as a stylistic device to elevate poetic writings to the "sublime" (ibid., 1:120).

36. Muilenburg, "Form Criticism and Beyond," 8–18.

37. In 1987 Croft notes that few authors had written on the importance of metaphor in Psalms or religious language (*Identity of the Individual*, 53). As a matter of fact, Watson offers a long list of books and articles on biblical metaphor during the 1950s to 1980s (*Classical Hebrew Poetry*, 253–54). Weiss devotes a long section to the imagery in Psalm 1 (*Bible from Within*, 130–63). See also Caird offers a book-length treatment of the subject (*Language and Imagery*). See also Alter, *Art of Biblical Poetry*, 231–54; Landy, *Paradoxes of Paradise*, 183–265. Since 1990s more works on biblical metaphor have appeared. E.g., collections of essays in Camp and Fontaine, eds. *Woman, War and Metaphor*; van Hecke, ed. *Metaphor in the Hebrew Bible*; Forti, "Bee's Honey," 327–41.

language would catch up with the development of metaphor theories in linguistics and philosophy. This in turn would make important contributions to the studies of biblical figurative language. One significant contribution is that recent biblical scholarship does not see figurative language as a mere rhetorical device, but an integral part of human cognition and therefore crucial for our understanding of biblical theology.

THE CLASSICAL CLASSIFICATION OF FIGURATIVE LANGUAGE: SIMILE AND METAPHOR

Having recognized the crucial role of figurative language, we are now ready to familiarize ourselves further with it. We will start with the classification of figurative language. The classification of figurative language can be traced back as early as the ancient Greeks. Aristotle, for example, divides figurative expressions into two categories: metaphor and simile. Today English literature critics offer more details and consequently more categories. They sum up figurative language into seven categories: simile, metaphor, synecdoche, metonymy, personification, allegory and symbol.[38] As for biblical figurative language, some scholars suggest that simile and metaphor are the basic and primary types, and the rest are elaborations or extensions of one of these two types.[39] We will focus on these basic types of figurative language in the following discussion.

Aristotle's Classification

As commented earlier, Aristotle speaks of figurative language in terms of two categories: metaphor and simile. For him, the difference between the two is minimal, as he observes:

> The simile is also a metaphor, the difference is but slight. When the poet says of Achilles that he "leapt on the foe as a lion," this is a simile; when he says "the lion leapt," it is a metaphor.[40]

According to this definition, the difference between metaphor and simile lies in whether or not "as" or "like" is used: the one with "as" or "like" is a simile, the one without is a metaphor. For Aristotle then, metaphor is

38. Friedman, "Imagery," 560.

39. Caird, *Language and Imagery*, 145; Watson, *Classical Hebrew Poetry*, 269.

40. Aristotle thinks that metaphor is a word whose usage is "altered from the everyday" (*Rhetoric* 1406b).

an abbreviated simile. This concept had been adopted by many for centuries until it was critiqued by philosophers such as Paul Ricoeur.[41]

Simile

Jacqueline Vaught Brogan defines simile as follows: "a figure of speech most conservatively defined as explicit comparison using 'like' or 'as.'"[42] Following this definition, simile can be identified by at least two indicators. The first one is *explicit comparison*; the second one is the *comparative marker* that makes it explicit: "like" or "as." So in English we have "His eyes are *like* saucers"; or "His eyes are *as* big *as* saucers." Here someone's eyes are *compared* to the size of saucers. In Chinese we have "strong as a cow," in which someone's strength is compared to that of a cow.[43] Similarly, in Hebrew simile is marked by comparison and the use of the Hebrew particle *kĕ* or *kĕmô* (like, as), *māšal* (to be like).[44] Ps 1:3 compares the righteous to a tree: "he is *like* a tree planted by the streams of water"; Ps 10:9 compares the wicked to a lion: "He lurks in a hiding place *as* a lion in his lair."

Metaphor

Compared with simile, metaphor is more difficult to identify. One reason is that it is more concise and vaguer than simile.[45] Following Aristotle's definition, simile gives the reader a clue by using comparative markers such as "as" or "like." But metaphor, being less explicit, does not offer the reader such explicit indicators. The reader is left to decide whether or not a particular expression is metaphorical.

In some cases, we recognize a metaphor as we see it. We know that "barking up the wrong tree" is metaphorical even without markers such as "like" or "as." However, in other cases, it is not so straightforward. It is one thing to say "Elina is *like* a rose"; it is another to say "Elina *is* a rose."

---

41. Ricoeur argues, among other things, that whereas metaphor involves transfer of meaning, no transfer of meaning occurs in a simile (*Rule of Metaphor*, 186). E.g., in the simile "Jim is as stubborn as a mule," every word retains its meaning; this is unlike the metaphor "Jim is a mule," in which the characteristics of the mule are transferred to Jim.

42. Brogan, "Simile," 1149.

43. In English, at times comparative markers such as "resemble," "seem," or "as if" are also used. So in English we have "She has eyes resemble dove"; "everyday seems a lifetime"; "He was stunned, as if dead."

44. Watson, *Classical Hebrew Poetry*, 257–58.

45. Ibid., 255.

In the former we can be certain that we have a simile (as indicated by the comparative marker "like"). But in the latter we are not sure if we have a metaphor, because there is a kind of rose named "Elina."[46] This case suggests that context is important for determining whether or not an expression is metaphorical and what it means. Song 2:2 is an example:

> *Like* a lily among the thorns,
> so is my darling among the maidens.

This simile is preceded by two metaphors in Song 2:1:

> I am the rose of Sharon,
> the lily of the valleys.

Note that in the latter example markers such as "like" and "as" are absent. But read in its context (especially in view of Song 2:2), we know that we have a metaphor. If anything, all these examples remind us of the importance of understanding how figurative language works.

UNDERSTANDING HOW FIGURATIVE LANGUAGE WORKS

Interestingly, though people use figurative language every day, not many of them know or care to know how it really works. However, since figurative language is part of the make-up of Hebrew poetry, it is necessary for the student of Hebrew poetry to understand how it works. A sketch of scholarly discussion of the subject is therefore in order.

The Binary Nature of Figurative Language

As the idiom goes, "It takes two to tango"; so does figurative language. Like parallelism, figurative language involves the relationship of two entities.[47] To be precise, two kinds of relationship are involved. The first kind is between two subjects, which Black calls *principal* subject and *subsidiary* subject.[48] The remark "Yahweh is my shepherd" (Ps 23:1) involves two subjects:

---

46. *Elina* is a light yellow hybrid rose introduced by Patrick Dickson of Northern Ireland in 1983.

47. Petersen and Richards, *Interpreting Hebrew Poetry*, 50. Johnson speaks of the two entities in terms of A and B, reminding us of Kugel's terminology of parallelism ("Introduction," 24).

48. Black, "Metaphor," 77.

Yahweh (the principal subject) and shepherd (the subsidiary subject). The second kind of relationship is between *the thing said* and *the thing meant*. In the remark "Yahweh is my shepherd," "shepherd" is the thing said, and divine provision is the thing meant.

Philosophers and literary critics use different labels in the second kind of relationship. Aristotle speaks of metaphor as "the application of a name belonging to something else,"[49] that is, applying the thing meant to the thing said. Paul Henle speaks of it in terms of the *literal* and the *figurative*.[50] I. A. Richards speaks of "two halves of a metaphor," calling the first half *vehicle* (the thing said) and the other half *tenor* (the thing meant).[51] So in the case of the metaphorical expression "Yahweh is my shepherd," "shepherd" is the vehicle, and divine provision is the tenor (see figure 1).

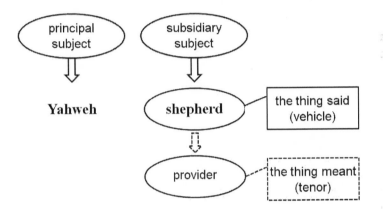

Likewise, in the case of "He is like a tree planted by streams of water" (Ps 1:3) the word "tree" is the vehicle, and the tenor is the idea of vitality (as elaborated in the rest of Ps 1:3). Whatever one calls the two entities, the mechanism between them is crucial to the workings of figurative language.

Figurative Meaning: A Mechanism of Binary Relationships

The figurative sense is created by the mechanism between two entities (i.e., in a binary relationship). The challenge for the reader is to decide what kind of mechanism it is. Principally, the debate in the past century has been whether it is a one-way mechanism or multi-way mechanism. The former

49. Aristotle, *Poetics*, 1457b.
50. Henle, "Metaphor," 84. Cf. Martin, "Metaphor," 760.
51. Richards, *Philosophy of Rhetoric*, 96.

assumes that figurative meaning is created through a transfer of characteristics from the subsidiary subject to the principal subject. When one says,
"God is my fortress," they transfer a characteristic of fortresses (defense or
protection) to God (i.e., applying the fortress's characteristic to God).

The latter, however, assumes a two-way or multi-way movement
between the entities, in which the characteristics of both subjects *interact*
with each other. Following this view, in the remark "God is my fortress"
the transfer of the fortress's characteristic is made possible by not just the
defensive function of the fortress, but also by God's ability of defending or
protecting people. This being the case, the transfer involves the characteristics of both subjects, not just one; thus it is a two-way rather than one-way
mechanism. Consequently, while the one-way position views metaphor
as a transfer of characteristics from one subject to another, the two-way
or multi-way stresses the dynamics between the two subjects in a broader
context. The former mechanism has led to approaches to metaphor on *the
surface level*, the latter mechanism to approaches on the *conceptual level*.[52]
We will first discuss the former. For argument purposes, we will call the
transfer approach.[53]

The Surface Approach: Metaphor as a Transfer of Comparable Characteristics

Transfer approaches analyze the mechanism between the two entities
on the surface level, treating it on the "syntactic, surface level of literary
composition."[54] In other words, this approach assumes that figurative meaning is created within the syntactical relationship of a single metaphorical
expression. Basically, such an approach focuses on two issues: *What makes
transfer possible? What is being transferred?*

The transfer view does not assume that figurative language works by
transferring *all* the characteristics of the subsidiary subject to the principal
subject. Rather it works on the basis that it transfers only some *comparable
characteristics*. In the simile "he is like a tree planted by the streams of water" (Ps 1:3), nobody assumes that all the characteristics of a waterside tree
are transferred to the righteous person, but only their comparable qualities
(such as life and vigor). In the case of the metaphor "the leg of the table,"

---

52. For these terms, see Jindo, *Biblical Metaphor Reconsidered*, 35.

53. This traditional approach has been variously called the comparison theory
(Johnson, "Metaphor: An Overview," 3:208), or the similarity position (Lakoff and
Johnson, *Metaphors We Live By*, 214).

54. Jindo, *Biblical Metaphor Reconsidered*, 35.

only one characteristic of animate legs is transferable to the inanimate table: the standing function. The comparable characteristics are normally based on images or observable features: the external characteristics of a healthy tree (as represented by green foliage and fruitfulness), or the visible function of a table leg.

Substitute and Comparison Views

The foregoing discussion highlights for us that the tenor (figurative meaning) is created by a transfer of comparable characteristics from the subsidiary subject to the principal subject. This fact has led to the question how exactly the transferred characteristics become the tenor. The question has been answered two ways. The first is called the *substitute view*. According to this view, when a characteristic of the subsidiary subject is transferred (or applied) to the principal subject, a *substitution* takes place: the subsidiary subject becomes the substitute for the transferred characteristic. In other words, for the substitute view, metaphorical meaning occurs as the vehicle becomes the substitute for the tenor. Aristotle's definition of metaphor seems to fit this view:

> Metaphor is *the application of a name belonging to something else*, either from genus to species, or from species to genus, or from species to species, or on grounds of analogy.[55]

In the same vein, Richard Whately defines metaphor as "a word substituted for another on account of the Resemblance or Analogy between their significations."[56] Take for example the metaphor "God is my fortress." When a characteristic of the fortress (e.g., protection) is applied (transferred) to God, "fortress" (vehicle) is a substitute for divine protection (tenor). In other words, instead of saying "God is my *protection*," one says, "God is my *fortress*." As such "fortress" (the subsidiary subject) is substitute for "protection" (tenor), as illustrated in figure 2 below:

---

55. Aristotle, *Poetics*, 1457b; italics for emphasis.
56. Whately, *Elements of Rhetoric*, 280, cited in Black, "Metaphor," 68.

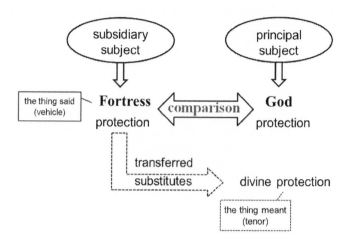

The second view is called the *comparison view*. This view also sees metaphor as the result of substitution, but draws attention to the *comparison of the shared characteristics* of the principal and subsidiary subjects. For this reason, Black calls the comparison view "a special case of a 'substitution view.'"[57] As it is also based on similarity (i.e., comparable characteristics), this view may also be another version of the Aristotelian definition of metaphor, for Aristotle speaks of metaphor as transference of meanings based on similarity: "Metaphor is the application of a name belonging to something else. . .on *grounds of analogy*." In a way, it is also reflected in Whately's definition: "a word substituted for another on account of the *Resemblance* or *Analogy* between their significations."

What distinguishes this view from the substitute view even more is perhaps its use of "like" or "as" to compare the principal and subsidiary subjects. This, then, results in explicit metaphor, that is, simile. As such, according to the comparison view, metaphor is "condensed or elliptical simile."[58] Also, perhaps for this reason Whately thinks that simile is different from metaphor *only in form*: in simile similarity is stated explicitly (by "like" or "as"), whereas in metaphor it is implied.[59] Black also notes that the main difference between the substitution view and the comparison view is like the difference between simile and metaphor. To express someone's bravery, for example, the substitution view would say, "David is a lion"; whereas the comparison view would say, "David is *like* a lion (in being brave)."[60]

57. Black, "Metaphor," 71.
58. Ibid.
59. Whately, *Elements of Rhetoric*, 280; cited in Black, "Metaphor," 71.
60. Black, "Metaphor," 71.

Application of Transfer Approaches to Biblical Studies

Studies of biblical figurative language in the twentieth century mainly follow the traditional substitute and comparative models. Petersen and Richards's discussion is one example. In *Interpreting Hebrew Poetry* they intriguingly focus on similes only, basing their argument on a small pool of data.[61] The fact that they follow the comparison view is evidenced by their definition of simile: "A simile is a figure of speech in which two entities are compared. The comparison is normally created . . . by an indicator of resemblance, such as the word 'like' or 'as,'"[62] as in Hos 6:3c:[63]

His going out is as certain as the dawn.

Also, the bicolon simile in Hos 10:7:[64]

Samaria's king will perish,
like a splinter on the surface of the waters.

Alonso-Schökel's detailed discussion of biblical "images" is another example of the comparison model. As the word "images" suggests, for him, metaphor is mainly derived from physical images.[65] He speaks of the mechanism of the two entities (what is said and what is meant) in terms of "two panels" of an image.[66] Alonso-Schökel is aware that the mechanism comes in a whole lot of variety: it may be a correlation between two perceived subjects, or between "the spiritual and the sensed object," or between "the abstract and the concrete," or between "the transcendent and the empirical."[67] All these pairs of panels create figurative meaning by comparing their similarities[68] which at times involves substitution.[69]

61. The sample data is limited to similes in Hosea. See Petersen and Richards, *Interpreting Hebrew Poetry*, 50–60.

62. Ibid., 50.

63. Ibid., 51.

64. Ibid.

65. Alonso-Schökel can be confusing at times. Sometimes he notes that metaphor is not necessarily based on images, yet frequently, his discussion and examples emphasize images captured by human senses (*Manual of Hebrew Poetics*, 95–97, 100, 114). One example is the metaphor of the fool in Prov 27:3. He contends that the metaphor is not "perceived by the senses, seen or touched"; yet in the same breath he comments: "The image is very clear, and presents very effectively the feelings we have towards such a person."

66. Ibid., 96.

67. Ibid., 95–96.

68. Ibid., 105–6.

69. Following Ricoeur, Alonso-Schökel mentions in passing that the substitute in

The transfer approach works well with figurative expressions that evidently involve comparison. A few examples from Alonso-Schökel will illustrate this. As a case of comparison, Alonso-Schökel cites the simile in Prov 25:13:[70]

> Like the coldness of snow in the time of harvest,
> a faithful messenger to those who send him.
> He refreshes the soul of his masters

Evidently, the comparative marker "like" suggests a comparison: a messenger who faithfully accomplishes his mission is likened to the refreshing coldness of snow in harvest time.[71] Following Alonso-Schökel, the refreshing coldness would be a substitute for "snow." Another example is the metaphor in Prov 25:18:

> A war club, and a sword, and a sharp arrow,
> a man bearing false witness against his neighbor.

Though without "like," it is evident that false witnessing is compared to the deadly weapons of war (club, sword, and arrow).[72]

Caird's approach is explicitly comparative. He speaks of biblical figurative language in terms of explicit comparison (i.e., simile) and implicit comparison (i.e., metaphor) between two entities.[73] But Caird stresses that it is important to identify what aspects of the two things are being compared, because "when two things are compared, they are not to be considered like [sic] in all respects."[74] When the psalmist of Psalm 133 says that a family unity is like oil dripping down Aaron's beard onto the collars of his robes (Ps 133:2), he does not mean that family unity is messy and greasy. The comparison does not involve what one sees, but what one smells (the fragrance of the anointing oil).[75] Therefore, for Caird it is important to identify the "points of comparison."

Caird goes further to propose that we should be familiar with points of comparison of the two entities. Caird divides points of comparison into four

---

fact brings in a whole set of new connotations (ibid., 108). But he stops short of elaborating it further.

70. Ibid., 106.

71. As harvest time in ancient Israel (between April and May) is not in winter, snow would be considered refreshing.

72. Alonso-Schökel, *Manual of Hebrew Poetics*, 106.

73. Caird, *Language and Imagery*, 144.

74. Ibid., 145.

75. Ibid.

classes: perceptual, synaesthetic, affective, and pragmatic.[76] By perceptual he means characteristics perceived by the five senses: the moon will turn "into blood" (sight, Joel 2:31); the laughter of the fool is like "the crackling of thorn bushes under a pot" (sound, Eccl 7:6). Synaesthesia is a subcategory of the perceptual, referring to a characteristic indirectly related to the senses: "He has made my mouth like a *sharp sword* (Isa 49:2); "His speech was *smooth as butter*" (Ps 55:21). Affective comparisons refer to the feel, value, impression, or effect of one thing compared to that of another: Jeremiah's heartache felt like an incurable wound (Jer 15:18); Belshazzar is weighed and "found deficient" (Dan 5:27). The pragmatic refers to comparisons of activity or effect: the throats of the wicked gape like an open grave (Ps 5:9); love is headier than wine (like the effect of alcohol, Song 1:2).

Caird's attention to points of comparison is helpful in dealing with some poetic figurative expressions such as the ones in Song 4:4:

> Your neck is like the tower of David,
>
> built in rows of stone.
>
> On it hang a thousand shields,
>
> all of them shields of warriors.

It is self-explanatory that taking the perceptual as the point of comparison would be disastrous. Instead, as Caird notes, the point of comparison is affective (impression). What the poet compares here is the *impression* of "tower," "stone," "shields," not *what they look like*. This is suggested by the context: the use of war metaphor (tower, shield and warriors). Read in this context, the poet seems to compare the girl's chastity to a strong defense system, suggesting her virginal inaccessibility.[77] This case suggests the importance of context for reading biblical figurative language, a subject we will now turn to.

Context and Transfer Approaches

Scholars recognize the importance of context for understanding figurative language. Richards argues that metaphor is fundamentally "a transaction between contexts."[78] Also, Ina Loewenberg notes that metaphor can

---

76. Ibid., 145–48.

77. Ibid., 148.

78. Though Richards speaks of this in the context of conceptual metaphor (*The Philosophy of Rhetoric*, 94), it is equally true for the traditional views of metaphor. See below.

be discerned only at the level of utterance in its total context.[79] Context is important for understanding figurative language for two reasons. Firstly, it helps us determine whether the sense of a given remark is literal or figurative. In the past this issue was addressed by following Aristotle's theory. Aristotle has suggested that the sense of an expression is figurative only when it is used in a way deviant from its normal sense.[80] Today, however, the theory is found inadequate. This is because we do not always know whether an expression is used in deviant way, unless we know the context.

Therefore, one way to determine if a remark is used in a deviant sense is to see if it is at odds with the context. For example, we know that "His eyes are like saucers" is figurative because it is at odds with the usually known context: "saucers" which belong in the kitchen are now used in the context of human organs (eyes). We also know that the statement "her eyes are as big as mine" is no simile, because it is not at odds with its context (a comparison of two set of human organs in the context of human organs). Similarly, we know "He lurks in a hiding place as a lion in his lair" is a simile because "lion" which belongs to the four-legged mammals is now used in the context of humans ("He").

It may be said that without context, an expression can either be literal or metaphorical.[81] So, "Elina is a rose" remains ambiguous until we are certain of its context. The sense is metaphorical when used in a non-horticultural context; it is non-metaphorical when used in a horticultural context (i.e., referring to the name of a rose in Northern Ireland).

The second reason why context is important is that figurative expression is capable of multiple meanings.[82] A metaphor can be used in various circumstances (contexts), so it has no one fixed meaning. For instance, in England, the expression "to table an item on the agenda" means to bring it up in a discussion; but in the United States, it means to remove it from a discussion.

Likewise, the same biblical figurative expression may mean one thing in one context, but mean another thing in another context. For example, water could mean source of life (Isa 55:1), trouble (Ps 46:3), as well as power (Amos 5:24). At times, a single metaphor can even be used in two opposite and contradictory senses: The wilderness may be a symbol of desolation and demonic power (Isa 13:20–22; 34:13–15), but because of its association with the exodus, it may also be a symbol of innocence, sincerity, liberation and

---

79. Loewenberg, "Identifying Metaphors," 322.

80. Aristotle, *Poetics*, 1458a.

81. Cf. Loewenberg, "Identifying Metaphors," 322.

82. Caird, *Biblical Language and Imagery*, 149.

security under God's providential care (Jer 2:1–2; 31:2). The question now: *How do we identify the context?*

Inter-colon Relationship as Context

There may be several contexts involved in a figurative expression: historical, cultural and literary contexts. As much of biblical Hebrew poetry is remote from its origins, often not much is known about the historical and cultural contexts. What remains fairly obvious to us is the context provided by the text, that is, the literary context. The literary context is especially important for those who take the surface level approaches to figurative language, thus it is no surprise that most commentators depend on it for understanding biblical metaphors.[83]

As figurative expressions are often constructed by more than one colon,[84] the relationship with one colon (in which the figurative expression occurs) with another often serves as context. Often inter-colon relationship (parallelism) helps us determine if an expression is figurative or literal. Zech 10:3 is a case in point:

> My anger is hot against the shepherds,
>
> and I will punish the *he-goats.*

Note that the first colon ("the shepherds," referring to human leaders) provides context for reading "*he-goats*" in the second colon. He-goat, a term usually used in the context of four-legged mammals, is now used to describe creatures in the context of human leadership, suggesting a metaphorical use.

Another example is "the daughter of Zion" (*bat-ṣiyyôn*), an expression with "considerable emotional and conceptual impact" in Hebrew poetry.[85] In some contexts, when it occurs in the singular (*bat-ṣiyyôn*), it is used as a collective term referring to the inhabitants (male and female) of Jerusalem, a personification of and simile for the city Jerusalem (thus metaphorical), as in Mic 4:10:[86]

---

83. For example, Petersen and Richards observe that the meanings of biblical similes depends on "their respective literary contexts" (*Interpreting Hebrew Poetry*, 59).

84. As Watson points out, while biblical figurative expressions may appear in one single colon, often they are constructed in bicolon, tricolon, even at times multi-colon format (*Classical Hebrew Poetry*, 258–60).

85. Follis, "The Holy City as Daughter," 174–75. This expression occurs twenty-six times, all in poetic texts.

86. Cf. Follis, ibid., 176.

Writhe and groan, O daughter of Zion,
like a woman in labor.

In other contexts, especially when it appears in the plural (*běnôt-ṣiyyôn*), the expression refers to the female inhabitants of Jerusalem (thus literal), as in the case of Song 3:11:[87]

Go out, O daughters of Zion,
and look upon King Solomon.

As inter-colon relationships are generally parallelistic in nature, here we see the synergy between figurative language and parallelism. Ps 17:8 may serve as a helpful illustration:

Guard me like the apple of your eyes,
in the shadows of your wings conceal me.

Here we have two figurative expressions ("apple of your eyes" and "shadows of your wings") parallel to each other (both refer to protection). As the second colon intensifies the first, it also provides supporting evidence that "apple of your eyes" refers to protection. At times, the second colon serves as the tenor as it clarifies, such as Song 2:2:

Like a lily among the thorns,
so is my darling among the maidens.

Notice that "lily among thorns" is not only parallel to "my darling among the maidens," but also compared to each other by the *like/so* formula. As such we have a simile built into two parallel cola. More importantly, the second colon serves as the referent (tenor) of the first (vehicle).

The relationship between vehicle (what is said) and tenor (what is meant) can be viewed as a semantic as well as a grammatical inter-colon relationship. Commenting on simile, Petersen and Richards note, "just as with all parallelism, [simile] may be paradigmatic or syntagmatic, that is, the vehicle or tenor in one simile may substitute for the vehicle or tenor in the next simile, or the similes may build upon each other."[88] Petersen and Richards cite an example from Hos 10:7:[89]

Samaria's king shall perish,
like a chip on the face of the waters.

87. So Follis, ibid., 174 n2.
88. Petersen and Richards, *Interpreting Hebrew Poetry*, 59.
89. Ibid., 51.

Here the first colon provides the tenor, and the second the vehicle. The following poetic text from Hos 4:16 may serve as an example of one metaphor built on another:

> Like a stubborn heifer,
> stubborn is Israel.
> Will Yahweh feed them,
> like a lamb in broad pasture?

Petersen and Richards observe the parallelism between the two similes on different levels. First, the two similes are expressed by a pair of bicola, with the second building on the first. As such, the two similes are in fact a parallelism constructed by a contiguous (syntagmatic) relationship. Second, in each simile the second colon clarifies the meaning of the second, suggesting a semantic progress. Third, in the first simile we have the vehicle ("like a stubborn heifer"), followed by the tenor ("stubborn is Israel"); in the second metaphor, the tenor comes first ("will Yahweh feed them"), the vehicle later. Thus the two similes are chiastically parallel: vehicle-tenor, tenor-vehicle. Fourth, the subject in the first simile (Israel) is equivalent (parallel) to the subject of the second simile (them). Finally, the subject of the second simile (them) is a substitute for the subject of the first simile (Israel), suggesting a grammatical (paradigmatic) parallelism between the two similes.[90]

Section Summary

Transfer approaches examine figurative language at the syntactic and surface levels of a poetic composition. Key to the approaches is the assumption that figurative meanings are based on the transfer of comparable/analogical surface features. As the approaches take figurative language on the syntactic and surface levels, context then is defined by syntactical and literary relationships. In poetry, such relationships often involve parallelism. In other words, for the transfer approach, context is to be found in parallelism.

Conceptual Approaches to Figurative Language

We will now turn to the second position about the mechanism between the principal and subsidiary subjects: it is a two-way or multi-way movement rather than a one-way movement. This position arose from the discovery

---

90. Ibid., 52.

that transfer approaches offer only a limited account for the mechanism within figurative language.

Limitations of Transfer Approaches

While helpful, transfer approaches have been found inadequate in providing a full account for the mechanism of figurative language in general and many metaphors in particular. Ricoeur, for instance, questions whether what happens between the two entities is a case of transfer. In fact, as he argues, instead of a transfer of some characteristics from one subject to another, what really happens is the creation of a new meaning. Moreover, for Ricoeur, metaphor is not a case of substitution either; rather it is semantic innovation.[91] Following his view, in the case of "God can heal a broken-heart," "broken-heart" is not a substitution for "sorrow"; rather it creates a new meaning. The literal meaning of "brokenness" (i.e., separating a physical object in two or more pieces) is now given a new meaning (sorrow, i.e., emotional pain). This being the case, what happens here is not a case of *transfer* (one-way movement), but of *interplay* between the two subjects that results in a new meaning (thus a two-way movement). Lakoff and Johnson's argument may confirm this observation. Granted that metaphor is grounded in similarities, they argue that the "similarities do not exist independently of the metaphor."[92] In short, it takes two to tango.

Nevertheless, the more significant limitation of transfer approaches is that they fail to explain metaphorical expressions which do not involve apparent transfer or comparison. For instance, in the remark "Your cellphone is cool," one cannot find any comparable characteristics between the electronic device and the term "cool" (low in temperature), also the metaphorical sense of "cool" (i.e., fashionable or attractive) is not the result of transfer. Instead, the meaning is grounded on what critics call conceptual experience, just like orientational metaphors such as "everything is *under* my control," "they are in *high* spirits," and "I'm feeling *down*."[93] Notably, the meanings of these metaphors are not apparent on the surface (not observable in their syntactical structure).

Even Caird's theory of points of comparison, helpful as it is, may sometimes be found inadequate. What point of comparison is at play in the metaphor "Your cellphone is cool"? The metaphorical sense "fashionable" is not based on perceptual points of comparison (e.g., the cellphone looks like

---

91. Ricoeur, "Metaphorical Process," 146, 158.

92. Lakoff and Johnson, *Metaphors We Live By*, 148.

93. Lakoff and Johnson, "Conceptual Metaphor," 461–62.

a cool drink), nor is it based on the affective (e.g., the gadget feels like the cool air from an air-conditioner), nor the pragmatic (e.g., it makes the user feel cool [lower in body temperature]). Obviously, none of these can serve as the grounds for its metaphorical meaning.

The same limitation is observable in the biblical simile "For as the crackling of thorns under a pot, so is the laughter of the fools" (Eccl 7:6), which Caird categorizes under the perceptual point of comparison (transfer of comparable acoustic similarity). Weiss argues that while acoustic effect may be involved, such a treatment misses much of the intended meaning. In light of the theme of vanity that dominates Ecclesiastes, the thorns simile has to be read in the context. Thorns have no value, thus they embody vanity. The flame is bright, the crackling deafens the ears; but at the end of the day, when burned off in smoke, thorns will be blown away by the wind. This is what the laughter of the fool is like: nothing, as indicated at end of the verse "This also is vanity."[94] These thoughts which are related to vanity, however, are not apparent on the surface, because they belong to a "network" that lies below the composition of the text. An analysis such as this highlights how much the traditional approaches miss the larger picture below the surface of the text.

Conceptual Approaches: Metaphor as a Mechanism of Conceptualization

In the last century, it was "the larger picture below the surface of the text" deliberated above that became the focus of some linguists and philosophers in their studies of metaphor. They point out that certain metaphorical expressions are connected by a conceptual network. For instance, the metaphor "Do not spend too much time in computer games" is conceptually connected with other metaphors such as "We should budget time" and "You are wasting my time"; and they are all connected by the basic metaphorical concept "Time is money."[95] Such a network is not immediately apparent on the surface of a text, as it exists below the text, and this explains why we cannot address them by the surface-level approaches (transfer approaches).

Such a notion marks a significant shift in the understanding of figurative language. It suggests that the figurative meaning of certain metaphors is not grounded on the *transference* of some characteristics within a single metaphor (one-way movement), but on an *interplay* within a network of

---

94. Weiss, *The Bible from Within*, 131.

95. See Lakoff and Johnson's discussion below.

metaphors (multi-way movement). This notion serves as the starting point for the conceptual approaches to figurative language.

INTERACTION VIEW

Discussions of conceptual approaches often begin with I. A. Richards and his *interaction* view.[96] Richards does not dismiss the validity of transfer approaches completely, only that he highlights the limitations we pointed out in the previous section. He contends that the comparison view accounts only for a few "modes of metaphor,"[97] failing to account for other modes in which metaphors do not involve comparison of similarities but other relations.[98] To tackle the problem, Richards revises and expands the understanding of the mechanism between the principal and subsidiary subjects. Firstly, instead of seeing the mechanism in terms of *comparison*, he understands it as *interaction*. Secondly, instead of speaking of the entities in terms of two subjects with *common characteristics*, he speaks of two sets of *corresponding thoughts*. Richards argues that metaphor happens when two sets of thoughts interact with each other. As he puts it: "In the simplest formulation, when we use a metaphor we have two thoughts of different things active together and supported by a single word, or phrase, whose meaning is a resultant of their interaction."[99] The interaction takes place in the mind of the reader, in which the reader "connects" the two sets of thoughts.[100]

To understand Richards's theory, it is important to know his view of human thought. For him, thought is a metaphorical process (meaning the mind processes things through metaphors); consequently, metaphor is conceptual.[101] He elaborates on this as he explains what happens in the interaction between the two subjects: the interaction is "*superimposed* upon a perceived world which is itself a product of earlier or unwitting metaphor."[102] This remark is significant in at least two ways. First, for Richards the world as we know it is a perceived world;[103] and it is perceived through metaphors

96. E.g., Johnson, "Metaphor: An Overview," 208.

97. Richards, *Philosophy of Rhetoric*, 94.

98. See ibid., 107–8, 117–18.

99. Ibid., 93.

100. Ibid., 124–25.

101. As Richards (ibid., 94) notes, "Thought is metaphoric," and "the metaphors of language derive therefrom."

102. Ibid., 108–9.

103. As he writes, "Our world is a projected world, shot through with characters lent to it from our own life" (ibid., 108).

(consequently, our world is "a product of metaphors"). Second, the inter-action involves the superimposition (conceptualization) of one conceptual metaphor upon another.

Richards illustrates his argument with John Denham's *Cooper's Hill*, which portrays the poet's mind like the Thames:

> O could I flow like thee, and make thy stream
>
> My great exemplar as it is my theme!
>
> Though deep, yet clear; though gentle, yet not dull;
>
> Strong without rage; without o'erflowing, full.[104]

Here the vehicle is a river (the Thames) and the tenor is the poet's mind. Following the comparison approach, the flow of the poet's mind may be compared to the characteristics of the river "deep, yet clear," "gentle, yet not dull," "strong without rage" and "without o'erflowing, full." But Richards argues that this "is not the whole mode of this metaphor."[105] In fact, one can get a deeper understanding of "deep," "clear," "gentle," "strong," and "full." For example, as far as a river is concerned, below the word "deep" is a set of implications (thoughts) such as "not easily crossed (or unfathomable), dangerous, navigable." When the reader conceives (conceptualizes) Den-ham's mind by these implications, they understand his mind as more than just "deep," but "mysterious, not easily accounted for, rich in knowledge and power."[106]

Metaphor then is an interaction between the metaphorical thoughts implied by "deep" and those of the mind, not just a comparison between the characteristics of the river and those of the mind. More importantly, in the process, thoughts such as "mysterious," "rich in knowledge" are *superim-posed* upon the poet's mind; in other words, the poet conceives the workings of his mind by those thoughts. In sum, for Richards, figurative language is a conceptualization of one set of metaphorical thoughts by another set of metaphorical thoughts.

Richards's theory is clarified as Black develops it further.[107] Black does so by refining the understanding of the principal and subsidiary subjects. First of all, he sees them not as individual subjects (e.g., "man" and "wolf" in "Man is wolf"), but as "systems of things."[108] In other words, each subject represents a system of related thoughts. The system encompasses thoughts

---

104. Denham, *Cooper's Hill*, 11.

105. Ibid., 123.

106. Ibid., 122.

107. See Black, "Metaphor," 72–73.

108. Ibid., 78.

which are not necessarily semantically similar but conceptually related. Also, these thoughts do not necessarily appear in the same passage. For instance, the word "wolf" in "Man is wolf" carries with it a system (bunch) of conceptually related thoughts such as "predator," "sly," and "fierce." These thoughts are not synonymous but associated. For Black, the system is culturally bound, and he calls it "associated commonplaces," that is, a conceptual system commonly shared by people in a particular community.[109]

Secondly, instead of transferring characteristics from one subject to the other, Black argues that what metaphor does is apply a system of "associated implications" belonging to the subsidiary subject (e.g., "wolf") to the principal subject (e.g., "man")[110] In other words, if the people of a community conceptualize man's behavior by wolf-like traits such as "predator," "sly" and "fierce," the remark "Man is a wolf" would evoke in the reader's mind someone who is sly, fierce and preys on others. In the Chinese community, the word "color" (which also means "sex") is added to "wolf" to form the Chinese metaphor "sexual predator" (*se lang*, lit. "colored wolf"), which means a man who preys on women. Such a conceptual approach would later open the door to what is now widely recognized as the *cognitive approach*, an approach closely associated with Lakoff and Johnson.

Cognitive Approach to Figurative Language

The cognitive approach is premised upon the notion that figurative language is inextricably bound up with human conceptualization of things. Lakoff and Johnson highlight the fact that our concepts structure what we perceive, how we relate to people and the world; and this conceptual system is "fundamentally metaphorical in nature."[111] It follows then, everything we do, experience, even the way we think and speak is metaphorical; the metaphors we use are therefore *conceptual metaphors*. For example, many people perceive and think of arguments in terms of war, therefore they use war language to describe arguments:[112]

He attacked every weak point in my argument.

His criticisms were right on target.

I demolished his arguments.

---

109. Ibid., 74.

110. Ibid., 78.

111. Lakoff and Johnson, "Conceptual Metaphor," 454.

112. Ibid., 454–55.

I have never won an argument with him.

He shot down all my arguments.

All these expressions suggest many of the things we do in arguing are structured by the concept of war. As Lakoff and Johnson write, "We talk about arguments that way because we conceive of them that way."[113] In a nutshell, figurative language is part of our cognition. As Lakoff and Johnson sum it up, "The essence of metaphor is understanding and experiencing one kind of thing in terms of another."[114]

One significant contribution of Lakoff and Johnson's cognitive approach is that unlike the previous theories, it does not speak of metaphor in terms of comparable characteristics of two subjects or two individual concepts, but two *conceptual networks* or *domains*.[115] In the case mentioned above, we used a concept from one domain (e.g., war) to structure a concept from another domain (e.g., argument). The first domain is called "source domain," the second "target domain," and the juxtaposition of the two domains "mapping."[116] The correspondences between the two domains (argument and war) can be mapped as follows:

War (source)		Argument (target)
enemy	→	opponent
battle	→	argument
tactic/strategy	→	methods of arguing
offensive	→	criticism
defense	→	response/counter-argument

As a result of the correspondences between the source and target, we have subcategorized metaphors such as "He attacked every weak point of my argument," and "I demolished his arguments."[117] Another example is "Love is a journey":[118]

---

113. Ibid.

114. Lakoff and Johnson, *Metaphors We Live By,* 5.

115. Lakoff and Johnson, "Conceptual Metaphor," 461.

116. So Johnson, "Metaphor: An Overview," 211; see also Holyoak and Thagard, *Mental Leaps,* 220–21.

117. Lakoff and Johnson, "Conceptual Metaphor," 457.

118. Cf. ibid., 470.

Journey (source)		Love (target)
traveler	→	lover
journey	→	love relationship
distance covered	→	progress of relationship
obstacles	→	problems of relationship
direction	→	decisions on developing relationship

The correspondences between the source and target are reflected in sub-categorized metaphors such as: "I do not think the relationship is going anywhere" (lack of direction); "Look how far we have come" (progress of relationship); "It has been a long and bumpy road" (problems of relationship).[119]

Lakoff and Johnson show us that such conceptual metaphors are rather plenty and commonly used in our everyday life: "Love is a patient (metaphors such as 'love sick,' 'healthy marriage,' and 'relationship in good shape')"; "Seeing is touching; eyes are limbs (such as 'I can't take my eyes off her,' 'His eyes are glued to the TV,' 'Her eyes picked out every detail')"; and "Life is a gamble (such as 'I'll take my chances,' 'play your cards right,' 'He is a real loser')."[120] Moreover, many conceptual metaphors can structure different aspects of a single concept. The different aspects of the single concept "love" can be structured as "Love is a journey," "Love is war," and "Love is madness."[121]

Application of Conceptual Approaches to Biblical Studies

Despite having been developed in the mid-twentieth century, the cognitive approach does not seem to have caught on in biblical scholarship as quickly as expected. Even as recently as the late 1990s, many biblical scholars seemed to think it suffice to apply the traditional theories. In their *Interpreting Hebrew Poetry*, Petersen and Richards do not mention such a possibility at all.[122] Alonso-Schökel only comes close to it, as he notes that "a series of

---

119. Ibid.

120. For these examples and more, see Lakoff and Johnson, *Metaphors We Live By*, 46–51.

121. Ibid., 108.

122. Interestingly, they seem to be aware of the current scholarship in the field of philosophy, as evidenced of their use of Richards' terminology: vehicle and tenor (*Interpreting Hebrew Poetry*, 50).

homogeneous images may be used to develop one panel of imagery alone."[123]
He mentions Ps 18:3 (ET Ps 18:2) in which a group of metaphors are used:[124]

> Yahweh is
>
> my rock,
>
> my fortress,
>
> my deliverer,
>
> my rock, in whom I take refuge,
>
> my shield,
>
> the horn of my salvation,
>
> my stronghold.

For those who are familiar with the cognitive approach, these metaphors can be seen as conceptualizing God's protection with the domain of military defense ("God is defense"). Yet, Alonso-Schökel fails to go further than referring to them as "a group of images." Likewise, he mentions how Psalm 23 uses "a series of elemental symbols" for the image of a shepherd and that of a host. But he stops short of stating that the elemental symbols in fact reflect the poet's conceptualization of Yahweh's providence with a shepherd's care of their sheep.[125]

Caird comes much closer to the cognitive approach as he speaks of "a group of metaphors" belonging to a "metaphor system."[126] He notes that the metaphors are connected together by "their common origin in a single area of human observation, experience" and has generated "sublanguage."[127] Among his examples is the group of metaphorical expressions drawn from the exodus experience of Israel. The Hebrew poets use the exodus experience to conceive of other forms of slavery of Israel, including the exile by Assyria (Hos 11:5); slavery by sin (Ps 130:7-8); and deliverance from it (Isa 43:16-20).[128] Caird could have noted that the poets conceptualize spiritual slavery with the historical exodus, but he stops short of using the terminology; neither does he develop the idea further.

In contrast to these scholars, some other began to pay special attention to the cognitive nature of biblical figurative language. Kirsten Nielsen, for

123. Alonso-Schökel, *Manual of Hebrew Poetics*, 115–17.

124. Ibid., 116.

125. Ibid.

126. Caird, *Language and Imagery*, 155.

127. Ibid.

128. Ibid., 155–56.

example, analyzed the conceptual metaphor of the tree in Isaiah.[129] Recently, Göran Eidevall applies Lakoff and Johnson's theory to the spatial metaphors, exploring how the poet conceptualizes life activities by the "dimension of space and movement" in Lam 3:1–9.[130] Likewise, applying Lakoff and Johnson's theory, P. Van Hecke explores the pastoral metaphor in Hos 4:16.[131]

A more recent and fuller treatment is Job Y. Jindo's *Biblical Metaphor Reconsidered: A Cognitive Approach to Poetic Prophecy in Jeremiah 1–24*, a reworked version of his PhD dissertation under the direction of Geller. Jindo examines the metaphors in Jeremiah 1–24 on two levels: global and local. The global level gives structure to the conceptual framework of Jeremiah 1–24, the local level conceptualizes the inner experiences of characters.[132] The global model is conceptualized by "the cosmos is a state," in which God carries out a royal lawsuit against Israel.[133] On the local level, many plant images used by Yahweh and Jeremiah are conceived by the metaphorical concept "Israel is Yahweh's royal garden."[134] Together the global and the local metaphors present a poetic reality, which is a cosmic drama which revolves around the dissonance between divine and human perspectives and the call to resolve the dissonance.[135]

Context and Conceptual Approaches: Conceptual Domains

Like the proponents of transfer approaches, Richards and Black recognize the importance of context.[136] Likewise, Lakoff and Johnson observe that how the correspondence of two domains is conceived varies from culture to culture. For example, different cultures have different conceptions of argument; it may be conceived in terms of war in one culture, but not in another culture.[137] Similarly, conceptualizing time in monetary terms (such as "time is money") is taken for granted in highly commercial societies, but would sound strange in less commercial societies.

As mentioned, given the temporal distance between us and the biblical poets, cultural context often poses a challenge to the reader. Eventually,

129. Nielsen, *There is Hope for a Tree*.

130. Eidevall, "Spatial Metaphors," 133–37.

131. Van Hecke, "Conceptual Blending," 215–31.

132. Jindo, *Biblical Metaphor Reconsidered*, 49–50.

133. Ibid., 71–147.

134. Ibid., 151–240; for a useful illustration, see p. 237.

135. Ibid., esp. 240.

136. See 95–96.

137. Lakoff and Johnson, "Conceptual Metaphor," 455.

the reader has to fall back to what the text offers. Unlike the substitute or comparison approach, however, for the conceptual approach, the context is not limited to inter-colon relationship (parallelism). The assumption of the cognitive approach is that figurative expressions that appear in different places of a text may be part of the same conceptual network, referring to the same "poetic reality."[138] As such, the context is below the surface, on the conceptual level, across passages, even across poems. So when exploring the meaning of "He attacked all my arguments," the reader should explore this expression in light of other figurative expressions within the whole conceptual domain of "argument is war." These expressions may be found across passages or poems.

Validity and Contributions of Cognitive Approach to Biblical Studies

While not without criticism,[139] the validity of the cognitive approach has now been established both by linguistic-philosophical and biblical scholars. Scholars such as Black, Lakoff and Johnson have presented solid evidence for the conceptual nature of figurative language. More importantly, conceptual figurative expressions are not just a secular (philosophical) idea, but a universal phenomenon found across cultures, including the culture of the biblical writers. This is evidenced by the example that the metaphorical concept "people are plants" is widely used in different cultures and eras, including in ancient Israel.[140] Furthermore, biblical scholars such as Van Hecke and Jindo have also demonstrated the significant contributions the cognitive approach can make to our understanding of biblical figurative language.

One significant contribution of the cognitive approach is its premise that figurative language reflects human concepts. As Lakoff and Mark Turner put it, "To study metaphor is to be confronted with hidden aspects of one's own mind and one's own culture."[141] It follows that we can access the concept of a person or a society by studying their figurative language. For instance, Lakoff and Johnson note that we can have an idea about couples' views of marriage by paying attention to their marriage metaphors. A mar-

138. Jindo, *Biblical Metaphor Reconsidered*, 34.

139. It is important to note that not everyone in the scholarly community welcomes their theory of conceptual metaphor, as reflected in Lakoff and Johnson's afterword (*Metaphors We Live By*, esp. 244–46, 273–74).

140. Lakoff and Turner, *More Than Cool Reason*, 5–6, 12–14, 223; Jindo, *Biblical Metaphor Reconsidered*, 32–33.

141. Lakoff and Turner, *More Than Cool Reason*, 214.

riage may go awry when one spouse conceptualizes love as partnership and the other spouse sees love as a haven.[142] Likewise, this notion allows us to look at the moral values of a certain society, as "our basic understanding of morality arises via conceptual metaphor."[143] The moral metaphors such as "strong," "weak," "upright" and "rotten" reflect how a particular community conceptualizes morality.[144] If so, by studying biblical metaphors we too can discover the values (theological or moral) of the biblical authors. This in turn would be a great contribution to the studies of Old Testament theology and ethics.

Biblical Figurative Language: Surface or Conceptual?

Having affirmed the contributions of the cognitive approach, by no means are we promoting it as the only way of looking at biblical figurative language. The fact that figurative language is diverse and fluid warrants such a cautious approach. Richards notes that metaphors come with many "modes." While one approach can deal with certain "modes," it takes another approach to deal with other "modes."[145] Also, Lakoff and Johnson would remind us that metaphors come to us with many physical, social and cultural experiential bases.[146] In light of this, Loewenberg's observation may serve as a good reminder: "Metaphorical utterances occur in such a variety of circumstances that any common characterization of them must necessarily be highly general."[147]

All this can be confirmed by our earlier discussion. The mechanism between the thing said and the thing meant is fluid and comes with a whole lot of variety. Perhaps for this reason, while some scholars advance a cognitive approach to figurative language, they are by no means dismissing the traditional views completely. So although Lakoff and Johnson contend that metaphor in general is conceptual and based on cross-domain correlations,[148] they also note not every metaphor is connected by network. Some figurative expressions may be conceptual, but they are "standalone," "isolated" and

---

142. Lakoff and Johnson, *Metaphors We Live By*, 243–44.

143. Ibid., 250.

144. Ibid. See more detailed discussion in Lakoff and Johnson, *Philosophy in the Flesh*, 290–334.

145. Richards, *Philosophy of Rhetoric*, 94.

146. Lakoff and Johnson, *Metaphors We Live By*, 18.

147. Loewenberg, "Identifying Metaphors," 335.

148. Lakoff and Johnson contend for this point particularly in their 2003 afterword (*Metaphors We Live By*, 244–45).

"unsystematic," such as the lexicalized metaphors "the leg of a table" and "the foot of the mountain."[149]

Likewise, while as a philosopher Black argues that only conceptual metaphors matter in philosophy, he also concedes that such "genuine" metaphors exist in a "very small number of cases."[150] The implication is that we have a larger number of conventional metaphors to interpret. He observes that these "trivial cases" are best analyzed by the comparison and substitute approaches, as these approaches are sometimes "nearer the mark than 'interaction' views."[151] More importantly, Black points out that the mechanisms between the principal and subsidiary subjects are diverse, so generalization is impossible. As he writes, "There is, in general, no simple 'ground' for the necessary shifts of meaning—no blanket reason why some metaphors work and others fail."[152] Therefore, instead of dismissing one to promote another, he proposes that we classify figurative language "as instances of substitution, comparison, or interaction."[153]

All these comments suggest that the traditional transfer approaches have not been abandoned completely in recent scholarship. This notion is reinforced by Ricoeur's defense of the principle of similarity in metaphor.[154] He argues that the problem with the traditional approach is not its principle of similarity but its association with the substitution view. He proposes to disassociate the principle from the substitution view and reinterpret it "within the guidelines of the theory of interaction."[155]

All this suggests the diverse views on figurative language, and it is wise to take a cautious stance on it. This may well be the stance reflected in Jindo's approach to biblical figurative language. Jindo strongly promotes the cognitive approach as a method that assumes a maximum substantive value "from the creative and cognitive function of poetic metaphor," but also stresses that other approaches are "equally legitimate."[156]

In brief, though we recognize the significant contributions of the cognitive approach, it is no reason to dismiss the validity of the traditional

149. Lakoff and Johnson, "Conceptual Metaphor in Everyday Language," 472–73; and Lakoff and Johnson, *Metaphors We Live By*, 54–55. Though this argument represents their early views on metaphor, Lakoff and Johnson do not seek to revise them in their 2003 afterword.

150. Black, "Metaphor," 78.

151. Ibid.

152. Ibid.

153. Ibid.

154. Ricoeur, *Rule of Metaphor*, 191–200.

155. Ibid., 173.

156. Jindo, *Biblical Metaphor Reconsidered*, 43, 47–48.

approaches completely. Instead, we should perhaps reexamine the traditional approaches in light of the cognitive nature of figurative language. For
example, we may revisit the biblical plant metaphors such as "the righteous
as a tree by the streams of water" and other tree metaphors in Ps 52:10 ("the
righteous as an olive tree") and Ps 92:13–15 ("the righteous as a palm tree")
and see if they in fact belong to the conceptual domain of "the righteous
as plants." Scholars such as Jindo have demonstrated such feasibility in his
discussion of the local metaphors in Jeremiah 1–24.[157] This suggests that the
same may also be applied to other biblical metaphors which seem isolated
but are actually related as a domain.

SUMMARY AND CONCLUSION

The long development of metaphor theories shows significant progress in
two aspects. Firstly, it is a progress from seeing figurative language as mere
stylistic decoration to understanding it as part of human cognition. Figurative expressions are not just some special rhetorical device exclusive to
poets, but also represent the way we perceive things in everyday life. They
are a mirror of our conceptualization. Having said so, by no means do we
deny a special relationship between poets and figurative language. There are
indeed figurative expressions which reflect a creative mind, such as the ones
used in the poetic texts we noted.

Secondly, it is a progress from seeing the mechanism of the two entities of metaphor as a mere transfer of comparable characteristics to viewing
it as structuring one conceptual domain with another domain. The latter
approach goes beyond surface similarity, and deeper into conceptual correspondences on the cognitive level. The major theories about how figurative
language works can be summed up as follows:

---

157. See the diagram of the metaphor "human life as tree" in Jindo, *Biblical Metaphor Reconsidered*, 33. Unfortunately, Creach speaks of the relationship between the
similes of "righteous as a tree" in Pss 1:3; 52:10; and 92:13–15 in terms of literary dependency ("Psalm 1:3," 35) instead of conceptual metaphors belonging to a domain.

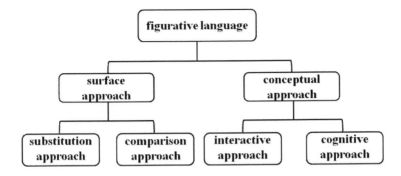

By now we have discussed the essential elements that form Hebrew poetry: colon, strophe, stanza, conciseness, ellipsis, parallelism, and figurative language. With these we are now ready to examine several poetic passages in the Old Testament and see how these elements work in the Hebrew poems.

5

Poetic Analysis and Interpretation of Psalm 1

IN THIS PSALM, THE psalmist versifies the profile of a "commendable person" (*'ašrê hā'îš*, often translated "blessed" or "happy"):[1] portraying him as a pious person who shuns evil and loves the torah of Yahweh. Before we proceed, it is necessary to make a number of preliminary remarks about this psalm.

PSALM 1 AS A POEM

Though Psalm 1 is a much cited and discussed biblical text, not everyone agrees that it is a poem. In his comprehensive introduction to Hebrew poetry, Watson lists Psalm 1 as one of the biblical passages whose poetic nature is questioned.[2] In the same vein, Sebastian Bullough argues that as the psalm is not metrical and uses Hebrew words and particles normally found in prose (among others, the relative particle *'ăšer* [who]), thus it is not poetry but a "rhythmic prose."[3]

We concur with Bullough that meter (as understood in its conventional definition) is nowhere to be found in the psalm, a view shared by

---

1. The present writer is indebted to Prof. Choon-Leong Seow for the analysis of this psalm. He is also grateful both to him and Dr. K. C. Hanson for discussions on the meaning of *'ašrê hā'îš*. For discussion on the translation of this phrase, see below, p. 132.

2. Watson does not offer any reason for this view (*Classical Hebrew Poetry*, 45).

3. Bullough, "Metre in Psalm 1," 42–49.

many scholars.[4] This, however, does not exclude the possibility of the psalm being poetic. As noted in chapter 3, while the metrical system of ancient Hebrew poetry remains elusive (if it ever existed), the presence of free rhythm is widely noted. Since Bullough considers Psalm 1 "rhythmic" (by calling it "rhythmic prose"), the psalm then should meet the criterion. Also, as argued in chapter 1, some of the prose-related words are also found in Hebrew poetry, so in and of themselves, they are not good indicators of poetry; to determine if a text is poetic, other factors have to be considered. Our analysis will show below that two primary elements that characterize Hebrew poetry (parallelism and figurative language) are present in the psalm in high concentration. Other poetic characteristics such as terseness and ellipsis are also found. Together, these are good grounds for treating the psalm as poetry.[5]

THE LINEATION OF PSALM 1

Exegetes have offered different proposals about the lineation of Psalm 1.[6] The reason for the diversity is due to different principles behind the division of the poem into cola, strophes and stanzas. The lineation of the present analysis will be based on the criteria noted in chapter 1, such as thought-content coherence, thematic flow and transition markers.[7] On the basis of these guidelines, we propose to divide this psalm into two stanzas (1:1–3 and 1:4–5 respectively) and a concluding bicolon (1:6).[8] The first stanza starts with the title ("commendable is the man") which is followed by three strophes. The second stanza consists of two strophes, which is followed by a concluding bicolon:[9]

---

4. E.g., Kraus, *Psalms 1–59*, 114.

5. Craigie argues that its parallelism and structure make this psalm "clearly and distinctively *poetry*" (*Psalms 1–51*, 59).

6. See Auffret, "Du psaume 1," 26–45; Fokkelman, *Psalms in Form*, 16.

7. See 17–19. Cf. the treatment of Psalm 3, 13 and 130 by Weber, "Toward a Theory," 174–76.

8. We agree with Kraus that the last verse is a concluding remark (*Psalms 1–59*, 114).

9. By and large the strophic division proposed here is similar to that of van der Lugt (*Cantos and Strophes*, 93, 96), but differs on our treatment of the opening phrase ("Commendable is the person," 1:1a). As Lugt and other scholars (e.g., Kraus, *Psalms 1–59*, 114) have noted, 1:1 and 1:3 have posed difficulties for scholars. Cf. Briggs and Briggs, *Psalms*, 3.

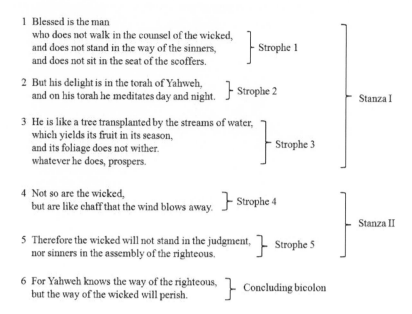

Strophes 1 and 2 are demarcated by the transition marker, that is, the adversative *waw* ("but") which begins the second strophe. Besides, Strophe 1 defines itself as a unit by its coherent thought-content: all the three cola speak of what the commendable person does not do. Likewise Strophe 2 sets itself apart from other strophes by the unified thought-content: what the commendable person does. Strophe 3 is defined by its distinctive thought-content: the whole strophe is a tree simile. These three strophes are regarded as a stanza (Stanza I) for a number of reasons. Firstly, the strophes are grouped by their common thought-content: they consistently speak of the commendable/righteous person. Secondly, they are grouped as a stanza for reason of thematic flow. The first strophes speaks of what the commendable person does not do, then the second strophe turns to what he does, and finally strophe 3 speaks of the outcome of his lifestyle. Thirdly, the contrastive particle "not so" (*lō-kēn*) in 1:4 serves as a transition marker that signals the beginning of a new strophe as well as a new stanza.

Whereas "not so" (*lō-kēn*) as a transition marker marks the start of Strophe 4, the boundaries of the strophe are also defined by its coherent thought-content (i.e., about the fate of the wicked). The particle "therefore" (*'al-kēn*) in 1:5 marks the beginning of Strophe 5, the strophe itself is also defined by the synonymous parallelism of its two cola (1:5a, b). This parallelism is indicative of coherent content, thus implying that the two cola are a unified unit.

Strophes 4 and 5 are grouped into a stanza by their common content and theme: the fate of the wicked. Strophe 6 is marked by the transition marker "for" (*kî*). In the strophe the poet speaks of the contrast between the righteous and the wicked (as he does in Stanzas I and II); therefore the strophe represents the concluding remark to the whole poem.

As Peter C. Craigie notes, the colon distribution of the psalm is "very uneven in length."[10] Particularly interesting is that Stanza I has more and longer strophes (three longer strophes) than Stanza II (two shorter strophes). This suggests that the psalmist has his focus on the righteous rather than the wicked.[11] As will be pointed out, this will have some implications for the message of the psalm. We will now examine the poem in detail.

STANZA I: THE PORTRAYAL OF A COMMENDABLE PERSON (1:1–3)

The commendable person is portrayed by three "does nots" (Strophe 1, 1:1), one "does" (Strophe 2, 1:2), and one simile (Strophe 3, 1:3). The first striking feature is the parallelism in the stanza, evident both in inter-colon relationships as well as inter-strophe relationships.

Parallelism

Strophe 1 (1:1)

This strophe consists of three cola. The first colon introduces the title ("commendable is the man," which at once serves as the theme of Stanza I), which is followed by a negating statement. The second and the third cola contain two other negating remarks:

> Commendable is the person (title),
>
> who does not walk in the counsel[12] of the wicked,

10. Craigie, *Psalms 1–50*, 59.

11. Tuell comments, "It is apparent that the Psalmist actually has no interest in the wicked; like chaff, they have no lasting destiny" ("Psalm 1," 280). It should be added, however, many exegetes have argued that the final redactor intends Psalm 1 and 2 to be read as a unit. If this is correct, we may see the continuation of the story of the wicked in Psalm 2, in which they rebel against the righteous king. See for example, e.g., Brown, *Psalms*, 112–33; for a fuller treatment, see Cole, *Psalms 1–2*.

12. The noun *'ēṣāh* refers to council or counsel; here we are with Craigie, *Psalms*

and does not stand in the way of the sinners,

and does not sit in the seat of the scoffers.

Notably, the cola are parallel to each other in several ways. Firstly, they correspond to each other by their use of the negating particle "lō'" (not). Next, the first half of each colon has a verb which parallels the verbs in the other cola. Each of them makes the same point about what the commendable person does not do: "does not walk"//"does not stand" //"does not sit." Likewise, the second half of each colon has a phrase which is also semantically parallel to each other: the counsel of the wicked//the way of the sinners//the seat of the mockers. Again, the phrases seem to speak of the same thing, all referring to a group of wicked people.[13]

For this reason, some commentators argue that the parallelism here is synonymous, that is, each colon says the same thing in a different way.[14] On this basis some scholars reject the view that the three consecutive verbs indicate climatic progression.[15] In our opinion, this may not be the case, especially not for the verbs.[16] In light of the more recent parallelism theories (such as that of Alter and Kugel), it is possible that the three verbs demonstrate the intensification of sin.[17] In other words, they were put together to highlight the element of motion, perhaps a morally downward movement from "walking" to "standing" to "sitting."[18] While in themselves the verbs may not indicate markedly divided phases of moral deterioration, together they may suggest a motion: someone who starts with just "walking" (a

---

1–50, 57.

13. As Dahood observes, the Hebrew for "scoffers" (lēṣîm) here is a synonym for "the wicked" (rešā'îm) (Psalms 1–50, 2).

14. So Anderson, Psalms, 58; Kidner, Psalms 1–72, 48; Craigie, Psalms 1–50, 60; Anderson, "Ps 1:1," 231. This suggests that these scholars follow a Lowthian view of parallelism.

15. So Anderson ("Ps 1:1," 231–33); agreeing with him is Craigie (Psalms 1–50, 60). Many other commentators, however, argue that the three verbs denote progressive movement to sin, such as Weiser (Psalms, 103–4); E. Beaucamp (Psautire 1–72, 41–42); and Kraus (Psalms 1–59, 115). Kirkpatrick has argued that the verbs intimate "successive steps in a career of evil" (Psalms, 3).

16. As André points out, the synonymous argument is generally based on the studies of the objects of the verbs (the "wicked," "sinners" and "scoffers") but ignore the verbs ("'Walk', 'Stand' and 'Sit,'" 327). For an example of synonymous argument, see Anderson, "Psalm 1:1," 232.

17. Literally or metaphorically the three verbs walk, stand and sit are not synonymous; because to argue so is to ignore the widely recognized "A is so, and what's more, B is so."

18. As Görg argues, the correlation of the three verbs "makes it sufficiently clear that the context emphasizes the element of motion" ("יָשַׁב yāšab; מוֹשָׁב môšāb," 6:426).

casual act) may slide down to "standing" (conforming to the way of the sinners) and finally "sitting" (becoming part of the scoffers).[19] In sum, a commendable person is someone who avoids going down the slippery road.

Our understanding of this strophe will be enhanced by an analysis of its grammatical parallelism. The commendable person (*ʾašrê hāʾîš*, 1:1a) is portrayed by the repeated negating particle (triple *lōʾ*), displaying parallelism at the word level. The word-level parallelism (triple negating particle) serves to emphasize what the blessed person *does not do*.

What follows may demonstrate Geller and Greenstein's idea of deep structure parallelism. "The blessed person" is portrayed in three cola. While the relative particle "who" (*ʾăšer*) in the first colon serves as the subject of the first cola (1:1a, in place of "the blessed person"), the other two cola have no subject except that each is preceded by a conjunction. Nevertheless, syntactically the conjunctions co-join the two cola to the subject of the first colon:

> and (the blessed person) does not stand in the way of the sinners
>
> and (the blessed person) does not sit in the seat of the scoffers

In other words, the other two cola (1:1b, c) share the same subject as the first colon (1:1a). As such, we have a case of ellipsis (gapping) here. This suggests that while not visible on the surface structure, the subject ("the blessed person") operates deep beneath the surface. The effect of this gapping is that the reader would pay more attention to the three "does nots"; and in doing so, it emphasizes the necessity of setting oneself apart from bad company.

Jakobson's principle of selection and combination may also be applied here. After the negative particle (not) the psalmist employs a selection of words to describe what the blessed person does not do: "walk," "stand" and "sit," words of the same class.[20] Likewise, terms such as "counsel of the wicked," "the way of the sinners" and "the seat of the scoffers" belong to another class.[21] Thus the verb matching (belonging to one class) is paired with the noun matching (belonging to another class).[22] The psalmist seems

---

19. Cf. Jacquet, *Psaumes*, 209; Goldingay, *Psalms 1–41*, 82.

20. It is noteworthy that elsewhere in the Old Testament, "walk" (*hlk*) and "sit" (*yšb*) also appear as a pair (Deut 6:7).

21. The nouns "counsel" and "the wicked" occur as a pair in various places denoting the wicked (Job 10:3; 21:16; 22:18).

22. In Syriac *ʿeṣāh* ("counsel"(in 1:1b is transposed with *derek* ("way") in 1:1c, probably assuming the verb *hlk* ("to walk") should be together with *derek*. We agree with Craigie (*Psalms 1–50*, 57) that this is unnecessary. Syriac's treatment reflects an interpretive decision rather than a variant Hebrew *Vorlage*; in contrast, the MT is supported by the LXX Psalm 1 (earlier than Syriac). More importantly, the separation of *hlk* and *derek* may be deliberate for reason of word class as argued here.

to demonstrate his creativity with the word matching. While the nouns heighten the idea of moral decay by referring to its various aspects, the verbs are employed to denote semantic progress.[23] In other words, while the verbs denote a gradual slipping down motion, the nouns suggest that ultimately they all lead to moral decay.

Strophe 2 (1:2)

After describing what the blessed person does not do, in the second strophe the psalmist tells us what the blessed person does:

> But his delight is on the torah of Yahweh
> And on his torah he meditates day and night

The parallelism between the first colon and the second colon is evident both semantically and grammatically. Semantically, the meaning of the first (the righteous person's delight is Yahweh's torah) corresponds to that of the second (his constant meditation on Yahweh's torah). As in Strophe 1, semantic progress is also observable: the second colon (the act of constant meditation on Yahweh's torah) intensifies the meaning of the first colon (that his delight is on the torah of Yahweh).

In terms of its relationship with the preceding strophe, a few observations may be made. Firstly, the adversative particles *kî 'im* ("but") introduces a clause which is antithetical to the negative clauses in 1:1. This being the case, the antithetical function results in a negative-positive antithetical parallelism between Strophe 1 and Strophe 2. The first speaks of what the person *does not do*, the second what he *does*. More importantly, Strophe 2 also heightens the meaning of Strophe 1. If the first strophe tells us only one aspect of the righteous person (the person's defensive measures), the present strophe intensifies it by offering more information about the person (his active pursuit).

On the grammatical level, the psalmist also demonstrates the principle of selection and combination. He matches "his delight is *on the torah of Yahweh*" with paradigmatic words: "*on his torah* he meditates day and night." Besides, students familiar with biblical Hebrew would notice the matching on word level, morphological level as well as phonological level:

bĕtôrat YHWH	On the torah of Yahweh (1:2a) //
bĕtôrātô yegeh	On his torah he meditates (1:2b)

---

23. As argued above, while these belong to the same class of verbs, their meanings are not necessarily synonymous.

The combined effect of the parallelism draws attention to the torah of Yahweh, highlighting where the interest of the blessed person lies.

Strophe 3 (1:3)

Following the three negatives and one positive in the first two strophes, the psalmist further intensifies his description of the righteous person by a tree metaphor in a tetra-colon strophe:

> He is like a tree transplanted by the streams of water,
>
> which yields its fruit in its season,
>
> and its foliage does not wither.
>
> Whatever he does, prospers.

In terms of its relationship with the previous strophe, the parallelism between the first colon of this strophe (1:3a) and the immediate foregoing colon (1:2b) is to be noted:

> And on the his torah he meditates day and night (1:2b) //
>
> He is like a tree transplanted by the streams of water (1:3a)

Here constant meditation on the torah of Yahweh is matched with constant supply of water, highlighting the connection of the two.

Within the present strophe, the parallelism between the second (1:3b) and the third colon (1:3c) is evident even at first glance: both describe the vitality of the tree. However, one would be hard pressed to find explicit semantic correspondence between the first colon ("he is like a tree transplanted by the streams of water," 1:3a) and the second colon ("which yields its fruit in its season," 1:3b) or the third colon ("and its foliage does not wither," 1:3c), though they are thematically associated. Thus here we have a classic example of the limitations of the Lowthian approach, and Kugel's "A is so, and what's more, B is so" would lend itself to treating the strophe.

Being thematically related, the semantic progress in the three cola is hard to miss. The first colon informs the reader that it is a well-watered tree; the second colon intensifies this by describing its seasonal fruition (as a result of being well watered, signifying vitality and a sign of good tree, cf. Isa 5:1–4). While the second colon is parallel to the third colon in a traditional (Lowthian) way, it also intensifies the idea of vitality in the preceding colon. The fourth colon (1:3d) heightens the third colon as well as the first colon. It specifies the foliage metaphor in the third colon ("its foliage does not wither") by explaining its meaning: the person prospers in all he does. Moreover, it intensifies the first colon ("he is like a tree transplanted by the streams of water") as well as the rest of the strophe: like the flourishing tree (described in cola 1–4), the righteous person prospers in all he does.[24]

Our understanding of the present strophe would be enhanced by an analysis of its grammatical parallelism. The third person masculine singular verb (*wĕhāyāh*) in the first colon is matched with another third person masculine singular verb (*yaṣlîaḥ*) in the last colon:

He *is* (*wĕhāyāh*) like a tree transplanted by the streams of water //

Whatever he does, *prospers* (*yaṣlîaḥ*)

Also, phonetic parallelism is displayed by the ending sound of each verb (*wĕhāyāh // yaṣliaḥ*). If the former begins the strophe, the latter ends it, forming an *inclusio*. The chiastic relationship is significant in that it stresses the close association between what the person *is* ("he is like a tree") and what he *does* ("whatever he does, prospers").[25]

Figurative Language

By way of parallelism, the psalmist puts together a number of metaphors and a simile to elucidate the blessed person in Strophes 1 and 3. They are the "way of life" metaphors (walk, stand and sit) and the tree simile.

The Way of Life Metaphors

As in many other places in the Old Testament, the "walk" and "way" metaphors are closely associated in the Psalms (e.g., Pss 81:3; 86:11; 101:2; 119:3; cf. Deut 5:33; 8:6; 30:16; 1 Kgs 15:26, 34; 16:2, 19). This suggests they belong to a common conceptual domain which conceives "human life as a journey."[26] On this journey, one encounters different counsels; one of them

---

24. BHS suggests that this colon is a gloss. However, this lacks support from textual witnesses. On the contrary, LXX Ps 1:3 has the colon. Poetically, this colon makes sense as it concludes what the preceding two cola say.

25. The third person singular verb of *'āśāh* (to do) may refer to the tree, as Dahood has noted (*Psalms 1–50*, 4). But as the tree is a simile of the righteous person and given its chiastic relationship to 1:1 ("Blessed is the person"), it is also legitimate to assume that it ultimately refers to the righteous person, as noted by Kraus (*Psalms 1–59*, 113) and Craigie (*Psalms 1–50*, 58).

26. Helfmeyer, "הָלַךְ *hālakh*," 3:391.

is the counsel of the wicked. Similarly, on a life journey, there are many ways (*derek*), that is, a wide range of choices.[27] Not every one of them leads to happiness; and certainly not the way of the sinners, as it puts people in peril instead (cf. 1:6). The blessed person therefore does not "stand" in such a way. As noted, "stand" here may refer to remaining in the way, that is, a more permanent action such as conforming to the lifestyle of the wicked.

The most prominent use of the sitting motif in the Old Testament is sitting at the city gate, which normally carries legal overtones (Gen 19:1; Ruth 4:1–12; Job 29:7).[28] Not every one of such occasions is positive, as the legal role may be abused (Prov 22:22). This seems to be the case here, as the sitting metaphor is associated with the "seat" of scoffers. "Sitting with" frequently connotes agreement and support (e.g., Ps 26:4b).[29] As such, "sit" implies something more than conformity, namely, permanent association and even participation in making false accusations with the wicked.

As a whole, the series of metaphors indicates a motion from passing by the counsel of the wicked to remaining in their way (conforming to their lifestyle) and to finally participating in their judicial decision-making. The change from accidental encounter to conformity and judicial participation suggests a downward motion (from a casual act to an intentional act). The righteous person avoids sliding down the way of the wicked.

If the route of the wicked is not an option, which way does the blessed person go? Just as their literal use does, the metaphorical use of "walk" and "way" normally involves space and direction. Significantly, in the Psalms the "walk" and "way" metaphors are closely associated with divine torah (Ps 119:1, 29), an association also found in many places in the Old Testament (Exod 16:4; 2 Kgs 10:31; Isa 2:3). The close association implies that "walk" and "way" have a direction, that is, in the direction of the torah.[30] It is of little wonder that soon the psalmist will highlight the fact in 1:2.

---

27. The metaphorical use of *derek* is especially prominent in Proverbs, where the term occurs 75 times. Clifford writes: "Proverbs is keenly aware of the social consequences of individual acts, and expresses these consequences by the metaphor of the way. One's choices place one on a path that has its own dynamic" (*Proverbs*, 21–22). One's choices are particularly highlighted in Proverbs 1–9, where wisdom and folly are metaphorically described as two ways. For a fuller discussion of the conceptual metaphor of "way" in Proverbs, see Van Leeuwen, "Proverbs 1–9," 111–44. Cf. Koch, et al., "דֶּרֶךְ *derekh*," 3:272, 286–88.

28. Görg, "יָשַׁב *yāšab*; מוֹשָׁב *môsāb*," 6:425.

29. Ibid., 426.

30. It is worth noting that the word *tôrāh* often connotes direction in the psalms (Pss 78:10; 89:31; 119:1).

In view of all this, the metaphor "life is a journey" in this strophe may be mapped as follows:[31]

Journey (source)		Life (target)
traveler	→	(blessed) person
intended distance	→	progress on the way of the torah
obstacles encountered	→	counsel, way and seat of the wicked
alternative distance	→	slippery way of the wicked
decision on the direction	→	to shun the counsel, way and seat of the wicked
destinations	→	blessedness or destruction

The preceding mapping shows two possible distances to cover: one is the intended distance (the progress toward blessedness), the other is the alternative distance (sliding down the way of the wicked). Consequently, there are two possible destinations: blessedness or destruction. The route to blessedness requires the pursuit of the intended distance and the avoidance of the alternative (undesirable) distance; to do that, one has to make right choices (decision to shun the counsel, way and seat of the wicked and to pursue the way of the torah).

The Tree Simile

If the conduct or lifestyle of the righteous person is conceived by a journey, its outcome is conceptualized by a plant: "He is like a tree, transplanted by the streams of water." The outcome implies that the intended distance has been covered and the destination is reached.

LIFE IS A PLANT

A very similar simile (coached in much of the same language) occurs in Jer 17:8, where the righteous is also portrayed as a tree by the streams of water. This has led to the debate of whether the psalmist borrows from Jeremiah or vice versa.[32] The possibility of compositional dependency should not be brushed aside easily. Nevertheless, it is also very likely, as some scholars

---

31. Cf. Jindo, *Biblical Metaphor Reconsidered*, 29.

32. See Creach, "Psalm 1:3," 36–39.

have argued, that the similarities are due more to the conventional nature of the simile rather than literary dependency in either direction.[33] This is supported by the parallel "righteous life as a plant" metaphors elsewhere within the Psalms (Pss 52:10; 92:13–15). The parallels suggest that the tree simile in our psalm is one of the subcategories of the conceptual imagery "Life is a plant" which can be mapped as the following domain structures:

Plant life (source)		Righteous life (target)
tree	→	righteous person
water	→	the torah of Yahweh
constant watering	→	constant meditation on the torah of Yahweh
fruit and healthy foliage	→	the result of a righteous life

Life is a Plant in God's Garden

It is also important to note that the tree simile is part of a broader conceptual domain widely attested in the ancient Near Eastern literature: the divine garden.[34] In such literature, the divine garden is understood as part of the royal manor of the deities.[35] In the Old Testament, the garden motif is often depicted as God's special place, where trees grow by the streams of water and humans are entrusted with the administration of the manor (Gen 2:8–15).[36]

More importantly, the tabernacle (or the temple) is often conceived of as a representation of the divine garden (Exod 25:31–40),[37] with water running through it (Isa 33:21; Ezekiel 47; Zech 14:8).[38] Moreover, the lampstand in the sanctuary is shaped in the form of a tree (Exod 25:31–40).[39] Also, the

33. So Brownlee, "Coronation Liturgy," 326; and Carroll, *Jeremiah*, 351.

34. Wallace, "Garden of God," 906–7; also by the same author, *Eden Narrative*. Though Stordalen rejects the theory of "divine garden" in the ancient Near Eastern literature, he notes that the gardens have a cultic (worship) function, symbolizing divine activity in the earthly realm (*Echoes of Eden*, 139–61).

35. Jacobsen, *Treasures of Darkness*, 81.

36. See Van Seters, "Creation of Man," 333–42; Greenstein, "God's Golem," 219–39; Walton, *Ancient Near Eastern Thought*, 203–6.

37. Wenham, "Sanctuary Symbolism," 399–404.

38. Stager, "Garden of Eden," 183–94.

39. Meyer, "Lampstand," 141–43; Meyer, *Tabernacle Menorah*.

first temple has pomegranate images on its columns (1 Kgs 7:18, 20; 2 Kgs 25:17; Jer 52:22–23). Jindo argues that all these plant images indicate that the *conceptual domain of God's royal garden* is being systematically mapped onto the *conceptual domain of the temple*.[40]

Significant to our discussion is that the righteous are often likened to trees planted in the temple (Pss 52:10; 92:13–15).[41] In light of this, the tree simile in Ps 1:3 could well be an example of such a poetic concept.[42] If this is correct, the tree simile here depicts prosperity in more than its usual sense. Instead of mere material prosperity, it denotes an intimate relationship with the source of life: Yahweh.

STANZA II: THE PORTRAYAL OF THE WICKED (1:4–5)

Parallelism

Strophe 4 (1:4)

A quick glance would notice the antithetic parallelism between the first colon of this strophe and the first colon of Strophe 3:

> He is like a tree (1:3a)
>
> *Not so* with the wicked (1:4a)

The phrase "not so" (*lō-kēn*) marks the contrast between the righteous and the wicked. As this is the beginning of the description of the wicked, perhaps it is also antithetic to the opening colon:

> Blessed is the person (1:1a)
>
> *Not so* with the wicked (1:4a)

Again, the antithetical parallelism here serves to contrast the wicked with the blessed person. The double contrast underlines the different fates of the two. The fate of the wicked is further specified in the second colon of the strophe (1:4b):

> But are like chaff that the wind blows away.

In turn, this second colon is antithetic to the first colon of Strophe 3:

---

40. Jindo, *Biblical Metaphor Reconsidered*, 160–62.

41. Cf. Creach, "Psalm 1:3," 35.

42. See Frymer-Kensky, "Planting of Man," 134.

He is like a tree transplanted by the streams of water (1:3a)
But [they] are like chaff that the wind blows away (1:4b)[43]

In the Hebrew the antithetic parallelism between the tree simile (*k'ṣ*, "like a tree") and the chaff (*kmṣ*, "like chaff") simile is evident, as the difference is just by one root letter (the middle root consonant). In terms of imagery, in contrast to the righteous (well watered, flourishing and heavy due to abundant fruit), the wicked is like chaff (dry, dead and light). However, within the strophe, the inter-colon parallelism in the Lowthian sense is not evident. Instead, it displays semantic progress: the chaff simile specifies the fate of "the wicked" mentioned in the preceding colon.

Viewed in the larger context, semantic progress is also present, though subtly. In light of the references to the wicked, sinners and scoffers in 1:1bcd, the present strophe indicates a specification/intensification. The shunning of the counsel of the wicked, way of the sinners and seat of the scoffers in the first strophe is now intensified by the description of their sad fate: like chaff, they are lightweights (lacking in substance and worth) and to be disposed. Such a fate is the reason why the blessed person shuns the ways of the wicked. As will be noted, this fate is further specified in the following strophe.

It should be noted that in the Hebrew, gapping is evident in this strophe: the subject is omitted in the second colon, but presumed to share the same subject with the preceding colon (*hārĕšāʿîm*, "the wicked"):

Not so with the wicked (1:4a)
but [they] are like chaff that the wind blows away (1:4b)

While ellipsis reflects the characterized terseness of Hebrew poetry in general, here it has the effect of drawing attention to the direct connection between the wicked and chaff, highlighting the consequence of the way of the wicked.

Strophe 5 (1:5)

The phrase "therefore" (*ʿal-kēn*) suggests that this colon (1:5a) states the consequence of the preceding colon, thus displaying intensification:

---

43. The LXX adds ἀπὸ προσώπου τῆς γῆς to רוּחַ ("from the face of the earth"). Against Kraus we do not think the LXX translator added the phrase as a "decorative appendage" (*Psalms 1–59*, 113); rather this avoids the abruptness of the MT. However, it makes 1:4b longer thus creating poetic asymmetry. Cf. Craigie, *Psalms 1–50*, 58.

But they are like chaff that the wind blows away (1:4b)

Therefore, the wicked will not stand in the judgment (1:5a)

Here the meaning of the chaff simile in the preceding colon is made plain: the lightweight chaff signifies the fate of the wicked before divine judgment; lacking substance, they will fail to measure up. This colon is equivalent to the following colon:

Therefore the wicked will not stand in the judgment (1:5a)

nor sinners in the assembly of the righteous (1:5b)

While one may note the synonymous parallelism between the two (the wicked//sinners; judgment//assembly of the righteous), there is also specification: the wicked (now called sinners) will not stand in the (judicial) assembly of the righteous. On the grammatical level, another case of gapping occurs here. The second colon has no verb, as the verb "will not stand" governs both cola. This way, the importance of judgment is underscored.

The relationship of Strophe 5 with the preceding strophe should also be noted, both on semantic and grammatical levels. Semantically, the first colon of Strophe 5 appears to correspond to the first colon of Strophe 4:

Not so with the wicked (1:4a) //

Therefore, the wicked (1:5a)

In fact, there is specification involved:

Not so with the wicked (1:4a)

Therefore, the wicked will not stand in the judgment
(1:5a, clarifying "Not so")

Whereas the former simply makes reference to the fact that the wicked is unlike the righteous, the latter specifies in what way the wicked is unlike the righteous.

On the grammatical level, in the Hebrew, matching is found on different levels, and the play on selection and combination is interesting:

lō'-kēn hārĕšā'îm	Not so with the wicked (1:4a)
'al-kēn lō'-yāqumû rĕšā'îm	Therefore will not stand the wicked (1:5a)

While the syntactical, morphological and phonological matching results in an almost complete repetition (notice the *lō'-kēn hārĕšā'îm* and *'al-kēn* . . .

rěšā'îm combination), the psalmist adds (inserts) a new element, that is, *lō'-yāqumû* in the latter:

> *lō'-kēn hārěšā'îm*
>
> *'al-kēn lō'-yāqumû rěšā'îm*

Such a play on selection and combination results in the clarification of 1:4a: "not so" (*lō'-kēn*) is clarified by "will not stand" (*lō'-yāqumû*). If the former prepares the reader for the fate of the wicked, the latter makes it clear what fate it will be.

Figurative Language: The Chaff Simile

The dynamics of the parallelism in Strophe 4 present us another kind of imagery. To elucidate his remark "Not so with the wicked," the psalmist uses the chaff simile. In several places in the Old Testament the chaff (*mōṣ*) is always used to describe God's judgment over the wicked (Job 21:18; Isa 17:13; 29:5 and Hos 13:3). All this suggests that the Hebrew authors have the metaphor "wicked people are chaff," mapping the domain of chaff onto the domain of the fate of the wicked:

Chaff (source)		Fate of the Wicked (target)
chaff	→	the wicked
blowing wind	→	judgment
being blown away	→	failing to stand before judgment

Perhaps chaff is chosen for its light weight, being easily blown away or disposed. As explicated in Strophe 5, the simile signifies the fact that before God's judgment, the wicked has nothing (no substance or power) to count on, therefore they will not stand.

CONCLUDING BICOLON (1:6)

The antithetic parallelism of this bicolon is immediately evident: the first colon is the opposite of the second:

> For Yahweh knows the way of the righteous,
> but the way of the wicked will perish.

Through this antithetic parallelism, the psalmist contrasts sharply the fates of the two ways. Whereas the way of the righteous is known to Yahweh, the way of the wicked will lead to perdition.

In doing so, the last strophe sums up the contrast between the preceding two stanzas (Stanza 1 and 2), alerting the reader to the corresponding relationship between this strophe and the two stanzas:

Stanza I : the portrayal of the righteous //

1:6a : the way of the righteous

Stanza II : the portrayal of the wicked //

1:6b : the way of the wicked

Upon a closer look, the concluding bicolon also further intensifies the respective stanzas. If Stanza 1 speaks of the prosperous life of the righteous, the first colon of the bicolon specifies that it is not about mere prosperity, but also about being known to Yahweh. Likewise, if Stanza 2 says that the wicked will fail to pass divine judgment, the second colon of the bicolon states that the failure will lead to perdition.

However, the summing up is done in more ways than one here. Notice the morphological parallelism between 1:1a (the beginning of the psalm) and 1:6b (the ending of the psalm): the former begins with the first letter of the Hebrew alphabet (aleph, *'ašrê*), the latter the last (*taw, tō'bēd*), forming an *inclusio* acrostically.[44] The end result is that the fates of the two ways are juxtaposed by placing them at the opposite end of the alphabet: one is beatitude, the other is perdition.

SUMMARY

The psalmist versifies the blessed person by two stanzas and one concluding bicolon. He portrays the blessed person in Stanza I and contrasts him with the wicked in Stanza II, then in the concluding colon he concludes the difference by contrasting the way of the righteous and the way of the wicked. We noted earlier that the psalmist devotes more and longer cola to the blessed person. This fact suggests where his interest is: the blessed righteous person.

Stanza I draws attention to the fact that the blessed person is a righteous person. By way of parallelism the psalmist tells the reader what the blessed person does not do in Strophe 1 and what he does in Strophe 2. In a

---

44. Van der Lugt, *Cantos and Strophes*, 97.

way, the three parallel "does-not cola" in Strophe 1 also function to contrast the righteous and the wicked. In other words, the righteous person is distinguished by contrasting his actions with those of the wicked.

The three parallel "does-not cola" also involve three "way of life" metaphors, which conceive life as a journey. Like a journey, life has a direction and distance to cover. The three parallel cola hint at the presence of a wrong direction and a wrong distance: a journey of gradually sliding down the road to perdition (moving from "walk" to "sit" and "stand"). The blessed person has discernment and makes wise decisions; he decides to avoid the slippery road.

Strophe 2 seems to explicate further why he avoids the slippery road. The blessed person knows the right direction and the right distance to cover: life should be oriented towards the torah and covering the distance of its way. Therefore he not only takes defensive measures (shunning evil) but also the proactive measure of meditating on the torah of Yahweh constantly. To the blessed person, to "meditate" (*hgh*) on the torah of Yahweh is a delight.[45] The parallelism in this strophe is such that the importance of this active measure cannot be missed.

In Strophe 3 the outcome of the active measure is delineated by the tree simile. As the semantic parallelism presents to us the vibrancy of the tree in a progressive manner, the simile itself maps vibrant life by a flourishing and prosperous tree. The tree simile is probably part of the broader divine garden metaphor, which conceptualizes God's dwelling (the temple) by a garden. If so, someone who constantly meditates on God's torah is like a tree in God's garden (his dwelling place) and enjoys the presence of God. The parallelism between the two cola suggests that the constant presence of Yahweh is in direct proportion to the person's constant meditation on the torah.

In Stanza II the portrayal of the blessed person is heightened by being contrasted with the wicked. Strophe 4 reveals that instead of being likened to a flourishing tree in God's garden, the wicked is conceptualized by the dry and light chaff. Then in Strophe 5 the reader is told that contrary to the vibrancy of the blessed person, the wicked will not withstand judgment; like chaff, being too light, they will be "blown away."

In the concluding bicolon, by antithetic parallelism the psalmist summarizes the versification of the blessed person by contrasting the way of the righteous and the way of the wicked. The contrast, however, focuses on the outcomes. The outcome of the righteous way is being known by God. Such

---

45. At times the verb *hgh* may denote audible meditation; see Negoiță and Ringgen, "הָגָה *hāgāh*," 321.

knowing is normally conceived in terms of relationship, an understanding reinforced by the fact that the righteous (the "tree") is in God's dwelling. In contrast, the way of the wicked leads to perdition. This contrast also summarizes the contrast between Stanza I (the portrayal of the righteous) and Stanza II (the portrayal of wicked). In a nutshell, God knows the person in Stanza I, not the one in Stanza II.

THEOLOGY

The psalmist begins his psalm with 'ašrê, a formulaic phrase used no fewer than thirty times in the Psalms (e.g., Pss 2:12; 32:1–2; 34:6; 40:5; 84:5; 119:1). Generally, 'ašrê is translated by "blessed." Unlike the more religious bārûk, 'ašrê is a general term that denotes a congratulatory sense (e.g., Pss 2:12; 32:1).[46] Furthermore, in the context of the Mediterranean value system, the congratulatory connotations may include "commendable" or "honorable."[47] In view of the piety of the person in this psalm, the congratulatory connotations may include "commendable (to God)."

Translated in the Old Greek Psalms (widely called LXX Psalms) as μακάριος, 'ašrê may be considered a beatitude (i.e., "Blessed is the person . . .").[48] As the psalm begins with the first letter of the Hebrew alphabet (aleph, 'ašrê) and ends with the last (taw, tō'bēd), the psalm may also be called "the A–Z guide to being a commendable person."

Theologically, this beatitude joins Psalm 119 in its orientation towards Yahweh's torah.[49] In keeping with Deuteronomic teachings, Psalm 1 expects the pious person to set himself apart from wickedness (cf. Deut 21:18–21; 25:1–2) and devotes himself to constant torah meditation (cf. Deut 5:33; 6:7; 30:16).[50] The setting apart suggests that the world is not conducive to torah living, but that such godly living is faced with a competing lifestyle, the lifestyle described by the metaphors of "walk," "stand" and "sit." The

46. See Cazelles, "אַשְׁרֵי 'ašrê," 1:445–48; Kraus, Psalms 1–59, 115.

47. This writer is grateful to K. C. Hanson for sharing his article on the meaning and cultural context of 'ašrê; see Hanson, "How Honorable! How Shameful!," 81–111.

48. From Latin beatus, equivalent to μακάριος; so Clifford, Psalms 1–72, 38.

49. Like this psalm, Psalm 119 also begins with 'ašrê: "Blessed are those whose way are blameless, who walk in the torah of Yahweh" (Ps 119:1).

50. The Hebrew word tôrāh may refer to the Mosaic law or the divine teachings in general. Some scholars aver that here the psalmist refers to the former, particularly Deuteronomy. Incidentally, as André points out, two of the verbs in this psalms (hlk and yšb) are found Deut 6:7, where Israel is taught to "talk about" God's torah "when you sit (yšb) in your house, walk (hlk) by the way" ("'Walk,' 'Stand' and 'Sit,'" 327). See also Kraus, Psalms 1–59, 116–17.

threefold "does not" and the semantic progress (from "walk" to "stand" to "sit") suggest that the powerful pull of this alternative lifestyle is not to be underestimated; it is no wonder that those who can escape such a pull are commendable to God.

Perhaps for this reason, it is inadequate to just passively resist temptations. To be a blessed person one also needs an active measure, that is, the constant meditation on the torah of God. The outcome of this active measure is delineated by the tree simile, which belongs in the metaphorical domain of the divine garden. In light of the divine garden metaphor, the "tree" is transplanted in none other than God's sanctuary, the closes one can get to the Source of "prosperity" (cf. "whatever he does, prospers"). By way of parallelism, the constant meditation on the torah (1:2) is matched with the constant supply of water ("tree transplanted by the streams of water," 1:3). Here lies the secret to "prosperity": constant connection with the Source by constant meditation on his torah.

To bring his message home, the psalmist contrasts sharply the preceding portrayals to the picture of the wicked (1:4–5). The fate of the wicked belongs to a different metaphorical domain, that is, the chaff domain. This implies that the wicked belong in the domain outside the divine garden (God's dwelling). Being outside God's domain, the wicked are found lightweight in God's sight; they will not stand in judgment.[51]

The beatitude is concluded by the final contrast: the way of the righteous and the way of the wicked. After reading through the psalm, it is obvious to the reader which way to go. For those who want to be a person commendable to God, there is only one choice: the way of the righteous, which is the way of Yahweh. Incidentally, in the theological scheme of Deuteronomy, this is also the only way to blessedness (Deut 5:33; 30:16).

It is universally noted that being placed at the beginning of the Psalms, Psalm 1 is intended to be the introduction to the whole book.[52] If so, becoming the commendable person in the psalm is important for understanding the rest of the Psalter. This may explain why the psalmist devotes more and longer lines to the righteous than to the wicked. His main interest is in the righteous, and wants the reader to place their focus on him.

---

51. The word "judgment" or "assembly of the righteous" here is open to different interpretations, such as the judgment of the last days; the judgment of Israel community, the messianic judgment etc.). For a discussion see Kraus, *Psalms 1–59*, 119–20. Regardless of one's view, the overall message here stresses the peril of the way of the wicked.

52. So Cole, *Psalms 1–2*, 46; Auffret, "Du psaume 1," 26; Craigie, *Psalms 1–50*, 59.

NEW TESTAMENT CONNECTIONS

Over the centuries, the commendable person in Psalm 1 has been identified with various biblical characters. Jewish interpreters identified him with Adam, Noah, Abraham, Moses, David and Josiah; the Church Fathers identified him as Christ;[53] Martin Buber identifies him with the paradigmatic wise portrayed in the wisdom literature.[54] However, some modern commentators have noted that the blessed person portrayed here is too perfect and thus "beyond human possibilities."[55] Indeed, it is difficult to imagine that flawed characters such as Adam, Noah, Moses or David would fit the description. From the point of view of the New Testament authors, however, Jesus certainly fits the portrayal of such a perfect person (e.g., Heb 4:15). In other words, he alone has been able to "fulfill" the expectations of the psalm.

Some scholars have observed the connection between this psalm and Jesus' Sermon on the Mount, in which Jesus begins with a series of beatitudes ("Blessed are . . ." especially Matt 5:1–12) and speaks of two gates (Matt 7:13–14).[56] However, it should be noted that Jesus' allusion reflects a new way of appropriating Psalm 1. His beatitudes include not only those who are like the ideal person of Psalm 1 (cf. "Blessed are those who hunger and thirst for righteousness," Matt 5:6 NAS), but also those who are "poor in spirit" (5:3 NAS), which among other things may refer to those who are imperfect but humble and have a contrite spirit.[57] Repeatedly, the Gospels tell us that Jesus' good news is for remorseful sinners (Matt 9:10–13; 11:19; Luke 7:34–35; 15:2–10), a theology in keeping with the beatitude elsewhere in the Psalter: "Blessed (ʾašrê) is the one whose transgression is forgiven, whose sin is covered" (Ps 32:1).

All this indicates that the authors of the Gospels present Jesus as the hope for those who are in "the way of the sinners" (cf. Ps 1:1). The door to becoming a commendable person is open to them provided they show contrition. As a matter of fact, according to the New Testament authors, this is the only door to being commendable before God. The reason is simple: only Jesus is the perfect and righteous One; only through him and being transformed into his likeness can one stand the chance of growing into a commendable person (e.g., Heb 5:9; 10:19–21).

---

53. See Cole, *Psalms 1–2*, 55, nn. 32–34.

54. E.g., Buber, *Right and Wrong*, 53–62. It is noteworthy that the psalm is regarded by many commentators as a wisdom psalm. See Craigie, *Psalms 1–50*, 61; Apple, "Blessed Man," 180.

55. So Eaton, *Psalms*, 31; Kraus, *Psalms 1–59*, 121.

56. Craigie, *Psalms 1–50*, 61–62; Gillingham, *Psalms*, 16.

57. See France, *Gospel of Matthew*, 165.

6

Poetic Analysis and Interpretation of Ecclesiastes 1:3–8

ECCLESIASTES 1:3–8 AS A POEM

ECCLESIASTES INTRODUCES ITS THEME by quoting Qoheleth: "Vanity of vanity! All is vanity!" (1:2).[1] The book proceeds to unpack this thematic statement by the poem in 1:3–8. The latter passage displays parallelism and rich metaphor; therefore, the majority of commentators have identified it as a poem.[2]

LINEATION OF ECCLESIASTES 1:3–8

The lineation of the present passage faces at least two problems. First of all, the boundary of is not easy to determine. Part of the problem is whether or not to treat 1:9–11 as belonging in the poem. Though parallelism is present

1. There are diverse views on the identity of Qoheleth and his relationship with Ecclesiastes. These issues are well covered in many critical commentaries (e.g., Crenshaw, *Ecclesiastes*, 32–33). See also Fox, "Frame-Narrative," 83–106.

2. Most commentators think that 1:1–11 is prose, because as a whole it lacks "parallelism, terseness and wordplays" which normally characterize Hebrew poetry (Barton, *Ecclesiastes*, 69; Rousseau, "De Qohelet 1:4–11," 201–3; Murphy, *Ecclesiastes*, 6–7; Ogden, *Qoheleth*, 34–35; Seow, *Ecclesiastes*, 113, 116; Bartholomew, *Ecclesiastes*, 109–10) agree that the section is poetic. Longman (*Ecclesiastes*, 59). As will be shown in this chapter, while 1:1–2 and 1:9–11 are indeed prosaic, 1:3–8 displays key poetic indicators such as metaphors and intensified use of parallelism.

in 1:9–11, it is not as consistent as 1:3–8. Furthermore, it lacks the high concentration of metaphors which characterize 1:3–8. This has led to different
treatments of 1:9–11. Some scholars see 1:9–11 as part of the poem,[3] while
other scholars exclude it.[4] The uncertainty is betrayed by the fact that even
some of those who include 1:9–11 have printed it as prose.[5] Perhaps the
uncertainty and diversity here are partly due to one's definition of Hebrew
poetry.[6]

Nonetheless, we argue that at least two indicators set 1:9–11 apart
from 1:3–8. First is the transition marker "what" (*mah*) in 1:9a, as it marks
the beginning of a new section. Second, as mentioned above, the lack of
consistent use of parallelism and low concentration of figurative language
leave one with the impression that 1:9–11 is more prosaic than poetic. This
by no means to say that 1:9–11 is unrelated to 1:3–8, but that the prose section serves as a commentary on the poem.[7]

Another problem is that while the strophes are recognizable, it is not
easy to identify the stanzas of the poem. This is where the criteria offered
by Watson, Muilenburg and van der Lugt encounter complication.[8] The
reason is that the thought-content of the strophes are so tightly cohesive
and interwoven with each other (especially from Strophe 2 onwards), that
their criteria can lead to more models than one.[9] Therefore, in our opinion,
dividing the poem into two or three larger sections (two stanzas or three
stanzas) is rather arbitrary.[10] As most strophes are tightly coherent, we treat
the poem as one compact unit comprising strophes rather than stanzas.

3. E.g., Rousseau, "De Qohelet 1:4–11," 201; Whybray, "Ecclesiastes 1:5–7," 105–6;
Murphy, *Ecclesiastes*, 5; Ogden, *Qoheleth*, 34.

4. E.g., Seow, *Ecclesiastes*, 111; Wright, "Riddle and the Sphinx," 333.

5. At least one of them has printed it "somewhat hesitantly in prose" (Murphy,
Ecclesiastes, 7).

6. For more discussion of this issue, see our analysis of 1:9–11 below.

7. In arguing so, we align ourselves with scholars who see 1:3 as the introductory
statement of the poem, 1:4–8 as the poem proper and 1:9–11 as the explanation of the
poem (see Wright, "Riddle and Sphinx," 333; Seow, *Ecclesiastes*, 111, 113, 116). The
argument of Fox is in agreement to this position except that he takes 1:10–11 as the
commentary prose (*Time to Tear Down*, 169).

8. See 17–19.

9. Thought-content wise, the cola in 1:4–8 are tightly connected by the theme of
circularity. Grammatically, as Murphy notes, the repetitive use of participles through
1:4–7 bonds them together as a compact unit (*Ecclesiastes*, 7).

10. For instance, Wright divides the poem into two sections: 1:4–6 and 1:7–8
("Riddle and Sphinx," 333). While 1:4–6 appears to be a unit, 1:7–8 seems arbitrary, as
it ignores the grammatical coherence of 1:7 and 1:4–6. Similarly, Rousseau breaks the
poem into three sections, arbitrarily breaking the two closely strophes in vv. 4–5 and vv.
6–7 apart ("De Qohelet 1:4–11," 202–3).

Here we propose to divide the poem into six strophes. The first three are bicolon strophes, the fourth is a tricolon strophe, and the fifth and the sixth are tetra-colon strophes:

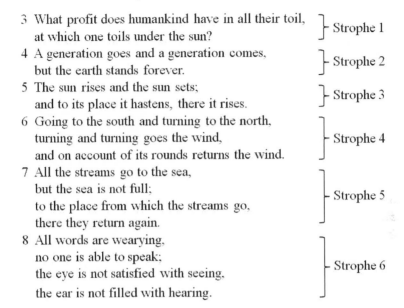

3 What profit does humankind have in all their toil,
  at which one toils under the sun?
                                    } Strophe 1

4 A generation goes and a generation comes,
  but the earth stands forever.
                                    } Strophe 2

5 The sun rises and the sun sets;
  and to its place it hastens, there it rises.
                                    } Strophe 3

6 Going to the south and turning to the north,
  turning and turning goes the wind,
  and on account of its rounds returns the wind.
                                    } Strophe 4

7 All the streams go to the sea,
  but the sea is not full;
  to the place from which the streams go,
  there they return again.
                                    } Strophe 5

8 All words are wearying,
  no one is able to speak;
  the eye is not satisfied with seeing,
  the ear is not filled with hearing.
                                    } Strophe 6

The boundaries of each strophe are identifiable primarily by their thought-content. Only one strophe is demarcated by a transition marker, that is, Strophe 1, which begins with the interrogative pronoun "What" (*mah*). Strophe 2 sets itself apart from the preceding and following strophes by its thought-content (i.e., the contrast between the generational cycles and the permanence of the earth), as do Strophes 3, 4, 5 and 6.

PARALLELISM

A close examination indicates that the poem is constructed by tightly parallel cola. The parallelism is employed to present Qoheleth's reflection on struggles with "vanity" (*hebel*) experiences.

Strophe 1 (1:3): Programmatic Statement

The poem is introduced by the rhetorical question: "What profit does humankind have in all their toil?" As widely noted, the rhetorical question serves as the thematic/programmatic statement of the poem.[11] The question is constructed as a bicolon, in which the first colon corresponds to the second in the subject matter (i.e., toil):

What profit does humankind have in all their *toil* //

at which one *toils* under the sun?

Semantically, the second colon intensifies and specifies the first: whereas the first colon speaks only of toil, the second intensifies/specifies that it is toil under the sun. The intensification effect is aided by the grammatical parallelism. In the Hebrew the parallelism in terms of word order is evidently shown by the inverted order of the root '*ml* ("to toil"):

mah-yyitrôn lā'ādām bĕkol-'ămālô // *šeyya'ămōl taḥat haššāmeš*

The inversion draws the reader's attention to '*āmāl* (toil), thus underscores its importance, which happens to be one of the keywords (*Leitworter*) of Qoheleth.[12] The implied answer to the rhetorical question is "no": "all toil" has no profit (i.e., it is futile). If so, the rhetorical question highlights the *hebel* of "all toil" (*kol-'ămālô*). The fact that this is the implied answer is evidenced by the subsequent analogies (which form the poem) and serve as the response to the question about toil.

Strophe 2 (1:4): The Life Cycle Analogy

The first analogy is taken from the cycle of life:
A generation goes and a generation comes,
but the earth stands forever.

The antithetical parallelism in the strophe is observable on two levels: the intra-colon and the inter-colon levels. The intra-colon parallelism in the first colon is too obvious to miss:

A generation goes // a generation comes

At first glance the colon seems to speak of the passing of generations. However, as recent scholarship has recognized, it in fact expresses a cyclical motion.[13] It is uncertain if the Hebrew word *dôr* here means "a period of

---

11. Seow, *Ecclesiastes*, 111; Bartholomew, *Ecclesiastes*, 107; Fox, *Ecclesiastes*, 4.

12. In Ecclesiastes, the noun of root '*ml* occurs 22 times, and the verb 13 times.

13. E.g., Ogden, "Interpretation of דור"; and Murphy, *Ecclesiastes*, 7.

time" or "a generation of people."[14] However, the cyclical idea is supported by the antithetical parallelism. Though the verb "goes" is the antonym of "comes,"[15] together they describe a repetitive to-and-fro motion, going on and on, forming a cycle.[16] Being cyclical, even though the repeated to-and-fro motion of generations indicates constant change, in reality it does not effect change at all.

Antithetical parallelism is also present in the inter-colon relationship. The adversative conjunction (*waw*, "but") sets the second colon in contrast with the first:

> A generation goes and a generation comes,
> *but* the earth stands forever.

Against the circularity in the first colon is the unchanging nature of the earth in the second colon.[17] The antithetic parallelism, however, also suggests semantic progress: the notion of the unchanging nature of the earth heightens the circularity of generations.

A number of observations on word matching reinforce this idea. While the word "generation" (*dôr*) is repeated, it is matched with a pair of antonyms ("going" [*hōlēk*] and "coming" [*bāʾ*]). This reinforces the circular nature of the movement of generations: whereas the participles "going" and "coming" already suggest repetitive/cyclical motion, their matching with "generation" (which originally means "cycle") intensifies the notion of circularity.

In turn the combination of "generation," "going" and "coming" in the first colon is matched with the combination of "standing" (*ʿōmādet*) and "earth" in the second colon. If the first colon's combination results in a circular motion, the second colon's combination heightens that sense by contrasting it with the unchanging state of the earth. It turns out that the circularity expressed by this strophe sets the pattern for the following analogies from nature.

14. Commentators variously take it to refer to time (so Freedman et al., "דּוֹר, *dôr*," 3:169–81 and Whybray, "Ecclesiastes 1:5–7," 106); generations of people (Lohfink, *Qoheleth*, 41; Murphy, *Ecclesiastes*, 7; Seow, *Ecclesiastes*, 114). Ogden ("Interpretation of דור") argues that it refers to cycle of nature; while Crenshaw (*Ecclesiastes*, 62) thinks that it encompasses both nature and people.

15. In the Hebrew they are participles ("going" and "coming").

16. As Isaksson and Crenshaw note, the use of the participles not only expresses repetition and also continuation. Isaksson, *Language of Qoheleth*, 66; Crenshaw, *Ecclesiastes*, 62.

17. The term "earth" (*hāʾāreṣ*) is open to different readings. While many commentators take it to mean the physical earth, Fox argues that it refers to humanity as a whole (*le monde*); see Fox, "Qoheleth 1:4," 109. For the meaning of *ʿōmādet* (standing) in 1:4b, see Whybray, "Ecclesiastes 1:5–7," 106; Seow, *Ecclesiastes*, 106.

Strophe 3 (1:5): The Sun Analogy

After pointing out the circularity of generations, the poet proceeds to the circularity of nature in Strophe 3:

> The sun rises and the sun sets;
>
> and to its place it hastens, there it rises.

The strophe speaks of the movement of the sun, which is the first of the series of natural routines. Just as in preceding strophe, the circularity of the solar movement is illustrated by way of parallelism. In fact, the word matching in the first colon gives the reader a sense of *déjà vu*: the poet repeats the thought of Strophe 2 by employing a set of corresponding parts of speech:

Strophe 2 (1:4a)	Strophe 3 (1:5a)
generation (noun)	the sun (noun)
goes, comes (verbs)	rises, sets (verbs)

The two strophes are also parallel on the intra-colon level; like Strophe 2, the present strophe demonstrates antithetical parallelism within the first colon:

A generation goes // a generation comes (1:4)

The sun rises // the sun sets (lit. comes, 1:5)

Also like the first colon of the preceding strophe, though the verbs "rises" and "sets" seem to refer to opposite movements, taken as a whole they in fact represent a circular movement.

Similarly, the semantic inter-colon parallelism is observable. The "rising-setting" movement is matched with the "hastening-rising" movement, demonstrating chiastic parallelism:

The sun rises, the sun sets

and to its place it hastens, there it rises

Notice that, as in Strophe 2, the foregoing parallelism (be it in terms of semantics or word matching) also demonstrates semantic progress. The first colon describes the sun's motion from the rising place to the setting place. To complete the depiction of the sun's circular movement, the second colon describes the sun's movement from the setting place back to the rising place.

In addition, it should be pointed out that while in many ways Strophe 3 corresponds to Strophe 2, in fact it intensifies the circularity theme of the latter. This is achieved by the second colon. If Strophe 2 speaks of the going and the coming of generations, Strophe 3 speaks of a hastening/rushing (*šô'ēp*) sun, suggesting a more intense action. Nevertheless, this intense action leads the sun back to the place where it rises. As such, the movement is circular, albeit more intensified than that of the preceding strophe.

Strophe 4 (1:6): The Wind Analogy

From the sun's circularity the poet now turns to another form of circularity in nature: the movement of the wind.[18] But here he employs a tricolon:

> Going to the south and turning to the north,
>
> turning and turning goes the wind,
>
> and on account of its rounds returns the wind.

The first colon (1:6a) corresponds to the preceding strophe (1:5a) in terms of intra-colon parallelism:

> Going to the south//turning to the north (1:6a)

Like the previous strophes, each of these half-cola appears to move in the opposite direction, only to end up moving in a circle; this thought is reinforced (intensified) by the following colon:

> Turning and turning goes the wind (1:6b)

This second colon is in turn intensified in the third colon:

> And on account of its rounds returns the wind (1:6c)

In terms of Strophe 4's relationship with the preceding two strophes (Strophes 2 and 3), we should pay attention to the semantic intensification. The circularity of the previous strophes is intensified by the repeated use of the participle "turning" (*sôbēb*) in the present strophe.[19]

An examination of its grammatical parallelism shows the poet's skillfulness in selection and combination. Though this strophe appears to be a

---

18. The wind turns up only in the second colon, some commentators therefore debate whether the subject of the first colon is the wind or the sun in the preceding verse; see below.

19. The intensity is evidenced by the repeated use of the participle *sôbēb*: four times in one single strophe (once in the first colon, twice in the second colon, and once in the last colon [translated as "rounds"]).

repetition of the previous two strophes, in fact it varies on two accounts. Firstly, unlike the previous strophes, the subject of the sentences does not appear until the end of the second colon. As such, the subject (the wind) governs both the first and the second cola (1:6a, b), indicating a case of gapping.[20] The delay heightens the sense of circularity expressed by the repetition of "going" and "turning" preceding the subject.[21]

Secondly, while the participle "going" (*hôlēk*) is used again here (as in Strophe 2, 1:4a), it is now joined with another participle, "turning" (*sôbēb*) instead of the earlier "coming" (*bāʾ*, cf. 1:4a and 1:5a). As a result, the parallelism here is not mere repetition. Rather the selection and combination brings out a heightening effect, because the repetition of the particle "turning" (*sôbēb*) intensifies the sense of circularity.[22] In brief, people and things in nature are not only "going" and "coming" (which is circular enough), they are in fact "turning" like a revolving door.

Strophe 5 (1:7): The Streams Analogy

Strophe 5 consists of four cola. Using the phenomenon of streams, the poet continues the theme of circularity. Compared to Strophe 4, it is less intensified, and more similar to the pattern of Strophes 2 and 3. As such it suggests that this is the beginning of the poem's denouement. We will first look at the strophe by itself:

> All the streams go to the sea (1:7a)
>
> but the sea is not full (1:7b)
>
> to the place from which the streams go (1:7c)
>
> there they return again (1:7d)

The third and fourth cola (1:7c, d) are no mere repetition of the first and second cola (1:7a, b). Rather, they intensify the latter pair by highlighting

---

20. In doing so we follow the majority view that the wind is the subject of the whole verse; see for example Carasik, 'Qoheleth's Twists and Turns,' 192–209; Ogden, *Qoheleth*, 34–36; Dell, "The Cycle of Life," 183–85; Samet, "Qoheleth 1:4," 93–94. Other commentators argue that the sun is still the subject of at least the first colon of 1:6; see Japhet, "Goes to the South," 289–322; and Weeks, *Ecclesiastes and Scepticism*, 47. In our opinion, such a reading fails to consider the literary technique of gapping and intensification in the text.

21. Scholars such as Good and Wilson argue that the delay is Qoheleth's rhetorical technique with the intention to spring a surprise on the reader; see Good, "The Unfilled Sea," 66–67; Wilson, "Artful Ambiguity," 357–58.

22. Seow (*Ecclesiastes*, 108) notes the unusual construction of this verse.

the circularity of the streams: the streams are not just going (1:7a, b), but also moving in a circle of "going" and "returning" (1:7c, d).[23]

Now we will study the strophe in light of the preceding strophes. A close look at the strophe shows many correspondences with Strophe 2. Firstly, like Strophe 2 (1:4), antithetical parallelism is present between the first and second cola of this strophe. As in 1:4b, the poet uses the adversative *waw* 1:7b:

> All the streams go to the sea (1:7a) // *but* the sea is not full (1:7b)

Secondly, in Strophe 2 generations come and go but the earth remains unchanged; similarly here, the streams move to the sea but the sea remains unchanged. Below is a comparison of the parallelism between Strophe 2 and Strophe 5:

Strophe 2 (1:4a, b)	Strophe 5 (1:7a, b)
A generation goes and a generation comes	All the streams go to the sea
but the earth stands forever	*but* the sea is not full

Nevertheless, unlike Strophe 2, the present strophe is longer by two more cola (1:7c, d):

> to the place from which the streams *go,*
> there they *return* again.

But the extension (as it were) repeats the pattern of Strophes 2 and 3 by presenting antithetical parallelism: "go" (*hōlĕkîm*) versus "return" (*šabîm*). Also like Strophes 2 and 3, the antithetical parallelism basically connotes circularity: the streams return to where they go. The similarities between this strophe and Strophes 2 and 3 imply that the present strophe returns to a less intense pattern. This in turn suggests that the poem's intensity highlighted in Strophe 4 begins to ease in the present strophe, intimating a denouement.

---

23. The Hebrew *'el-mĕqôm šehannĕhālîm hōlkîm* may mean "to the place *from* which the streams go" or "to the place *to* which streams go." The former would mean the streams go cyclical, whereas the latter would mean they flow continuously. The problem is in part lies in the meaning of the *šābîm* + *lālāket* construct which follows immediately, whether it means 'return' or 'do something once again' (Joüon-Muraoka §102g). Commentators follow either the former (e.g., Lohfink, *Qoheleth*, 39, 41; Seow, *Ecclesiastes*, 100, 108–9) or the latter (e.g., Barton, *Ecclesiastes*, 74; Murphy, *Ecclesiastes*, pp. lxxi, 8). However, considering the cyclical nature of the preceding analogies (and especially the *šûb* in v. 6), it is more likely that *šābîm lālāket* means "return" (so Whybray, *Ecclesiastes* [NCBC], 42).

Strophe 6 (1:8): Wearying Effects of Words

From analogies taken from the natural world, the poet now switches back to the human world to discuss the effects of human words on speaking, seeing and hearing. In the Hebrew the two cola are corresponding to each other by the root *dbr*, and the word order forms inverted parallelism. The first colon has the noun *haddĕbārîm* ("the words," 1:8a),[24] whereas the second has the infinitive construct *lĕdabbēr* ("to speak," 1:8b):

> *kol-haddĕbārîm yĕgē'îm* // *lō-yûkal 'îš lĕdabbēr*

> All words are wearying // no one is able to speak

By matching the two forms of *dbr*, attention is drawn to "words" and their wearying effect. This notion is further elaborated in the following two parallel cola (the third and fourth):

> The eye is not satisfied with seeing //   The ear is not filled with hearing
> (1:8c)   (1:8d)

Here semantic parallelism is demonstrated by the corresponding thoughts: "words fail to satisfy one's seeing (reading)" corresponds to "words fail to satiate hearing." Also on the semantic level, we notice word pairing:

1:8c		1:8d
eye (human organ for seeing)	–	ear (human organ for hearing)
satisfied	–	filled/satiated
seeing (visual sense)	–	hearing (audio sense)

Grammatically, word matching is also evident:

1:8c		1:8d
eye (3 fs noun)	–	ear (3 fs noun)
negation particle *lō'*	–	negation particle *lō'*
Qal Imperfect 3 fs *śb'*	–	Niphal Imperfect 3 fs *ml'*
preposition + Qal infinitive construct *r'h*	–	preposition + Qal infinitive construct *šm'*

---

24. The Hebrew word *dĕbārîm* means "words" or "things." Throughout Ecclesiastes, most often it refers to "words" (5:2; 6:11; 7:21; 10:14). Here "words" fits well with the immediate context, in which the poet speaks of being "not able to speak" (1:8b) and the activity of hearing (1:8d). See Murphy, *Ecclesiastes*, 6 n8a; and Seow, *Ecclesiastes*, 109.

All these correspondences are intentional and thus more than just repetition. Drawing on Jakobson's principle of selection and combination and Alter's semantic progress we will point out their poetic function. The poet begins with the statement: "All words are wearying," As the particle "wearying" suggests, words have wearying power.[25] To elaborate the meaning of this term, the poet selects and combines three parallel negations. The word choice of each negation is deliberate and serves a purpose. Each begins with the negation particle *lō'* ("not"), followed by a verb, a noun and an infinitive construct verb which is related to *dĕbārîm* (i.e., to speak, see and hear). Translated literally, the cola will be as follows:

> One[26] is *not* able to speak
> The eye is *not* satisfied with seeing
> The ear is *not* filled with hearing

The correspondence is to alert the reader to the connection of the respective colon as to demonstrate the semantic progress of the three negations. The first negation clarifies by stating the extent of the wearying power: no one is able to speak. Likewise, the second and third negations intensify the wearying effects of words: the eye is not satisfied with seeing (reading) words, the ear not satiated by hearing words. In sum, the second, third and fourth cola intensify the first colon by stating the wearying power of words on speech, sight and hearing. Read in its immediate context, Strophe 6 also enhances the points made in the preceding strophes. If the preceding strophes speak of the ceaseless activities in the natural world, this last strophe adds that ceaseless words can make humankind weary.

Section Summary

The poet answers the rhetorical question "What profit does humankind have in all their toil?" by a series of life and natural phenomena. By way of parallelism, the poet intimates that life and things in nature experience endless activities or change, yet the apparent change is ultimately circular. It should be noted that while the semantics progresses from one strophe to another, the description of circularity is carried out in varying degrees of intensity. The intensity may be illustrated below:

---

25. As many commentators note, here *yĕgē'im* is used as a participle (wearying) rather than an adjective (wearisome); see Seow, *Ecclesiastes*, 109; Ogden, *Qoheleth*, 37.

26. Lit. "man" (*'îš*).

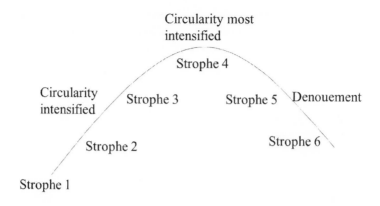

The thematic rhetorical question in Strophe 1 (that one's toil is futile, 1:3) is elaborated by the illustrations of circularity in the strophes that follow. Strophe 2 begins by citing the circularity of the cycle of life. Strophe 3 intensifies the sense of circularity by employing the participle šōʾēp (hastening/rushing), resulting in the "hastening" of the circular motion. Circularity is most intensified in Strophe 4, where the participle "turning" is used repeatedly on the "turning and turning" of wind in its cycle. Such intensity eases in Strophe 5, where the sense of circularity is described in the pattern of Strophes 2 and 3 again. This suggests the beginning of a denouement. The denouement leads to the end of the poem in Strophe 6. Here circularity is delineated by human activities, suggesting a return to where the poem starts (Strophe 1, i.e., the futility of human activities).

This analysis reinforces Alter's argument that parallelism is no mere repetition. The observations above suggest that the poet does not just repeat the circularity theme by merely running through similar illustrations. Rather, he does so by increasing the intensity till it reaches its climax, then heads for a denouement.[27] Ironically, such non-monotonous portrayal is intended to demonstrate the monotony of human experience.

FIGURATIVE LANGUAGE: THE HEBEL METAPHOR

Ecclesiastes is known for its rich use of figurative language.[28] The book is filled with metaphors such as darkness (2:14; 6:4; 11:8), shadow (6:12; 7:12), light (11:7–8; 12:2), dreams (5:2 [ET 5:3]; 5:6 [ET 5:7]), and the much de-

---

27. This reminds us against assuming that Hebrew poets always present their poems in a chiastic pattern, as Rousseau does to the poetic text in question ("De Qohelet 1:4–11," 202–3).

28. See Miller, "Qohelet's Symbolic," 444.

bated images of death (12:1–8). Even a cursory reading would pick up the metaphorical rendering of the participles "coming" and "going" in the present poem (1:4), which are widely recognized to be metaphors for birth and death.[29] Likewise, the recurrent phrase "under the sun" is metaphor for the present transient life.[30]

We will focus only on the most significant metaphor in the poem, *hebel*, for a few reasons. First, it serves our limited purpose (to demonstrate how to do poetic analysis); second, hebel as a metaphor is not only the main theme of the poem in question, but also programmatic to the rest of the book. As we will see soon, several other metaphors (such as those in the analogies) are in fact subsumed under this key metaphor.

Hebel as a Metaphor

As we mentioned above, the poem is meant to validate the thematic statement of Ecclesiastes: "All is vanity" (1:2b). The word "vanity" (*hebel*) literally means "breath" or "vapor."[31] Obviously, the author employs the word beyond its literal connotations.[32] As a matter of fact, recent studies have emphasized the metaphorical nature of *hebel* in Ecclesiastes.[33] Of interest is Douglas B. Miller's argument that Ecclesiastes uses *hebel* as a symbol (metaphor).[34] Miller argues that instead of picking up stock metaphors such as "the way" or "the tree of life" known in the wisdom tradition, the author uses a "live

29. The verb *hlk* (to go) is frequently used as a metaphor for death in Ecclesiastes (3:20; 5:14–15 [ET: 5:15–16]; 6:6, 9; 7:2; 9:10; 12:5) and elsewhere (Ps 39:14 [ET 39:13]; Job 10:21; 14:20; 2 Sam 12:23). See Crenshaw, *Ecclesiastes*, 62; Seow, *Ecclesiastes*, 106; Enns, *Ecclesiastes*, 33.

30. The phrase *taḥat haššemeš* ("under the sun") is unique to Ecclesiastes, as it is not found elsewhere in the Old Testament. In the book, the expression is preferred (occurs 29 times) to the usual "under the heavens" (occurs only 3 times in Ecclesiastes). Seow notes that the expression refers to the present life, the world of the living (as against the netherworld). Seow, *Ecclesiastes*, 105.

31. See Seybold, "הֶבֶל *hebhel*," 313–20.

32. The meaning and the use of *hebel* is a much discussed subject. For a survey and critique of the various proposals on the meaning of *hebel*, see Miller, "Qohelet's Symbolic," 437–43.

33. Fox points out that in the Hebrew Bible *hebel* is almost always used in metaphorical sense; the only occasion on which the word is used in a non-figurative sense is found in Isa 57:13 (*Qoheleth and His Contradictions*, 29). See also Fredericks, *Coping with Transience*, esp p. 12; Farmer, *Who Knows What is Good?*," esp. pp. 143–46; Perdue, *Wisdom and Creation*, 206–8.

34. For the relationship of symbol and metaphor, see his more recent publication, which is a revised and updated version of his Ph.D. dissertation: Miller, *Symbol and Rhetoric*, 44–46.

metaphor," *hebel*.[35] He also contends that *hebel* is a multi-meaning metaphor which holds three basic "referents": insubstantiality, transience and foulness.[36]

If Miller is correct, his insights shed light on the figurative language of the poem in question. As mentioned, the rhetorical question in the first strophe (1:3) elaborates *hebel* in 1:2, which Miller argues to be a metaphor for insubstantiality.[37] Unpacking this metaphorical sense, the rhetorical question implies the futility of one's *ʿāmāl* (i.e., various struggles in human experience[38]). Besides two illustrations from the human world (1:4 and 1:8), we note a series of analogies (metaphors) from nature intended to illustrate such futility. Relevant to our present analysis is the question: how do the analogies function in achieving the illustrative purpose? More pointedly, how do the analogies contribute to the reader's understanding of the *hebel* metaphor?

Mapping the *Hebel* Experience by Nature's Cyclical Phenomena

Miller argues that in order to "guard" the meaning of a live metaphor, among other measures, Ecclesiastes illustrates it by synonyms, synonymous phrases or contraries.[39] Since *ʿāmāl* in 1:3 is intended to illustrate the live metaphor *hebel*, to understand *hebel* one should first understand the meaning of *ʿāmāl*. Contrary to Miller, in this poem, the meaning of *ʿāmāl* is explained not by synonyms or contraries but by parallel analogies from nature.[40] To be precise, the poet conceptualizes *ʿāmāl* (human struggles) by natural phenomena. In other words, Qoheleth presents the metaphor "Human struggles are natural phenomena." The analogies from natural phenomena are then the

---

35. Miller, "Qohelet's Symbolic," 444–45.

36. Ibid., 446–52; also Miller, *Symbol and Rhetoric*, 91–95.

37. Miller, "Qohelet's Symbolic," 447; Miller, *Symbol and Rhetoric*, 101–3.

38. As some scholars point out, in Ecclesiastes *ʿāmāl* is more than just toil or work (e.g., Fox, *Time to Tear Down*, 101–2; Seow, *Ecclesiastes*, 104). It also covers a wide range of struggles in human experience, including efforts to seek wisdom, wealth, and pleasure.

39. Ibid., 445. By contraries, Miller means words negated because they are opposite to the intended sense of the metaphor). Another measure is extension (author's use of literary context).

40. Contra Miller, who observes that the analogies are contraries (i.e., they are opposite to the metaphorical sense of *hebel*); see Miller, *Symbol and Rhetoric*, 102–3. As will be shown, these analogies express the *very* sense of *hebel*.

vehicle (and source domain), and human struggles are the tenor (and target domain):[41]

Natural Phenomena (source)		Human Struggles (target)
coming and going	→	birth and death
hastening (panting)	→	vigorous and exhausting
nature's constant change	→	constant change in life
nature's cyclical change		the cycle of life
sea not filled	→	unfulfilling struggles
nature's change makes no ultimate change	→	change in life makes no ultimate change

The preceding mapping shows how the poet conceives the human world by the natural world. The ever coming and going in the natural world refers to birth and death in the human world. The strenuous activity of the sun refers to the vigorous and exhausting human activities.[42] The perpetual change effected by the coming and going in nature reflects the constant change in life; the ceaseless cyclical motions refer to the constant cycles of life; and the unchanging character of nature conceptualizes the unchanging character of life under the sun. As Graham S. Ogden sums it up well, the perpetual change exemplified in the natural world is "true also of the human world."[43]

Given that ʿāmāl is a commentary on hebel, it follows that the poet also conceptualizes hebel by the natural phenomena. In many ways, the insubstantiality and fluidity of hebel (whose literal meaning is "breath" or "vapor") is conceptualized by the ever changing character of nature:

Natural Phenomena (source)		Hebel of human experience (target)
coming/going/blowing/flowing[44]	→	fluidity

41. Cf. ibid., 103.

42. The root šʾp also means "panting" and carries two possible senses in the Hebrew Bible. In Ps 119:131, it refers to anticipation (positive sense), but in Jer 14:6 it expresses exhaustion (negative sense). Whybray argues for the former and asserts that the poem speaks positively of nature ("Ecclesiastes 1.5–7," 108–110;cf. Lohfink, Qoheleth, 40). But read in the negative context of 1:1–11, we agree with Seow and Crenshaw that it carries a negative connotation here; see Seow, Ecclesiastes, 107; Crenshaw, Ecclesiastes, 64.

43. Ogden, Qoheleth, 37.

constant change	→	constant change
cyclical motions	→	repetitive
sea not filled by water	→	unfulfilling struggles
nature's change makes no ultimate change	→	insubstantiality

The metaphorical rendering here indicates that as if mimicking nature, the *hebel* of human experience is fluid, going through endless change, yet remains insubstantial.

Section Summary

Qoheleth offers his answer to the question "What profit does humankind have in all their toil?" partly by the conceptual metaphor "Human struggles are natural phenomena." The answer is a solid negative: "No profit. All humankind's struggles can be conceived by the day to day natural phenomena around them. Just like many things in nature, they are rigorous without profit (*yitrôn*). Ultimately, like many things, life is circular, and thus ultimately futile." Interestingly, the conceptual metaphor is such that the reader comes away with the impression that while human struggles are unfulfilling, they are as bustling as nature's activities. This reinforces the irony drawn from our study of the parallelism earlier: the poet describes monotony without being monotonous.

Qoheleth's mapping of human struggles by natural phenomena reinforces what we discussed in chapter 4: one's conceptual metaphor reflects their theology.[45] By highlighting the futility of natural activities in the universe, Qoheleth betrays a pessimistic outlook on creation.

READING THE POEM IN LIGHT OF 1:9–11

As mentioned at the beginning of this chapter, 1:9–11 serves as a commentary on the meaning of the poem in 1:3–8. The nature of this prose section is rather distinct from 1:3–8. For example, parallelism is practiced in the section, albeit not consistently. Besides, the passage is written in plain language, lacking the figurative language that characterizes the poem in 1:3–8. This may have given some scholars reason not to treat it as part of the poem

---

44. As commentators point out, especially corresponding to the *hebel* is the wind analogy (Fox, *Ecclesiastes*, xx). The word *rûaḥ* ("wind") also means breath, just as *hebel* also means "breath."

45. See 109–10.

(1:3–8). To understand how this prosaic passage functions as an explanation for the poem, a literary analysis is in order.

Analysis of 1:9–11

The prose sections begin with two remarks which are mutually corresponding:

What has been is what will be // What has been done is what will be done
(1:9a)   (1:9b)

Grammatical parallelism is more evident in the Hebrew text. Word matching is noticeable within 1:9a itself:

> *mah-ššehāyāh*
>
> *hû' šeyyihyeh*

As shown above, the interrogative pronoun *mah* (what) is matched
with the personal pronoun *hû* ("it," translated "what"); and the combination of the relative pronoun *še* (which, translated "what") with the verb *hyh*
(to be) is repeated but not without variation, for the Qal Perfect (*ššehāyāh*,
"what has been") in the first half of the remark is matched with the Qal
Imperfect (*šeyyihyeh*, "what will be") in the second half. Syntactically, the
matching is constructed as follows:

interrogative pronoun *mah*   relative pronoun *še* + Qal perfect *hyh*

personal pronoun *hû*   relative pronoun *še* + Qal imperfect *hyh*

The juxtaposition shows that while *mah* and *hû* represent the same subjects
(translated as "what"), the former refers to the past and the latter to the
future. The effect of the juxtaposition is that the past *is* the future and vice
versa: what has been = what will be. Such a matching is repeated in the following statement but with variation:

> *ûmah-ššenna'áśāh*
>
> *hû' šeyyē 'áśeh* (1:9b)

Notice that the construction of interrogative pronoun + personal pronoun
+ relative pronoun in 1:9a is repeated here, but the verb *hyh* (to be) has been
replaced by *'śh* (to do). Syntactically the juxtaposition of the constructions
of the second remark (1:9b) is as follows:

interrogative pronoun *mah*   relative pronoun *še* + Qal perfect *'śh*

personal pronoun *hû*   relative pronoun *še* + Qal imperfect *'śh*

Again, in this matching both halves share the same subject (represented respectively by antecedents *mah* and *hû*), and both are joined with the same verb but in different aspects: *mah* is used with the Qal perfect *'śh* (referring to the past), *hû* with Qal imperfect *'śh* (referring to the future). This results in the same effect as the preceding statement (1:9a) albeit expressed by a different verb (*'śh*):

> What has been done in the past = what will be done in the future

This observation is reinforced by the subsequent statement, which seems to be the summary of 1:9a, b:

> There is nothing new under the sun (1:9c)

At first glance, 1:9b is a repetition of 1:9a (syntactically and semantically). A closer look at the remarks, however, indicates otherwise. Firstly, 1:9b is more than just a repetition of 1:9a; for whereas 1:9a uses a general verb *hyh* ("to be" or "to happen"), 1:9b intensifies it by using a more specific verb *'śh* ("to do" or "to make").[46] Though the remark in 1:9c breaks the parallel pattern of the previous statements (1:9a, b),[47] it in fact clarifies what the statements express. If the two statements say "The past is the same as the future," this statement says "There is nothing new under the sun." The last statement reminds us that thought correspondence does not necessarily require parallelism by word matching, syntax or semantics.

The assertion that nothing is new in 1:9c continues to be deliberated in 1:10. Compared to 1:9c this verse is more distinctly prosaic, as it lacks the usual parallelism noticed above, be it semantically or grammatically: "If there is something which one says, 'Look, this is new!'; that already existed in ages that have gone before us." But it does heighten (emphasize) the thought of 1:9: the future is the past, there is nothing new; because what is new today has in fact existed in the past already.

The same idea is reiterated and heightened in 1:11, albeit expressed with parallelism and intensified by some words. In terms of parallelism, the first remark (1:11a) matches "those before" (*rišōnîm*, referring to those of the past) with "those afterward" (*'aḥărōnîm*, referring to the future), but is constructed elliptically:

> There is no remembrance of those before or of those afterward

---

46. So Longman, *Ecclesiastes*, 72; contra Murphy, *Ecclesiastes*, 8.

47. Perhaps this is one reason some exegetes treat 1:9 as prose.

The antecedent of the object in the second half of the remark is omitted, as it shares the same antecedent ("There is no remembrance") with the first half. This remark is parallel to the second remark (1:11b):

> There is no *remembrance* of *those before*, or of *those afterward* (1:11a) //
>
> Of *those who will be* there will not be *remembrance* among those who *will be afterward* (1:11b)

The second remark repeats the word *zikkārôn* ("remembrance"), but as in the previous verses, it is used with variation in word combinations. Firstly, if in 1:11a *zikrôn* (construct form *zikkārôn*) is negated by the use of the particle *ʾēn* ("there is no"), in 1:11b it is negated by a negation particle *lōʾ*+ Qal imperfect *hyh* ("there will be no"[48]):

ʾēn	*zikrôn*	there is no remembrance (1:11a)
lōʾ—yihyeh	*zikkārôn*	there will be no remembrance (1:11b)

Secondly, if in 1:11a *zikkārôn* is employed with "of those before" (*rišōnîm*) and "of those afterward" (*ʾaḥărōnîm*), in 1:11b the same word is used with a play on the different combinations of the verb *hyh*:

ʾēn zikrôn	*rišôn*	*ʾaḥărôn*	*še*—Qal imperfect *hyh* (1:11a)	
lōʾ—Qal imperfect	*zikkārôn*		*še*—Qal imperfect *hyh*	*ʾaḥărôn* (1:11b)

The variation in the combinations effects intensification. The combination of *lōʾ*—Qal imperfect (1:11b) intensifies the negative particle *ʾēn* (1:11a). Likewise by the repeated *še*—Qal imperfect *hyh* combination (1:11a, b) the poet heightens the meaning of "those before" and "those afterward." We should also note the semantic progress from 1:11a to 1:11b. If the former says, "There is no remembrance of those in the past and of those in the future," the latter takes a step further and says, "There will be no remembrance of those in the future among those who will come after them." This suggests that the absence of remembrance applies not only to the past generation, but also to the future generation and the generations to come. As Craig G. Bartholomew comments, "As generations come and go, people are forgotten, and so it will continue to be."[49] In sum, harking back to the theme of *dôr* ("generations") in the poem (1:4a), in the prose section non-remembrance runs perpetually through life cycles.

---

48. Lit. "it will not be to them."
49. Bartholomew, *Ecclesiastes*, 111.

Ecclesiastes 1:9–11 as a Commentary on Ecclesiastes 1:3–8

We will now discuss how Eccl 1:9–11 functions as a commentary/explanation for 1:3–8. In some ways the passage elaborates and emphasizes the points made by the poem. This is indicated by the correspondences between the two passages. Firstly, the language in 1:9 corresponds to the introduction to the poem (1:3). The strophe begins with the rhetorical question that uses the interrogative particle *mah* ("what") and ends with the expression *taḥat haššemeš* ("under the sun," 1:3):

> What (*mah*) profit does humankind have in all their toil?
>
> which one toils under the sun (*taḥat haššemeš*)?

The commentary in 1:9 corresponds to the question as it uses the same particle *mah* and ends with the same expression *taḥat haššemeš*. The particle *mah*, however, is used as a subject rather than interrogative.

> What (*mah*) has been is what will be (1:9a)
>
> What (*mah*) has been done is what will be done (1:9b)
>
> There is nothing new under the sun (*taḥat haššemeš*)

The connection implies that 1:9 answers the question posed in 1:3: "There is no profit in toil under the sun." As noted in our analysis, 1:9 basically asserts that what has happened or been done (toiled) in the past *is* ultimately what will happen and be done (toiled) in the future; and for this reason there is nothing new.

Qoheleth's assessment is reiterated and emphasized in 1:10. If in 1:9 he says, "There is nothing new," in 1:10 he stresses, "If there is something considered new, it in fact already existed in the past." The thought corresponds to the point made in the poem: human struggles bring no ultimate change. However, 1:9–10 heightens the thought at the same time: "Yes, neither do they achieve anything new."

Furthermore, as a response to the question in 1:3, 1:11 speaks of non-remembrance. To the question "What profit (*yitrôn*) does humankind have in all their toil?" 1:11a responds by "There is no remembrance (*zikrôn*) of those before, or of those afterward." By matching *yitrôn* ("profit") with *zikrôn* ("no remembrance"), the reader is expected to catch the phonological correspondence and make the connection: the profit of human struggles is cancelled by non-remembrance.

The passage in 1:9–11 also responds to the rhetorical question in 1:3 by picking up the circularity theme underscored by the series of analogies. If the analogies are used as metaphors for circularity, here in 1:9–11 "plain language" is used to make the same point. This is especially clear when we put 1:4 and 1:11 side by side. The reference to generations (*dôr*) in 1:4 corresponds to "those before" (*riˀšōnîm*) and "those afterward" (*ˀaḥărōnîm*), which refer to past and future generations respectively.[50] While 1:4 speaks of the going and the coming of generations, here 1:11 clarifies by referring to generations of the past and generations of the future. Also, as 1:4 speaks of countless generations going through a cycle, 1:11 also equalizes the past and future generations (those before are those afterward), intimating cyclicality (1:11b). But it is no mere repetition of 1:4, for 1:11 adds a new element to life cycle: "non-remembrance." This additional element not only clarifies 1:9-10, but also 1:4, explaining why life is circular. As everything each generation has done is cancelled by non-remembrance, they and their toils are just going through the same process.

Section Summary

The preceding analysis has demonstrated that Eccl 1:9-11 reiterates (at once heightens) the points made by the poem, only without the consistent use of parallelism and imagery that characterizes the latter.[51] All this makes the passage prosaic rather than poetic. The correspondences between this passage and the poem function more as thought-connecting device rather than the poetic indicators of the passage. The poem expresses the view that there is no profit in struggles under the sun, because life, like things in nature, is constantly cyclical thus effecting no real change. The commentary echoes and intensifies that assertion. There is nothing new under the sun, because the human life cycle results in non-remembrance. As one generation passes, what they have done will be forgotten by the next generation. This non-remembrance continues, forming a cycle of non-remembrance.

---

50. It is possible, as Fox argues, that *riˀšōnîm* and *ˀaḥărōnîm* refer to things or events of the past and the future respectively (*Time to Tear Down Time to Build Up*, 169). But with Crenshaw and Seow (respectively, *Ecclesiastes*, 68, *Ecclesiastes*, 111), we argue that elsewhere in the Old Testament *riˀšōnîm* refers to generations of the past (Lev 26:45; Deut 19:14; Ps 79:8). Likewise, elsewhere in Ecclesiastes *ˀaḥărōnîm* refers to people in the future (4:16). It is noteworthy that in the Old Testament things of the past are expressed by *riˀšōnōt* (feminine form) instead of *riˀšōnîm* (masculine form), such as Isa 41:22; 42:9.

51. Cf. Enns, *Ecclesiastes*, 34.

THEOLOGY

The poem in question is part of Eccl 1:1–11, which is generally recognized as the preface to Qoheleth's discourse in Ecclesiastes.[52] The poem therefore plays an important role in understanding Qoheleth's theology in the whole book. The book wastes no time in telling us Qoheleth's theological outlook. Right from the start the preface states the book's thesis by quoting Qoheleth's motto: life is *hebel* (1:2). In its deliberation of the motto, the book chooses versification instead of propositional statements. By citing the "Poem on Toil"[53] the author seeks to elucidate the *hebel* metaphor with the poem about *ʿāmāl*. Drawing from our preceding poetic analysis, we will now examine what the poem says about Qoheleth's theology.

Qoheleth's View of Life

Through the preface the book announces to the reader that Qoheleth subscribes to a pessimistic outlook on life: "All is *hebel*" (1:2). His pessimism is expressed as early as the poem begins, where it questions the value (*yitrôn*) of all human effort: "What profit does humankind have in all their toil, which one toils under the sun?" The pessimistic spirit is made all the more evident by the words used. They are the keywords (*Leitworter*) of Ecclesiastes: *yitrôn* (profit), *ʿāmāl* (toil) and *taḥat haššemeš* (under the sun). In Ecclesiastes, all three words represent the major theological themes associated with *hebel*. Packed in the first two cola of the poem, the keywords set the stage for Qoheleth's discussion of *hebel*. This being the case, the question offers context in which the reader is expected to understand the poem as well as the book.[54] While *ʿāmāl* and *taḥat haššemeš* signify various vigorous struggles made in our transient life, *yitrôn* refers to the value of those efforts. In sum, the thematic remark in 1:3 questions the value of all which one does in their transient life.

In keeping with the motto in 1:2 ("All is *hebel*"), the answer to the question in 1:3 is "no." By way of metaphor, the poem seems to say that one does not have to go far to find the answer, for it is right in the daily routine, in the very nature in which humankind lives. Qoheleth's pessimism is betrayed also in the analogies used in the poem. The analogies indicate

---

52. Seow, *Ecclesiastes*, 100; Crenshaw, *Ecclesiastes*, 68; Batholomew, *Ecclesiastes*, 101.

53. To borrow Ceresko's terminology ("Function of Antanaclasis," 565).

54. As Enns rightly observes, paying attention to the key words (theological lexemes) would help the reader see the connections of the Ecclesiastes' major themes and understand what the author seeks to put across (*Ecclesiastes*, 26–27). For a list and discussion of the keywords in Ecclesiastes, see Fox, *Ecclesiastes*, xvii–xxi.

that Qoheleth conceives much of life by a bleak view of creation. This view is strikingly different from Israel's tradition on two accounts. Firstly, unlike Genesis or Psalms, which views order in creation as something positive (cf. Gen 1:31; Ps 104),[55] the poem points out a conundrum: order is not necessarily good, because it is repetitive and monotonous.[56] Secondly, in the portrayal of the sun, the poem lacks the celebrative mood known to Israel's tradition.[57] Instead of speaking about the sun happily running its course (Ps 19:5 [ET 19:5]),[58] the book speaks of a "panting" sun rushing through its circuit (1:5). Contrary to what some commentators aver,[59] the portrayal here is not about nature's wonders, but its struggles. Qoheleth's pessimism is heightened by irony in the metaphors. Monotony according to the poem is not lethargic, but energetic, as articulated by the repetitive use of participles *hōlēk* and *sôbēb* (1:6). As Seow notes, it is at once vigor and monotony.[60]

The outlook carries over into 1:9–11, only made clearer in plain language. Pessimism is now directly applied to what humankind does. For Qoheleth, when each generation exits the scene, what they have done will vanish with them. Qoheleth points his finger at two culprits. First is the problem of non-remembrance. Humankind tends to forget what has been accomplished. The language in 1:11 is such that even non-remembrance is part of the circular phenomenon observed in nature. As a result, whatever achievements or contributions, great or small, will not bring anything new. It follows then, in the eyes of Qoheleth, ultimately there is no such thing as a "golden age" in history, for the past, the present and the future are unified as one and the same cycle. This notion harks back to the phenomena which appear in the poem: Just like streams never fill the sea and words never fill the ear, humankind's efforts achieve nothing new.

The second culprit is death. The references to "going," "those who have been before" and "those who will be afterward" imply not only the change of generations, but also death. Death puts all human achievements to an end, for the value of any achievement is cancelled by death. Later in his discourse, Qoheleth repeatedly underscores death as the limit of what one can profit from their toil (2:12–23; 4:16; 9:1–10).

55. See Crenshaw, *Ecclesiastes*, 66.

56. Whybray is correct in asserting that the analogies from nature are intended to show their regularity ("Ecclesiastes 1.5–7," 105). But we should add that the regularity here is circular.

57. Crenshaw, *Ecclesiastes*, 63; Brown, *Ecclesiastes*, 23–24.

58. In Ps 19:6 (ET 19:5) the sun is portrayed in a celebrative mood: leaving its chamber like a bridegroom, a strongman running its course with joy.

59. Particularly Whybray, "Ecclesiastes 1.5–7," 105–12.

60. Seow, *Ecclesiastes*, 115.

In sum, in the theological schema of Qoheleth, life runs like a clock; as he says later, "There is a time for everything" (3:1–8). Every generation moves around the clock regularly but circularly. It is like the English idiom "it runs like clockwork," but not in a positive sense; for on this clock, yesterday is no different from today and today is no different from tomorrow. Naturally, the question which arises from this would be: What is the value (*yitrôn*) in what we do (*ʿāmāl*)? Qoheleth's answer is already given right from the beginning: "*Hebel*. All is *hebel*" (1:2). Life is in a perpetual circular motion. You have a journey, but no destination; so there is nothing to look forward too.

The Scope of Qoheleth's View

The present poem is just the first of the many passages which Ecclesiastes uses to unpack Qoheleth's *hebel* thesis. It turns out that the word "all" (*kōl*) here is a cryptic expression which will be unpacked soon in Qoheleth's following discourse. There Qoheleth will show us that "all" includes achievements in terms of wisdom (1:16–18; 9:13–16), career, wealth and pleasure (2:1–11), and religious life; all of them will come to naught (7:15–18; 8:14–15; 9:1–2).

The question is: How inclusive is Qoheleth's *kōl*? Are there limits to his *kōl*? Perhaps the answer is imbedded right in the question about *kōl* (1:3):

> What profit does humankind have in *all* (*kōl*) their toil,
> which one toils *under the sun*?

By way of semantic progress, the poet defines *kōl* in the second colon: all human efforts or struggles *under the sun*. Qoheleth's *kōl* therefore has limits to it: it is confined to experience *under the sun*. As already discussed, the expression "under the sun" (*taḥat haššemeš*) refers to the present life, which is transient as it terminates at death. In other words, Qoheleth's *kōl* is limited to empirical experience, that is, things observable in the present life.[61] If so, Qoheleth does not claim that his view of life is absolute. This explains why Qoheleth has more questions than answers in his discourse. Those issues fall outside the radar of his "under the sun," beyond what he can comprehend.[62]

---

61. Seow comments on the scope of "all" in the passage, "So it is not that everything that is known to humanity is *hebel*, but that toil and other human activities and earthly experiences are" (*Ecclesiastes*, 103).

62. Qoheleth is troubled by many anomalies in life and find them absurd. For the discussion of the issues see Fox, *Qoheleth and His Contradictions*; Berger, "Exigencies

Interestingly, the empirical nature of Qoheleth's theology is the very appeal of Ecclesiastes. The reason is that the "under the sun" experience is universal. The reader therefore can identify with Qoheleth's view of things. Qoheleth's sayings, pessimistic as they are, ring true with people of every culture. The ancient Greeks immortalized their observations on the futility of life by the story of Sisyphus.[63] The ancient Chinese drew on the constant cyclical change in life and nature, and came up with the *Book of Changes* (*Yi Jing*).[64] The Buddhist tradition is known for its observation that there are no essences and reality is not permanent.

Today we ourselves witness the irony of the impermanence of things every day. Technology moves forward rapidly, but ultimately it moves in a cycle. As technology advances, yesterday's new technology is old technology today, and today's new technology will be old technology tomorrow. This "cyclical advancement" results in electronic devices changing from new to old, old to new and new to old again. Consumers may echo Qoheleth's complaints in 1:9–11. The latest cellphone today will soon completely vanish not only from the market but also our memory. Likewise, those in the entertainment industry can identify with Qoheleth's lament. Actors or singers who are popular will soon be called "*has beens*," just as Qoheleth says (1:9). Qoheleth's words would also strike a chord with those who want to change the world. Some persons may have made tremendous impact on humanity in the past century, but that has become irrelevant to today's generation. This explains why children find history so boring; they would gladly say with Qoheleth: "Nothing is new under the sun."

Qoheleth's Theology and The New Testament Perspective

However appealing it is, being limited, Qoheleth's outlook is just one of the lenses through which we can view life. The Bible provides us other lenses as well. Within the wisdom texts, we have the lens of Proverbs, which offers a view which is optimistic.[65] Likewise, Psalm 1, as discussed in the previous chapter, gives the reader a challenging yet promising view of life.

---

of Absurd," 141–79.

63. Some philosophers of the last century used the myth of Sysyphus to illustrate their philosophy of absurdity. See Camus, *Myth of Sisyphus*.

64. Recently Jarick made some interesting observations on the parallels between the concepts of change in Ecclesiastes and the *Yi Jing* ("Book of Changes," 79–99). However, in our opinion, it is equally important to identify the differences.

65. Fox, "Proverbs 1–9," 622; Clifford, *Proverbs*, 19, 22.

More important is the lens provided by the New Testament writers. This lens transcends Qoheleth's empirical view. For them, death is not the end of all. All the four Gospels testify to Christ's resurrection, and death—Qoheleth's nemesis—fails to cancel what Christ has done on the cross. Christ himself assures the believer the same experience: "I am the resurrection and the life. The one who believes in me shall live even though they die" (John 11:25). This conviction allows Paul to stare at death and challenge it: "Where, O death, is your victory? Where, O death, is your sting?" (1 Cor 15:55).

The hope of resurrection breaks the circularity that Qoheleth laments. For the New Testament authors, there are indeed new things. As Paul says, "If anyone is in Christ, the person is a new creation" (2 Cor 5:17). As death is no more the "terminator" of what we do, our has-beens and will-bes count (they will have *yitrôn*). For this reason Jesus tells his followers to work for things which last (John 6:27), and elsewhere Christians are told that their earthly wealth will have enduring value in eternity (1 Tim 6:17–19).

Nevertheless, as these authors speak of the reality of "the other world," they do not dismiss Qoheleth's reality. In the New Testament even the most spiritual ones are engaged in some "toil": carpentry (Jesus), tent-making (Paul), or business (Lydia). In their "already but not yet" theological framework, every Christian still toils under the sun like the rest of world. The difference is that they do not toil in vain. Given the assurance of resurrection, what they toil (*'āmāl*) will reap profit (*yitrôn*) that lasts through eternity. For the New Testament authors, Christ has transformed the ephemeral into the eschatological.

7

Poetic Analysis and Interpretation of Job 42:2–6

JOB 42:2–6 IS JOB'S speech, his response to the divine speeches in Job 38–41. The speech is introduced by the narrator's formulaic expression "X answered Y and said" (42:1, as with Job's first response in 40:3). This passage is universally recognized to be a poem,[1] the tail end of the book's poetic section.

LINEATING JOB 42:2–6

Following the guidelines for delimiting a poetic text in chapter 1, we propose to delimit the poem in Job 42:2–6 as follows:

Job 41:2–6

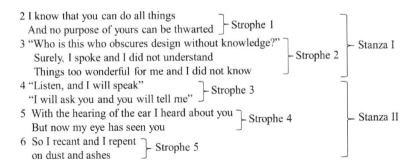

---

1. E.g., Whybray, *Job*, 170; Clines, *Job 1–20*, xxxv.

The stanzas are not of equal length, neither is each colon which forms the strophes. The first stanza comprises two strophes, the second stanza three strophes.[2] The reasons for the division are as follows. The first demarcation marker is verbal repetition. The verb *yd'* ("to know") appears in the beginning of Strophe 1 (42:2a) and the end of Strophe 2 (42:3c), forming an *inclusio*. In doing so, the verb *yd'* marks the beginning and the end of Stanza I.[3] Furthermore, words related to knowing occurs repeatedly in the first two strophes.[4] All this suggests the content is coherently about knowing. In sum, both verbal repetition and content coherence bind Strophes 1 and 2 together as a stanza.

The boundaries of the two strophes in the stanza are also definable. The transition marker "who" (*mî*, interrogative pronoun) in 42:3a marks the beginning of Strophe 2 (thus separating it from Strophe 1). The first colon of the strophe (42:3a) is bound with the subsequent cola (42:3b, c) as a single strophe by content (which is concerning Job's response to the question in 42:3a).[5]

The beginning of Stanza II is marked by the transition marker "Listen" (the imperative of *šm'*, 42:4a) and its ending is marked by the return of the narrator's voice that follows 42:6 (i.e., 42:7). More importantly, the stanza is unified by its thought-content, which centers on quotations of God's earlier remarks and Job's response to them. The transition marker "listen" (the imperative of *šm'*, 42:4a) marks the beginning of the first strophe (Strophes

---

2. Guided by the assumption that Hebrew poetry is constructed with logical and symmetrical syllable or word counting, both Fokkelman (*Major Poems IV*, 318–25) and van der Lugt (*Rhetorical Criticism*, 407–8) have broken the poem into two parts with equal length (3 "verses" on each part, i.e., in a 3 + 3 pattern). As discussed in chapter 3, syllable or word counting remains debatable. Besides, such a neat treatment is complicated by a number of issues, as will be shown below.

3. See Fokkelman, *Major Poems IV*, 318; van der Lugt, *Rhetorical Criticism*, 407.

4. Qal Perfect 1cs *yd'* ("I know," 42:2a); common noun *da'at* ("knowledge," cognate of *yd'*, 42:2b); and Qal Imperfect 1cs *yd'* ("I will know," 42:3c). In addition, another verb, Qal Imperfect 1 cs *byn* ("I did not understand,") in 42:3b share connotations with *yd'*, thus associated with the theme of knowing.

5. Van der Lugt (*Rhetorical Criticism*, 407) breaks the remark into two:
    Who is this that obscures design
    without knowledge?
Fokkelman rightly contends that van der Lugt has left the second colon too short (in fact, syntactically cumbersome); see Fokkelman, *Major Poems IV*, 318 n40, 320. However, Fokkelman's strophic treatment is also problematic, as he treats 42:3a as a separate colon by itself. This is in keeping of his assumption that Hebrew poetry can be divided by syllable count into a symmetrical 3 + 3 pattern (three verses in each strophe). But such a decision is arbitrary, because it ignores the fact that the colon in 42:3a is a question and the following two cola (42:3b, c) are its answer. It stands to reason that the question in 42:3a is an integral part of the answer in the following cola.

3) as it does Stanza II. The first strophe ends in 42:4c, right before the occurrence of the parallel cola in 42:5a,b. Strophe 4 (42:5a,b) comprises a bicolon bound by its parallelism and content. Finally, Strophe 5 begins with the transition marker "so" (*al-kēn*) in 42:6a.

STANZA I (42:2–3): CONTRASTING JOB'S OLD AND NEW KNOWLEDGE OF GOD

As mentioned, Stanza I comprises two strophes. The first one is a bicolon (42:2), the other is a tricolon (42:3). Also pointed out above, in terms of content, the cola in Stanza I are unified by the theme of "knowing." More to the point, the stanza lays before us Job's old and new knowledge/perceptions of God.

Strophe 1 (42:2)

Ellipsis

Even a cursory reading of Strophe 1 will detect the ellipsis in this strophe:

> I know—you can do all things
> and no purpose of yours can be thwarted.

What follows the verb "I know" is the clause "you can do all things," suggesting that the clause is the verbal predicate (object) of "I know." In turn, the verbal predicate is connected with another clause in the second colon by the conjunctive *waw*: "and [*waw*] no purpose of yours can be thwarted." The use of the conjunction indicates that the two clauses are to be read as the verbal predicates (i.e., "double objects") of "I know."[6] It follows that the verb "I know" governs both the first and the second cola, hence a case of ellipsis. In doing so, the poet draws attention to what Job *knows*.

Parallelism

The content of what Job knows, the double objects (the two verbal clauses), are constructed by what is traditionally called synonymous parallelism:

> I know that *you can do all things*
> And *no purpose of yours can be thwarted*

---

6. Cf. Fokkelman, *Major Poems IV*, 329.

In the Hebrew, matching is seen in the poet's choice of verbal and non-verbal words. The first one is the matching of a verb in the first person and a verb in the second person:

I know (*yāda'tî*)[7]

you are able (*tûkāl*)

Next is the matching of the verb in the first person and a second person pronominal suffix:

I know (*yāda'tî*)

[no purpose] of *yours* (*mimměkā*)

In both cases, the first person represents Job, the second person represents Yahweh. The "I-Thou" matching indicates a Job-Yahweh relationship in terms of knowing. Moreover, *tûkāl* (lit. "you are able") is matched with the expression *lō'-yibbāṣēr* (lit. "cannot be thwarted"):

yāda'tî kî-kōl tûkāl // wělō'-yibbāṣēr mimměkā mězimmāh

I know you are able [to do] all things // purpose of yours cannot be thwarted

What appears to be synonymous here in fact intimates semantic progress. The expression "you are able to do all things" is a general statement of God's omnipotence, whereas "no purpose of yours can be thwarted" is its elaboration or implication. In sum, in Strophe 1 Job confesses that he now knows something about God, that is, his omnipotence and its implication.

Strophe 2 (42:3)

If Strophe 1 is Job's confession of what he knows, Strophe 2 is his confession of what he did not know previously. The strophe comprises three cola (tricolon). It begins with Job's citation of Yahweh's earlier question in 38:2,[8] which is followed by Job's response to the questioning (42:3b, c):

7. The Ketib is *yāda'tā* ("you know"). But many ancient versions and modern commentators agree with the Qere (*yāda'tî*, "I know"). See Dhorme, *Job*, 645; Clines, *Job 38–42*, 1205 2a.

8. 42:3a is an almost verbatim repetition of Yahweh's words in 38:2 (with one different word and one omission). For this reason some scholars have regarded it as a scribal error and left it out or placed it in brackets (e.g., Dhorme, *Job*, 645; Pope, *Job*, 347). But here we follow the majority of commentators (Gordis, *Job*, 491–92; Clines, *Job 38–42*, 1214–1215; Gray, *Job*, 487) who regard it as Job's quotation of God's remark. For this reason, translations or commentators (e.g., NIV; Gordis) have added "You asked" or "You have said" (though this is not in the Hebrew).

Job's quotation: "Who is this who obscures design[9] without knowledge?" (42:3a)

Job's response: Therefore, I spoke and I did not understand (42:3b)

Things too wonderful for me and I did not know (42:3c)

Ellipsis

Before we analyze its parallelism, we will comment on the terseness in the second and third cola. Of course, generally terseness characterizes Hebrew poetry, but in this particular case, it deserves more attention. In the Hebrew, the first clause of the second colon ("Therefore, I spoke") has no object; while the term "wonderful things" (*niplā'ôt*) in the third colon appears to be an object without a verb. Naturally, such terseness has left the two cola shrouded in ambiguity. Translators and commentators have taken different approaches to the issues. Some of them regard the term "wonderful things" as the object of the verb "I spoke" (*higgadtî*).[10] Other translators take either the verbal clause "I did not understand" as the object[11] or both this clause and "wonderful things" as the objects of "I spoke."[12]

While these conjectures are tenable, we should ask whether they are necessary. Elsewhere in the book of Job, the Hiphil of *ngd* ("to make known" or "speak") does not need an object.[13] 42:3b is probably a similar case. However, it is also likely that the object is absent for a different reason, especially when read in the wider context. As this strophe is Job's confession about the wrong speech he made previously, it is likely that the expression "I spoke" points back to all the speeches he made in the dialogue (Job 3–37). Such a connection is supported by Job's use of the same verb (also Hiphil of *ngd*) in one of his speeches (31:37),[14] where Job uses the verb to demand a legal suit of God. Now, using the same verb, Job admits his ignorance then. Given the connection between "I spoke" and the previous speeches, the reader would understand the reference even without the object. If this notion is correct, the reference to "I spoke" is not to be found on the surface of the text (42:3),

9. The Hebrew noun *ʿēṣah* may mean "counsel" or "advice." It is translated "design" here as it probably refers to the complexity of God's cosmic design elaborated at length in God's speeches. See Habel, *Job*, 575, 578; Clines, *Job 38–42*, 1205 3d, 1214.

10. E.g., NJPS; Habel, *Job*, 575; Fokkelman, *Major Poems IV*, 321.

11. E.g., NAS.

12. KJV; NIV; ESV; Pope, *Job*, 347; Hartley, *Job*, 534.

13. As Clines observes, the use of the verb without object is also found in Job 15:18 and 38:18 (*Job 38–42*, 1206 n3g).

14. See Clines, *Job 38–42*, 1215.

because it runs deep back through the previous dialogue. In doing so, the intention is probably to link Job's confession to his speeches which he made "without knowledge."

Parallelism

Semantically the parallelism of the tricolon is evident even to those unfamiliar with the Hebrew:

> "Who is this who obscures design *without knowledge?*" (42:3a)
>
> Therefore, I spoke and *I did not understand* (42:3b)
>
> Things too wonderful for me and *I did not know* (42:3c)

Interestingly, parallelism is conspicuous at the "tail" of each colon. In doing so, the poet underscores Job's knowledge deficiency. This understanding is further supported by a study of the parallelism on the syntactical level. At the end of each colon the poet pairs a negative particle with a word associated with "knowing" (*yd'* ["to know"], *byn* ["to understand"] and *da'at* ["knowledge"]), resulting in what O'Connor calls "line-match":

negative particle *bĕlî*	noun *da'at* (without knowledge, 42:3a)
negative particle *lō'*	verb *byn* (did not understand, 42:3b)
negative particle *lō'*	verb *yd'* (did not know 42:3c)

The poet places the line-match at the end of each colon:

mî ze ma'lîm 'ēṣāh bĕlî dā'at (42:3a)

lākēn higgadtî wĕlō' 'ābin (42:3b)

niplā'ôt mimmennî wĕlō' ēdā' (42:3c)

The line matching at the tail ends of the cola highlights the lining up of the negation of the three words of "knowing," reinforcing what we have mentioned earlier: Job's lack of knowledge.

Upon a closer look, one may also discover word matching between the first colon and the subsequent two cola:

First colon (42:3a)	Second and third cola (42:3b, c)
"Who is this who obscures design" //	I spoke
"without knowledge" //	I did not understand
"without knowledge" //	I did not know

Notice the interrogative pronoun ("Who" [*mî*]) in the first colon (42:3a) is paired with a verb in the first person singular ("I spoke" [*higgadtî*]) in the subsequent colon (42:3b). Both end with the same vowel sound, indicating phonological parallelism. The effect of the pairing is to associate Yahweh's question of "who" with Job's confession of "I" (i.e., referring to himself). The fact that this is the case is evidenced by the use of *lākēn* as the connecting particle between the two cola, indicating that the second colon is the continuation of the first.[15] Job's confession is expressed to the effect: "You asked, 'Who is this who obscures design without knowledge?' Well, surely you were right. I am the one." In saying so, Job admits that he is the one who is guilty of Yahweh's accusation in 38:2.

This admission is intensified by pairing the noun *da'at* (in "without knowledge") in this colon with two semantically overlapped verbs in the second and third cola (*yd'* "to know," *byn*, "to understand"). The meaning of "without knowledge" in 42:3a is heightened by Job's confession that he did not understand and he did not know (42:3b,c). Put in another way, these word pairings highlight for the reader what Job owns up to: "Yahweh is right; I have indeed spoken without knowledge."

We will now turn our attention to the relationship between the second and third cola. Here Job's confession of his knowledge deficiency is intensified by semantically parallel verbs:

> Therefore, I spoke of things and *I did not understand* (42:3b)
>
> Things too wonderful for me and *I did not know* (42:3c)

At first glance, the two cola appear to be a classic case of synonymous parallelism; for semantically, the connotations of "understand" (*byn*) and "know" (*yd'*) are closely overlapped that no significant semantic progress is immediately apparent. However, we should not ignore the fact that the clause with the verb "know" (*yd'*) is joined with the preceding phrase, "Things too wonderful for me." Regardless of what one thinks the syntactical function of this phrase is,[16] its inclusion not only heightens but also offers a reason for the preceding colon: Job did not understand because those things are wonderful and beyond his comprehension. In terms of their relationship with the first colon, these two cola also demonstrate semantic progress. If the first colon poses Yahweh's questioning Job's knowledge deficiency (42:3a), the second and third cola present Job's confession that Yahweh is right.

15. So van Wolde, "Job 42,1–6," 230.

16. Whether "wonderful things" is the object of the verb: "I spoke about wonderful things" (e.g., Pope, *Job*, 247; Clines, *Job 38–42*, 1204, 1206, 3g), or just a complement the verb: "I spoke about things I did not know, things too wonderful for me" (Dhorme, *The Book of Job*, 645–46).

To fully appreciate Strophe 2 and the whole stanza, we should also examine in what respects it corresponds to Strophe 1. Semantically, Job's citation in 42:3a antithetically corresponds to the first colon of Strophe 1 (42:2a). The former says Job knows something, whereas the latter says Job had no knowledge:

> *I know* that you are able to do all things (42:2a)
>
> "Who is this who obscures design *without knowledge?*" (42:3a)

Furthermore, both semantically and grammatically the Qal Perfect first person singular of *yd'* ("I know") at the beginning of 42:2a is parallel to the related noun *da'at* ("knowledge") at the end of 42:3a, forming an *inclusio*. By connecting the two by the *inclusio*, Job contrasts his knowledge before and after Yahweh's theophany. He admits that Yahweh was right in saying that he was without knowledge before Yahweh's appearance (42:3a). Now, after Yahweh's theophany, Job knows something (i.e., Yahweh's omnipotence, 42:2a).

Also, on the grammatical level, there is an inverted line-match between the last colon of Strophe 1 (42:2b) and the last colon of Strophe 2 (42:3c):

particle *lō'* + Niphal Imperfect of *bṣr* + preposition-suffix + noun //

verbal noun + preposition-suffix + particle *lō'* + Qal Imperfect of *yd'*

42:2b:
  x particle *lō'* + Niphal Imperfect of *bṣr*
  y preposition-suffix
  z noun
42:3c:
  z' verbal noun
  y' preposition-suffix
  x' particle *lō'* + Qal Imperfect of *yd'*

The word order is such that the line-match results in chiastic correspondences: We have a number of important observations to make here. The negation of the passive form of *bṣr* ("cannot be thwarted") corresponds to the negation of the active form of *yd'* ("I did not know"). The connection suggests that Job's confession of his past ignorance is related to his realization of Yahweh's omnipotence (that no purpose of God can be thwarted). Next is the correspondence between the preposition + second person suffix (*mīmĕmkā*, literally, "from you") and the preposition + first person suffix (*mimmennî*, "for me"). By connecting the second person suffix (referring to Yahweh) and the first person suffix (referring to Job), the poet associates Job's re-alization of Yahweh's omnipotence with Job marvelling at things beyond his comprehension. Finally, the noun *mĕzimmâ* in 42:2b corresponds to the verbal noun *niplā'ôt* in 42:3c. Again, by associating the two the poet suggests that Job's realization of God's omnipotence has led to the realization of the incomprehensiveness of things.

Section Summary

By way of ellipsis, parallelism and metaphor Stanza I focuses on the theme of "knowing God" and contrasts what Job knows before and after his en-counter with God. The first half of the stanza (Strophe 1) speaks of Job's confession of "I know" after the theophany. The experience has opened his eyes to Yahweh's omnipotence in a fresh way. The new awakening results in his realization of what he did not know in the past. So in the second half of the stanza (Strophe 2) attention switches to Job's knowledge prior to the encounter. By quoting God's earlier remark, Job draws attention to the inadequacy of his previous knowledge. The inadequacy led to his demand for a lawsuit against God. Now Job realizes that the lawsuit was based on deficient knowledge; in other words, he has no case. For this reason Job retracts the lawsuit in the followig stanza.

STANZA II: CONTRASTING THE "HEARING" AND "SEEING" EXPERIENCES

Stanza II consists of three strophes, each being a bicolon (42:4, 42:5 and 42:6). In terms of thought-content, it continues the contrast between Job's knowledge before and after the theophany. If the preceding stanza contrasts Job's old and new knowledge of God, the present stanza contrasts his old and new modes of knowing God: the "hearing" mode versus the "seeing" mode. The comparison is sharper here as the stanza highlights the powerful effect of the theophany (new mode). As in the first colon of Strophe 2 in the first stanza, the first strophe of Stanza II (42:4) comprises quotations of earlier remarks of God.[17] In the first colon of Strophe 3 Job quotes seem-ingly Elihu's remark in 33:31.[18] Intriguingly, as most commentators recog-

17. Some commentators and translators treat 42:4 as a gloss; e.g., (Dhorme, *Job*, 646; Pope, *Job*, 347–48; NEB). They have either omitted the verse or put it in brackets. But the majority of commentators and translators regard it as part of the poem; e.g., Clines, *Job 38–42*, 1215–16; Habel, *Job*, 545; Gray, *Job*, 486; NIV; NAS; ESV.

18. In the Hebrew, Job's quotation omits two words from Elihu's remark, i.e., "to me"

nize, this remark is now regarded by Job as Yahweh's remark as well.[19] In the second colon, he partially quotes another remark of Yahweh (38:3; 40:7).[20] By quoting all these remarks Job is preparing a "legal" response, as it were. Much is transpired in the earlier long dialogue, but here it is referred to only in two concise cola. Thus such terseness represents omission; the purpose is to direct the reader's attention to the contrast between Job's old and new experiences of God and the ensuing transformation.

Strophe 3 (42:4)

A close examination of the parallelism of the two strophes will show that the poet's choice of quotations and the words therein are deliberate and intended for a purpose: to draw attention to the powerful effect of his new experience and his subsequent retraction of his lawsuit.

Parallelism

What catches our attention first is the intra-colon antithetical parallelism in both cola. The first colon puts "listen" and its antithetical counterpart "speak" side by side:

> "Listen, and I will speak" (42:4a)

Similarly, within the second colon the verb "ask" is placed next to the antithetically parallel "tell" (lit. "make known"):

> "I will ask you and you will tell me" (42:4b)

The parallelism between the two cola on the semantic level is also apparent:

> "Listen, and I will speak" (42:4a) //

> "I will ask you and you will tell me" (42:4b)

Grammatically, the verb "listen" is paired with "ask," and "speak" paired with "tell." The pairings suggest a two-way communication between two individuals. In the first colon the communication moves from "I" to "you": "I speak, you listen"; in the second colon it is from "I" to "you" and

---

(*lî*) and "keep silent" (*haḥărēš*).

19. For discussion of this issue, see Clines, *Job 38–42*, 1215–16. It is also possibly a quotation of Job's remark in 13:22. Though not put in exactly the same Hebrew words, the remark expresses the same idea.

20. Job quotes only the second half of Yahweh's remark in the two passages.

"you" to "I": "I will ask you, you will tell me." This understanding is reinforced when examined on the syntactical level. The syntactical structure shows a line-match similar to that of 42:2a and 42:3c, but with a simpler chiasm:

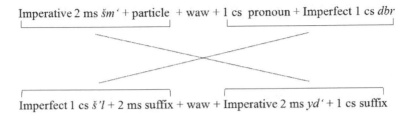

Imperative 2 ms *šm'* + particle + waw + 1 cs pronoun + Imperfect 1 cs *dbr*

Imperfect 1 cs *š'l* + 2 ms suffix + waw + Imperative 2 ms *yd'* + 1 cs suffix

In terms of grammar and syntax, the first half of the first colon is chiastically corresponding to the second half of the second colon; the second half of the first colon is chiastically corresponding to the first half of the second colon. The former chiastic pair comprises two imperatives, both in the second person singular ("you"): you listen—you tell me. The latter chiastic pair comprises two imperfect verbs, both in the first person singular ("I"): I will speak—I will ask you. This reinforces the two-way communication highlighted earlier. The conjunctive *waw*s which join the two halves of each colon are directly parallel to each other. Their parallelism suggests a corresponding function: both connect "I" (referring to God) and "you" (referring to Job). Such syntactical constructions show that God is doing the questioning and Job is at the receiving end. As such, it strikes us as a cross-examination in a courtroom in which God is the judge or prosecutor and Job is the defendant. It is to this kind of language we will now turn.

Figurative Language

It is well recognized that the book of Job is full of imagery; in fact, its imagery is one factor that makes Job "an exquisite work of literary art."[21] Of interest are its legal metaphors relevant to the present poem. Legal imagery in the Old Testament has been a subject of discussion in biblical scholarship for decades, especially metaphors involving the *rîb*, a term which refers to judicial dispute or controversy.[22] In recent years, some scholars have shown a particular interest in its use in the book of Job.

21. So Seow, *Job 1–14*, 84–87; see also Habel, *Job*, 54–60.

22. Gemser, "*Rib*," 120–37; Limburg, "Root 304–291 ",ריב; for a survey, see Harvey, "Le RIB-Pattern," 172–196; Harvey, *Le plaidoyer*. More recently, see Bartor, "'Juridical

LEGAL METAPHORS IN JOB

Given the prominence of the justice theme (theodicy) of the book, the legal language does not come as a surprise. One of the issues in Job's dispute with his friends and Yahweh is over whether Job's suffering is fair. Job's friends argue that Job's suffering is justifiable, because it is the very evidence of his guilt. Based on their retribution theology, they assume that Job's guilt has resulted in a *rîb* (controversy or dispute) with God, hence his suffering.[23] In his defense, Job shares his friends' retribution theology,[24] but turns to God for justice, and even initiates a hypothetical/metaphorical lawsuit against him in many of his speeches (9:27–35; 13:17–22; 23:3–7; 31:35).

The fact that a metaphorical lawsuit is involved is evidenced by the language of Job and his friends' speeches. The legal overtone is detected for example in Job's words: "How many are my offenses and sins? Tell me my crime and my sin" (13:23).[25] Some scholars have pointed out that in the dialogue the phrase *mšpṭ* is used in judicial terms (e.g., 9:19, 32; 14:3; 19:7; 32:9), as used in court proceedings in the Old Testament as well as other ancient Near Eastern societies.[26] More to the point, Job also repeatedly uses the root *ryb* (10:2; 13:6, 19; 23:6; 31:35); in fact, in one of his key litigation statements, he calls God "my legal adversary" *rîb* ('*îs rîb*, literally, "my man of dispute," 31:35).[27] In his response to Job, Yahweh picks up Job's language (38:3; 40:2, 7). Some scholars observe that all this suggests that Job and God are engaged in a metaphorical or hypothetical legal proceeding and the poetic speeches are therefore courtroom poetry.[28]

Dialogue,'" 445–64.

23. Biblical scholars generally note that the metaphors are set against the background of ancient Near Eastern legal systems. For recent discussion, see Magdalene, *Scales of Righteousness*; Magdalene, "Legal Impairment," 37–38.

24. So Scholnick, "*Mišpaṭ* in Job," 524; and Iwanski, *Job's Intercession*, 184; see also Bovati, *Re-establishing Justice*, 171–73.

25. Dick notes that such a pattern of questioning is similar to that of ancient Near East legal texts ("Legal Metaphor," 38–39 n10).

26. Roberts, "Job's Summons," 159–64; Scholnick, "*Mišpaṭ* in Job," 521–29. For such a use outside Job, see for example Num 35:12; Deut 17:8; Isa 28:6.

27. Dick contends that 31:35 is "the key to the legal metaphor in Job" ("Legal Metaphor," 38).

28. For reason of the legal language here, some scholars have go so far as to take the genre of the book of Job or a large portion of it as courtroom drama; see for example Alonso-Schökel, "Dramatic Reading," esp. pp. 52–59; Scholnick, "Poetry in Courtroom," 185–204. However, as Newsom has cogently reminded us, forensic language does not occur throughout the book, but in certain passages (*Contest of Imaginations*, 150–51). So the legal language is no indication of the genre of the whole book, and one should discern whether or not a particular passage carries legal overtones.

While reading the whole book as a courtroom drama goes beyond what the text warrants, Yahweh's remarks quoted by Job here evidently hark back to the metaphorical lawsuit in the dialogue section of the book. Of interest is the fluidity of the legal metaphors. At times Job is portrayed as the plaintiff and prosecutor, while God is the accused and defendant;[29] at other times, God is described as the plaintiff, the judge or the witness, and Job is the defendant.[30] Such a metaphor reflects the legal dispute language conventional to the prophetic books, where Yahweh plays a dual role, that is, he is both the plaintiff and the judge (e.g., Isa 1:18–20; 3:13–14).[31] Job protests against the unfairness of the "system" (9:12–20, 32), demands a third party, variously called "umpire/arbiter" (*môkîaḥ*, 9:33), "witness" (*ʿēd*, 16:19) and "redeemer" (*gōʾēl*, 19:25).[32] The difference between the conventional model of legal metaphors and that of Job implies two conceptual metaphors.

Two Models of Conceptual Metaphors

As pointed out in the earlier discussion, both Job and his friends conceive his suffering in terms of a judicial dispute. Thus we have here a conceptual metaphor that "suffering is a judicial dispute." Nonetheless, Job and his friends differ on the judicial model. His friends' is the conventional model which conceives suffering by a straightforward retributive judicial system. The friends' suffering-is-a-judicial-dispute metaphor can be mapped as follows:

Earthly Judicial Dispute (source)		Job's Suffering (target)
criminal code	→	moral/religious laws
crime	→	sin
judge	→	God

29. See Greenstein, "Forensic Understanding," 245.

30. Dick observes that in the scheme of the ancient *rib*, there is no sharp distinction of roles of plaintiff and defendants ("Legal Metaphor," 38). See also Gemser, "Rib," 135; Iwanski, *Job's Intercession*, 184–86.

31. Roberts ("Job's Summons," 160–65) notes that the prophetic *rib* language is based on covenant treaty, which is modeled after ancient Near Eastern treaties. In those treaties, deities both serve as witnesses and judges. Scholnick argues that in the creation poetry in Job 38–41 is God doubles up as a witness ("Poetry in Courtroom," 200). See also Harvey, *Le plaidoyer*, 55.

32. Roberts, "Job's Summon," 165; Dick argues that seeking a third party in a legal dispute is attested in ancient Near Eastern documents ("Legal Metaphor," 38–50).

plaintiff	→	God
witness	→	God
defendant	→	sinner
forensic evidence	→	suffering
punishment	→	suffering

In his argumentation, Job does not think some of the typical corresponding elements are applicable to him, such as "crime à sin" and "punishment à suffering," because he believes he is innocent. Neither does Job agree with the judicial system in which God is both judge and plaintiff. For this reason he requests for an arbiter, which also means that he seeks to *reconfigure* the metaphorical model.[33] Job's model of conceptual metaphor may be mapped as below:

Earthly Judicial Dispute (source)		Job's Suffering (target)
criminal code	→	moral/religious laws
judge	→	God
plaintiff	→	God
witness	→	God
defendant	→	Job
forensic evidence	→	suffering
third party	→	arbiter

The two models of conceptual metaphors betray the gap between Job's perception of divine justice and that of his tradition. It is not that Job dismisses the validity of the traditional retribution concept. In fact, the concept is the very reason for him to go into the dispute with God. As he believes that he is innocent, he argues that making an innocent person suffer runs against the law. Also, he believes that God's dual role (as the judge and plaintiff) undermines a fair judicial proceeding; a third-party arbiter is therefore needed.

In his response to Job, God picks up Job's legal metaphorical language and challenges him with the following remarks:[34]

---

33. As Newsom has pointed out, the reconfigured model allows Job to expose the problematic assumptions of his friends (*Contest of Imaginations*, 155).

34. For fuller discussion of the legal metaphors in the divine speeches, see Greenstein, "Forensic Understanding," 248–53.

Who is this who darkens design with word without knowledge? (38:2)[35]

I will ask and you will tell me (38:3)[36]

To this Job also adds what he assumes to be God's remark:

"Listen, and I will speak" (cf. 42:4a)[37]

God makes these remarks as a response to Job's demand for a lawsuit. Now, Job goes back to the divine response by quoting the words (42:3a; 42:4a,b). In doing so, Job is responding to God's challenge as his legal opponent: he concedes that he has "therefore" obscured God's cosmic design with his ignorance (42:3a), just as God has said (38:2). This confession implies not only Job's retraction of the lawsuit, but also the abandonment of his modified model of conceptual metaphor. In his own words, the legal conceptual model is based on ignorance (42:3). In the following strophe Job explains the reason for this change of attitude.

Strophe 4 (42:5)

Strophe 4 is a bicolon that expresses Job's response to God's challenge quoted in Strophe 3. The response marks his new theological stance concerning Yahweh and his justice.

Parallelism

The bicolon demonstrates antithetical parallelism; the antithetical notion is indicated by the use of *waw* in the second colon (translated "but"):

With the hearing of the ear I heard about you (42:5a)

But now my eye has seen you (42:5b)

Against Clines, we argue that the *waw* here is adversative or contrastive; contrasting Job's old cognitive mode ("with the hearing of the ear I heard about you") with his new cognitive mode ("but now my eye has seen

35. Interrogative pronouns *mah* and *mi* ("what" and "who") are formulaic interrogative forms of accusation in legal proceedings in the Old Testament. See Bovati, *Re-establishing Justice*, 75–77.

36. This expression, as Scholnick notes, is also part of the Old Testament legal language ("Poetry in Courtroom," 187).

37. Bovati notes that in the Old Testament *šmʿ* ("listen") and *dbr* (Piel, "speak") are two fundamental dimensions of a judge's activity (*Re-establishing Justice*, 187).

you").[38] The two cola also demonstrate semantic progress. The first colon speaks of perception by distant contact ("with the hearing of the ear"), whereas the second colon speaks of perception by close contact ("now my eye has seen you").[39]

We also note word pairing between the two cola:

42:5a	42:5b
ear (*ʾōzen*)	eye (*ʿayin*)
hearing and *heard*	*seen*

In view of the adversative *waw* between the two cola, the word pairing suggests that Job puts perception by "hearing" and perception by "seeing" in contrast.

On the grammatical level, we also note the morphological and word order equivalence, particularly in their second halves:

Preposition	verbal noun *šmʿ*	noun	Qal Perfect 1 cs *šmʿ*	2 ms suffix
Disjunctive	particle	noun	Qal Perfect 1 cs *rʾh*	2 ms suffix

In light of the disjunctive *waw*, such correspondence suggests Job compares and contrasts his old and new modes of perception.

Parallelism with the preceding strophe is also evident. Both the first colon of Strophe 3 and the first colon of Strophe 4 use the root *šmʿ* (the former as "to listen" and the latter as "to hear"):

Listen (*šmʿ*) and I will speak (42:4a)

By the hearing (*šmʿ*) of the ear I have heard (*šmʿ*, 42:5a)

Notice also that the verb "I will speak" (42:4a) is matched with "I have heard" (42:5a), indicating word pairing. By matching them the poet may intend to show the connection or, more precisely, the progress from 42:4a

---

38. Dhorme, *Job*, 646; Pope, *Job*, 347; Gray, *Job*, 486. Against this majority view, Clines contends that the *waw* is not adversative, thus the two cola are equivalent instead of contrastive, i.e., no distinction of then and now or hearing and seeing (*Job 38–42*, 1206 n5b, 1216–17). Given the poem's emphasis on Job's new knowledge/realization, it only makes sense to contrast his past (perception by hearing) and his the present (perception by "seeing").

39. Carasik argues that in Deuteronomy (e.g., Deut 7:19), perception with the eye represents direct and undeniable experience ("To See a Sound," 259). Though Clines objects the argument, he concedes that the expression "my eye has seen you" is "an idiom for a close or authentic encounter" (*Job 38–42*, 1216). For more discussion of Hebrew concept of human perception modes of seeing and hearing, see our discussion of figurative language below.

to 42:5a. The former quotes Yahweh's challenge to Job's lawsuit; the latter implies Job's admission that his lawsuit was based on knowledge by hearing (i.e., it is inadequate to mount a suit). In effect Job is saying, "You said,[40] 'Listen and I will speak.' Now after hearing what you spoke I realize the inadequacy of my perception by hearing." The idea of the inadequacy of hearing is reinforced by contrasting it with the advantage of the cognitive mode of "seeing" mentioned in the subsequent colon (42:5b). To further understand the advantage of "seeing" over "hearing" we will now turn to the conceptual metaphor behind the terms.

Figurative Language

In his intensive discussion of Hebrew modes of perception, Meir Malul observes that the process by which the ancient Hebrews formed their concepts of the world was often couched in graphic and concrete terms taken from everyday life, "where the physical body plays such a prominent role."[41] As is customary of the culture, the author of Job turns to sensory metaphors for the description of human perception of the transcendent God. In this strophe Job's means of knowing God is couched in sensory terminology: ear, eye, hearing and seeing. Elsewhere, as in the present poem, biblical authors speak of hearing and seeing God (Deut 4:36; Ps 17:15). The psalmist invites the reader to "taste" Yahweh: "O, taste and see that Yahweh is good" (Ps 34:9, ET 34:8), and Yahweh's word tastes like honey: "How smooth are your words to my palate, like honey in my mouth!" (119:103). Elsewhere God is said to "smell" the pleasing odor of sacrifices (Gen 8:21).[42]

Put together, all these metaphors appear to be subcategorized metaphors of a conceptual metaphor: "Knowing God is sensory perception." The conceptual metaphor involves two domains: human sensory perception and perception of God:

Human Sensory Perception (source)		Human Perception of God (target)
taste	→	pleasant experience
smell	→	pleasant experience

40. As mentioned, some translators have in fact added "You said" before Job's quotations of Yahweh's words (NIV; Clines, *Job 38–42*, 1206 n4b).

41. Malul, *Knowledge, Control, and Sex*, 257.

42. For a fuller discussion of process of knowing by taste and smell in the Old Testament, see Malul, *Knowledge, Control, and Sex*, 130–34; Ritchie, "The Nose Knows," 59–73.

seeing   →   perceiving

Chief among these are human sensorial functions of seeing and hearing, which Malul calls "higher" senses.[43] Generally, the Old Testament views visual and audio modes as equally important for perceiving the divine.[44] In fact, the line between the two modes is often obscure, because in some cases, the meaning of "see" is not limited to a visual experience but also an audible one.[45] This is attested in the Sinai theophany in Exod 20:18, where the Israelites are said to *see* lightning and the *sound of thunder*. As U. Cassuto correctly notes, the word "seeing" here refers to perceiving with the senses (for one cannot see sound).[46] Thus seeing, like hearing, is a metaphorical terminology referring to a wide range of perception.

Nonetheless, in other passages the Old Testament does distinguish the two perception modes in terms of priority. As George Savran observes, while in some theophany passages hearing seems to be the primary mode of perceiving God (Deuteronomy 4),[47] in other cases, visual encounter is presented as a "lethal" thus superior experience (Gen 28:16–17; 32:24–32; Exod 24:11).[48] This is the case with Job's experience, when he contrasts the hearing and seeing modes (42:5).[49]

Many commentators note that "hearing" here is understood as "primarily in the sense of passing on traditions from the elders," whereas "seeing" refers to a more personal and authentic experience.[50] The tradition inherited by Job primarily defines God by his workings in the nature and moral laws. Job used to follow the mode; however, in times of crisis, he seeks to perceive God in a more direct way. Taking God as his tormentor, repeatedly, Job requests for a face-to-face dialogue with God (e.g., 13:22–24; 31:35; most explicitly in 19:25–27).[51] The purpose is not so much to

43. Malul points out that in the Old Testament hearing and seeing are regarded as the most common ways of perceiving God (*Knowledge, Control, and Sex*, 144–51).

44. Savran, "Seeing is Believing," 322.

45. Carasik, "To See a Sound," 261–62; for more of his discussion of hearing and seeing, see his *Theologies of the Mind*, 32–43.

46. Cassuto, *Exodus*, 252.

47. Savran points out that this is especially so in the Deuteronomic re-telling of the Sinai theophany in Deuteronomy 4 ("Seeing is Believing," 323–26).

48. Ibid., 328–29.

49. Ibid., 329; Utzschneider, "Aesthetic Theology," 92.

50. Ibid., 338–50. A great many scholars view the contrast as between conventional assertions about God and Job's personal experience with God; see Whybray, *Job*, 170–71; Gray, *Job*, 488; Hartley, *Job*, 536–37; Utzschneider, "Aesthetic Theology," 99.

51. Savran, "Seeing is Believing," 350–55.

know what God looks like physically, but to vindicate Job once and for all in person.[52] As such the request for a face-to-face visual experience is both a perception as well as forensic metaphor.[53]

The dialogue between Job and his friends, therefore, presents two models of conceptual metaphors regarding human perception of God. First is the old model, a model Job used to follow and still held by his friends. The model forms concepts of God by a less direct sensory perception, that is, "hearing" from the wisdom tradition:

Human Sensory Perception (source)		Job's Friends' Perception of God (target)
hearing	→	perceiving God through tradition

Next is Job's model as represented by his speeches before the theophany, a model which desires to perceive God by a direct communication, so as to vindicate himself:

Human Sensory Perception (source)		Job's Desired Perception of God (target)
seeing	→	perceiving God through direct contact

Now God has eventually spoken to him directly; Job has indeed "seen" God, as he says:

---

52. So Savran, ibid., 360. This notion accords well with what we have concluded early that throughout his speeches, Job asks for a face to face meeting with God to prove his innocence.

53. Clines, *Job*, 1217.

> With the hearing of the ear I heard about you.
>
> but now my eye has seen you.

In our analysis of the strophe's parallelism we have pointed out that Job views "seeing" as having advantage over "hearing." The question that arises from this is: in what respects is "seeing" better than "hearing"? The question is especially pertinent because even in his direct encounter with God Job does not exactly see God. Instead he *hears* his speeches "out of the whirlwind" (38:1). As such, by "seeing" Job actually refers to hearing God's words, albeit in a direct way. So, as in the Sinai theophany, for Job hearing God in a face-to-face encounter is as good as "seeing" him.

Since for Job "seeing" means hearing God's speeches, the content of the speeches is then essential for understanding Job's view that "seeing" is better than "hearing." The divine speeches are a presentation of how God sees his own workings in the cosmos. The picture which God presents is morally much more complex than Job and his friends have ever conceived. After "viewing" God's 'presentation,' Job now says, "now my eye has seen you." This implies that now Job perceives God through his workings in the universe and the complex morality therein. This kind of "seeing" is more powerful than "hearing" because how God operates and the moral complexity are far beyond what Job has heard from tradition. It should also be noted that being able to see God in that light suggests that Job is able to see things through God's perspective. If so, this marks a paradigm shift from seeing God through Job's own perspective (which is shaped by his tradition) to seeing God through God's own perspective.[54]

The paradigm shift has also resulted in a metaphorical shift. Before his encounter with God, Job uses "seeing" as a forensic metaphor, namely, demanding God to appear in "court" to vindicate him. After his encounter with God, Job now stops using "seeing" with such legal overtones. Instead, "seeing" is used to express his willingness to view things through the eyes of God.

Strophe 5 (42:6)

Strophe 5 begins with the first expression, "so" (*'al-kēn*),[55] which indicates that what follows is the consequence of the preceding strophes. If the

---

54. Savran, "Seeing is Believing," 359; see also van Wolde, "Job 42,1–6," 233.

55. The adverb comprises two prepositions: *'al* and *kēn*; it may mean "Therefore" or "That is why."

preceding strophes represent Job's verbal response to his awakening, this strophe represents his practical response.

This strophe is notorious for its exegetical problems, as its grammar and semantics are fraught with ambiguities and have led to diverse translations.[56] Lineation has also proven difficult and "cannot univocally be determined."[57] The following reflects the lineation of most commentators:[58]

> So I recant and I repent
>
> on dust and ashes

The division keeps the two verbs ("I recant" and "I repent") together in the first colon, thus breaking the strophe at "on dust and ashes."[59]

Parallelism

The first thing that strikes us is the parallelism within each colon. The two halves of the first colon displays grammatical parallelism: the first person verb "I recant" ($m\mathring{s}$)[60] corresponds to the first person verb "I repent" ($nḥm$).[61] Semantic correspondence is also noticeable. Though the absence

---

56. There has been no consensus on the translation of this strophe, as reflected by the diverse treatments by ancient as well as modern translators. See Morrow, "Job 42:6," 211–25.

57. Van der Lugt, *Rhetorical Criticism*, 408–9.

58. See the lineations of various scholars listed by van der Lugt (ibid.).

59. Such a division has two advantages. First, it is in keeping with the function of the MT Atnach below *nḥm* ("I repent"), which marks the midpoint of the verse. Second, as will be shown in our discussion of parallelism, it results in equivalent/balanced division. Guided by his syllable counting schema, Fokkelman breaks the two verbs apart (i.e., placing "I repent" in the second colon), so to ensure the second colon of each strophe in Stanza II will have 9 syllables (*Major Poems IV*, 322–23). Gordis gives the same treatment to the two verbs, though no reason offered (*Job*, 491). This treatment is disadvantaged by its disregard for the MT Atnach and imbalanced division. Cf. Habel, *Job*, 575.

60. The basic meanings of the verb *m's* is "reject" and "despise" (so BDB 549b §2). Scholars have variously rendered the verb "reject," "retract," "recant," "melt," "sink down," "contempt," or "loath." In our opinion, "recant" or "retract" fits well with the context of Job's confession of having said ignorant words. For fuller discussion, see Patrick, "Translation of Job xlii," 369–71; Morrow, "Job 42:6," 211–25; Muenchow, "Dust and Dirt," 597–611; Wolters, "Child of Dust," 116–19; Clines, *Job 38–42*, 1207–8 n6b.

61. The MT pointing may either suggest the Piel or Niphal of *nḥm*. Many scholars take the Niphal reading, as the Piel does not fit the context (contra Scholnick, "*Miš paṭ* in Job," 528). The Niphal of *nḥm* may mean "repent." Following this translation are KJV; NIV; RSV; BDB 637a §2; Dhorme, *Job*, 646; Pope, *Job*, 47.

of an object for "I recant" has left us uncertain about what Job recants,[62] in light of his confession in the preceding strophes he may well refer to the speeches he uttered before the theophany.[63] If so, it corresponds to the following verb "I repent." As the Hebrew word *nḥm* ("repent") may mean to change one's mind, the expression is used here to suggest that Job changes his mind about his previous speeches about God.[64] As such, "I repent" also clarifies "I recant."

The two nouns in the phrase "on dust and ashes" in the second colon are a word pair; both refer to a kind of fine and powdery substance.[65] It is difficult to see any semantic progress in the combination of the two nouns, so this may be a case of what Clines calls "strict parallelism."[66]

In terms of inter-colon relationship, the two cola correspond to each other by syntactical matching:

preposition + verb + waw + verb (42:6a)

preposition + noun + waw + noun (42:6b)

As shown above, the poet matches prepositions in the two cola and verbs in one colon with nouns in another colon. Such a correspondence indicates the close association of the two cola as well as semantic intensification: the expressions "I recant" and "I repent" are intensified by the phrase "on dust and ashes." To know in what sense the latter intensifies the former, a discussion of the meaning of "on dust and ashes" is in order.

Figurative Language: "Dust and Ashes"

As mentioned in our discussion of Black's theory of metaphor, certain metaphors represent the way by which people conceptualize human behavior in

---

62. While the verb may be used absolutely (without an object), normally it is followed by an object (BDB 549b §2). Some translators ascribe the absence of the object as sign of textual corruption. As its absolute use may be read as a reflexive, the Old Greek (often called LXX) has supplied the object ἐμαυτὸν ("myself"), which is followed by KJV and RSV.

63. So Pope, *Job*, 348; Gray, *Job*, 488.

64. The Niphal of *nḥm* is often used to denote God changing his mind (e.g., Gen 6:6; 1 Sam 15:29); but at times it also refers to his people changing their minds (Exod 13:17; Jer 31:19); thus contra Clines, who argues that it refers to people changing their minds only once (*Job 38–42*, 1208 n6c). Janzen translates the strophe "Therefore I recant and change my mind concerning dust and ashes" (*Job*, 251).

65. The two nouns are at times used as synonyms. For further discussion, see the metaphorical use below.

66. Clines, *Job 38–42*, 1211.

a culture.[67] Such conceptualization is not confined to verbal communications, but extended to nonverbal communication such as gestures. In many modern societies placing the index finger on one's lips means "keep quiet," and a thumbs-up means approval ("it is good"). Like their modern counterparts, ancient Near East societies also have commonly understood gestures. Relevant to the present study are gestures of mourning that involve dust and ashes.

In his study of nonverbal communication of the ancient Near Eastern peoples, Mayer I. Gruber points out that the mourning rites of the ancient Canaanites and Israelites are characterized by the use of dust (ʾāpār) or ashes (ʾēper). In the Old Testament, it is described in various ways: throwing dust (ʾāpār) upward over their heads (Job 2:12); throwing dust on their heads (Josh 7:6; Lam 2:10); rolling in ashes or in dust and ashes (Jer 6:26; Ezek 27:30; Mic 1:10).[68]

While such a practice is widely attested in the Old Testament as well as ancient Near Eastern literature, applying it to the phrase "[sitting] on dust and ashes" (al-ʾāpār wāʾēper) in the present poem has proven problematic for several reasons. Firstly, whereas according to Gruber's study, mourners either put dust or ashes over or on the head or roll in them, here Job is on dust and ashes (al-ʾāpār wāʾēper). However one takes the preposition ʿal, be it as "on/upon" ("I am sitting upon dust and ashes")[69] or "in" ("I am in dust and ashes," as in wearing them like mourning clothes)[70] or "of" ("I repent of dust and ashes"),[71] it will not fit the description.[72]

Secondly, when used as a gesture of mourning, frequently in the Hebrew Bible, the words "dust" (ʾāpār) and "ashes" (ʾēper) occur either separately or together without being joined side by side. Elsewhere in Job, mourning gestures are expressed either by sitting on ashes (2:8) or applying dust (2:12; 16:15). Here, however, the two expressions appear as a word

---

67. See 104.

68. Gruber, *Nonverbal Communication*, 456–57.

69. E.g., Driver and Gray, *Job*, 373; Dhorme, *Job*, 646; Scholnick, "Poetry in Courtroom," 201.

70. E.g., NIV; RSV; Pope, *Job*, 247.

71. Patrick has argued that ʿal is part of the idiom nḥm ʿal rather than the preposition of the subsequent nouns; and the phrase to be translated: "I repent of dust and ashes" ("Translation of Job xlii 6," 369–70); also, Habel, *Job*, 575 and Dailey, "On Job 42.6," 205–9. This, however, has been refuted by Muenchow ("Dust and Dirt," 609–10 n53).

72. Wolters has proposed to re-vocalized the MT ʿal to ʿul, a noun which means "child" ("Therefore I recant and repent, a child of dust and ashes"); see Muenchow, "Child of Dust," 117–19. In our opinion this rendering lacks support of the immediate context.

pair, "dust and ashes" (ʿāpār wāʾer). This is not in keeping with the practice discussed earlier, for as Clines notes, normally mourning does not involve sitting both on dust and ashes at the same time.[73]

Thirdly, the idea of mourning runs counter to the general thrust of the poem, which emphasizes Job's new understanding of God's omnipotence. Such a positive experience is no reason for mourning. Furthermore, mourning also runs against the thrust of the book. We are told that at the beginning of his suffering, Job already makes gestures of mourning by sitting on a heap of ashes (bĕtôk-hāʾeper, 2:8). Making more mourning gestures after the transformative experience and his positive confession would not only be redundant, but also strange.

It becomes clear that the phrase "[sitting] on dust and ashes" here represents not a gesture of mourning; therefore its significance as a gesture is to be found elsewhere. We should note that ʿāpār and ʾeper as a word pair is rare in the Old Testament. It occurs only here (42:6b) and two other passages in the Old Testament (Gen 18:27; Job 30:19). In the latter two occurrences, the word pair is used denote one's humble or demeaned status. In 42:6b the word pair may well connote the same meaning.[74] A gesture which expresses one's humble status before God would fit the general thrust of the poem. Having been awed and made speechless by the complexity of God, conceding his insignificance would be an appropriate gesture.[75]

Section Summary

By way of parallelism and metaphors, Stanza II continues to contrast Job's old and new knowledge of God. However, the stanza highlights a different aspect of the contrast. If Stanza I draws attention to how the theophany makes Job realize his ignorance, this stanza points at the new perspective the theophany has brought about. Job admits that he used to perceive God

---

73. Clines, *Job 38–42*, 1210 n6e. It is probable, as Gruber has argued, that the two words are used as synonyms here (*Nonverbal Communication*, 457–60). In Numbers (Numb 19:9, 10) and some other passages (Jer 6:26; Ezek 27:30), the Hebrew word for "ashes" (ʾeper) refers to the by-form of "dust" (ʿāpār, i.e., "dirt"), and is used interchangeably. Nonetheless, as will be discussed below, the word pair is rare. Other than here it appears only in Gen 18:27; Job 30:19. As such one still has to explain why it is not explicitly associated with mourning rituals in its two other recurrences.

74. So Whybray, *Job*, 171; Muenchow. "Dust and Dirt," 609.

75. We agree with Patrick who notes that 42:6b means that Job will "remove himself from the physical setting associated with mourning and lamentation and cease what he has been doing from ii 8" ("Translation of Job xlii 6," 370). However, we base this interpretation on the use of "dust and ashes" in the other two passages rather than reading *nḥm ʿal* as an idiom.

and his justice through the eyes of the wisdom tradition (the "hearing" experience). Now after his face-to-face encounter with God (the "seeing" experience), Job is able to see justice through the eyes of God. Finally, Job gives a practical response to such a transformative experience. He recants his attack against God, repents and concedes his humble status. The latter actions represent a formal retraction of his lawsuit and mark the climax and the resolution of Job's dispute with God.[76]

THEOLOGY

Repeatedly the poem contrasts Job's old and new experiences. The old experience is associated with the metaphor "hearing," whereas the new is associated with "seeing." "Hearing" in Job is a metaphor for the perception of God shaped by traditional wisdom. "Seeing," on the contrary, represents the perception of the divine by a special encounter. Initially, the poem just highlights how the "seeing" experience exposes the limitations of Job's knowledge of God. Later, it brings the effect of "seeing" into sharp focus by showing its transformative power. The new experience turns Job's views around and makes him align with God's perspective; it also marks the turning point and resolution of Job's dispute with God.

The gap between "hearing" and "seeing" does not emerge from nowhere, but is already hinted right from the start of the book. The narrative section of the book portrays Job and God as beings in two different realms: earthly and heavenly. Being confined to the earthly realm, Job and his friends can only "hear" about God through their common tradition. Job's suffering exposes the limitations of the "hearing" theology. As the ultimate reason of the suffering comes from outside the earthly realm (the heavenly conversation between God and the Satan in 1:6–12; 2:1–6), it is beyond the comprehension of the earthlings.

The subsequent poetic dialogue not only further demonstrates the limitations of "hearing," but also reveals a whole heap of unresolved issues it can generate. One of the issues is God's justice (theodicy). Based on the tradition which Job has learned, God created a moral universe in which he rewards the righteous and punishes the wicked. He can do no other because of who he is and what he is. Job, the innocent man, is therefore baffled when he finds himself groaning in suffering. Not only does the traditional theology fail to explain the experience, the very theology also makes God appear to have contravened his own moral system.

---

76. Habel, *Job*, 579; Scholnick, "Poetry in Courtroom," 200; Clines, *Job 38–42*, 1218.

The failure of the traditional theology leads to another problem: a dispute (*rib*) between Job and God. The traditional doctrine of retribution makes Job feel he has been wronged. Being overwhelmed by the sense of injustice, Job initiates a lawsuit against God. Furthermore, having found the shortcomings of the traditional theology, Job realizes he needs a more direct way of interacting with God: a face-to-face contact. Therefore he presses God to appear in person in "court" and hopes for vindication.

The resolution does come through a face-to-face contact. God grants Job's wish to "see" him face to face, only that it is not the kind of "seeing" Job has demanded. Instead of vindicating him, God challenges Job's assumptions by presenting a far more complex moral universe. Job calls such an experience "seeing" (42:5). The transformative nature of the "seeing" experience is such that not only does it expose the limitations of Job's traditional theology, but also results in Job gaining a new perspective, enabling him to see things through the eyes of God.

In sum, the book of Job tells its reader that limitations of the earthly realm can be overcome only by an experience in which God enters the human realm so as to allow a personal experience of him. In doing so, the book of Job by no means diminishes the significance of traditional theologies. In fact, the book ends by going back to the traditional doctrine of retribution: God blesses the pious man Job again, in fact doubly (42:10–17). Such an ending is significant as it implies that Job embraces his tradition again. In view of this, the book's emphasis on "seeing" here is unlikely an encouragement to abandon one's theological tradition. Rather it is a critique of its limitations and highlights the need for a constant reforming process.

Furthermore, the book of Job does not view the "seeing" experience as a silver bullet. As reflected in the protracted scholarly debate, the ending of the book is ambiguous and leaves many issues unanswered.[77] Instead of promising a silver bullet, the book invites the reader to experience God in a personal way and get their theology renewed. The dissonances left by the book's ending reinforce its claim that certain life experiences are just too wonderful for humans to comprehend (42:3). Though Job is now willing to see things through the eyes of God, there are no indications that he understands everything he "sees." On the contrary, God's presentation makes him realize that God is beyond his comprehension. This awakening makes him

---

77. Among others are issues such as whether or not the ending adequately addresses the issue of suffering, the moral issues regarding God's use Job as a wager. For a summary of the ethical issues and discussion, see Clines, "Job's Fifth Friend," 233–50; for other recent discussions, Shelley, "Job 42:1–6," 541–46; LaCocque, "Job and Religion," 131–53; Wiley, "Faith and Loss," 115–129; Tollerton, "Reading Job," 197–212; O'Rourke, "Job's Final Response," 58–71.

look so small and insignificant in the vast universe, that he concedes his humble status (by sitting on dust and ashes). In other words, by showing Job the complexity of his creation, God puts Job in his place. Willingly, Job accepts it. After all, he is just a "man from Uz," one of the multitude creatures in the whole wide universe.

JOB AND THE CHRISTIAN

Readers from every walk of life can identify with Job and his experience. Being confined to finiteness, relating to the infinite God is always a struggle. Such awareness is all the more conspicuous in times of crisis. Crisis pushes the sense of inadequacy to the fore, exposing even more the limits of their perception of God (i.e., theology).

However, the poem in 42:2–6 not only echoes the reader's experience but also holds out hope to them. Firstly, the poem reminds the reader what theological traditions *can* and *cannot* do. As commented earlier, the poem is not against existing theological traditions, but reminds the reader about their limitations. Regardless of how sound one thinks it is, nobody's theology is to be equated with God himself. Christians tend to craft a water-tight theology of God, a theology that allows them to understand God's workings in the universe. Yet Job reminds us that in times of crisis, such theology is reduced to nothing but beautiful wrapping paper. One cannot wrap the living God in a beautifully crafted theology. John Calvin was so fascinated with Job that he preached 159 sermons on the book in a year. One reason for this was Calvin's belief that the book is about God's incomprehensibility.[78] Indeed, by showing Job the complexity of his operation, God signals that Job should not confine his God to his water-tight theology, but to let God be God.

Secondly, the poem points out that our theology is capable of creating a dispute with God. Theological traditions have the ability to shape people's perception of God, just as Job's tradition does. Over time, people in turn shape a certain kind of image of God. When God's actions fail to conform to the image, it gives rise to what biblical scholars call the *rîb*, a dispute with God. What Christians often call "disappointment with God" is in fact a reflection of such a dispute. Without resolution, such a dispute will lead to alienation. Today the *rîb* does not lead to lawsuits against God, but betrays itself in different forms of behavior: giving up on one's ministry, church, or even the faith. The poem tells the reader that such a dispute is due more to their perception of God rather than who God really is. Their theological

78. Thomas, *Calvin's Teaching*, 13.

traditions cannot help them break their finite perception, because this perception is the very child of those traditions. Like Job, a person locked in such a predicament needs a more direct way of knowing God. This leads us to another important point of the poem: a way of knowing God which goes beyond traditions.

Our poetic analysis shows that the poem emphasizes the importance of the "seeing" experience. As noted, "seeing" is Job's metaphor for an experience which is beyond the wisdom tradition. In the Old Testament the "seeing" experience is essential for two reasons. Firstly, it is a facet of Israel's theological tradition. In the Sinai narrative (Exodus 33–34) and the prophetic books "seeing" is a special prophetic mode of perceiving God (e.g., Isaiah 6; Ezek 1:27).[79] It is also a desired mode of knowing God in times of crisis. Using language similar to the prophetic books, the psalmists seek such an experience with God as they grapple with the problem of suffering (Ps 11:7; 17:15; 27:4, 13; 42:3; 63:3 [ET 63:2]).[80] The poet of Job 42:2–6 picks up this element from the tradition and highlights the fact that to break out of the limitations of his theological tradition, Job needs such an experience.

The priority of the "seeing" experience is no dismissal of traditions as a whole. As a matter of fact, the "seeing" experience is an integral part of traditions themselves. Within the biblical traditions, both "seeing" and "hearing" are viewed as important. So instead of undermining traditions, Job speaks of their renewal and reformation. It reminds the reader that a personal experience with God is necessary to prevent their theology from limiting God and calcifying the faith. Having been confined to the earthly realm, the earthlings need to experience the transcendent God's intervention.

The reformative power expressed in the poem culminates in the incarnation of Christ. The "seeing" experience is unequivocally expressed in the language of the Gospel of John: "The Word became flesh and dwelt among us. We *saw* his glory, the glory as the only Son from the Father, full of grace and truth" (John 1:14, italics for emphasis). In fact, the incarnation represents the kind of experience the Old Testament authors dream of: a multi-sensorial experience of God: "Which was from the beginning, which we have *heard*, which we have *seen* with our eyes, which we *looked* at and our hands *touched*—about the Word of life" (1 John 1:1). Christ's incarnation represents God's breaking into the realm of the finite so as to allow humans to know him in a personal way.

79. On the theological role of Moses' encounter with God in Exodus 33–34, see Childs, *Exodus*, 596–97; Savran, "Seeing is Believing," 329–32; on the prophetic traditions, Wilson, *Prophecy*, 254–71.

80. For a discussion of "seeing God" in the Psalms see Weiser, *Psalms*, 182; Smith, "Seeing God," 171–83; Savran, "Seeing is Believing," 327.

History has proven that such a face-to-face encounter with God did not lead to the diminished significance of existing traditions, but their new appropriation.[81] As in Job, the face-to-face encounter with Christ reformed the way the New Testament writers viewed Scripture and traditions. The end result is the hermeneutical-theological paradigm shift attested by their writings. Their experience with Christ became the framework in which they appropriated Scripture and applied their tradition. The hermeneutical-theological paradigm shift resulted in a fresh way of looking at issues such as God's salvation, kingdom, suffering, love, ethics, and so on. In other words, they came to see those things through the eyes of the incarnate God.

Some scholars have lamented that religious experience is a "missing dimension" in modern biblical scholarship.[82] It rings true to us once we enter biblical scholarship. Modern scholars have the tendency to rationalize and explain away the religious experience of biblical texts, which is an unfortunate excess of the Enlightenment. As a result, God is often confined to intellectual exercise of developing authoritative works and traditions. In the Joban terminology, these are the "hearing" mode of knowing God. Though the contributions of such mode to biblical studies are undeniable, theologically it is limiting as it fails to consider the religious dimension of the biblical texts. The New Testament writers offer the way to break out of the limitations. As Richard B. Hays writes: "Rather than giving us a set of authoritative teachings, the NT offers us 'models of receptivity to the work of God's Spirit.'"[83] The models will allow modern interpreters to appropriate their rich theological traditions by responding "freshly and authentically to the work of God in our own living experience."[84]

81. The appropriation of the Second Temple traditions in the writing of the New Testament books is widely noted in New Testament scholarship. See for example, Wilcox, "Promise of the 'Seed,'" 2–20; Beaton, *Isaiah's Christ*, esp. pp. 23, 44–85, 144; Huizenga, "Obedience unto Death," 507–526. See also Hays' works such as *Echoes of Scripture* and *Conversion of Imagination*.

82. Johnson, *Religious Experience*, 1–37; Dunn, "Religious Experience," 3–15.

83. Hays, "Kerygma and Midrash," 124.

84. Ibid.

Epilogue

IN THIS BOOK WE have learned how biblical poets bring across their theological message by their poetic skill. On the theory level, the present author has decided to take a diachronic approach. The first four chapters show that the study of Hebrew poetry has a long history. For centuries Bible interpreters of every generation have attempted to understand the literary elements and the dynamics of Hebrew poetry, such as parallelism, rhythm and figurative language. Their contributions to our understanding of Hebrew poetry are undeniable. At times, scholars' taxonomies may sound complicated and difficult for beginning readers to follow. This is not because they deliberately make it esoteric so as to show off their scholarship. Rather, Hebrew poetry is, in fact, a complex art, and providing an explanation is always challenging. The studies of generations have helped clarified issues and provided us with a better understanding about how the poetic elements work. So, if we persevere, the benefits are almost guaranteed.

On the practical level, the last three chapters have demonstrated how the poetic elements work in selected passages. At the same time these examples would also demonstrate how we apply the theory learned in the preceding four chapters to biblical poetic passages. Our analysis of the three poetic passages shows the dynamics between parallelism, ellipsis, figurative language, and other features. The parallelism involves multi-level relationships: semantics, grammar, syntax, even phonology. The dynamics interconnect every colon, strophe and stanza as to form cumulative significance. The poets weave parallelistic relationship with other poetic elements such as ellipses and figurative language. Our analysis highlights the fact that far from being mechanical or monotonous, such dynamics vary from strophe to strophe, displaying the poet's creativity and literary finesse. The final outcome is that we have a lively play of words, vivid similes and metaphors, presenting the poet's thought and emotions, and most significantly his theological conviction.

Evidently, given its complexity and creative dynamics, there is more to Hebrew poetry than what this book (or any other book) can cover. Also, the three sample passages do not exhaust the poetic artistry of the biblical poets and the richness of their works. As noted in Preface, this book has a modest aim: to provide the reader with the basic concepts of biblical poetry, so as to help them read and appreciate the poetic texts of the Bible, and that in turn this will lead them to a deeper understanding of the theology of the texts. Finally, it is also the hope of the present writer that after tasting the beauty and the rich theology of biblical poems, the reader is motivated to explore further. If so, they may refer to the bibliography at the end of this book.

Bibliography

Aaron, David H. *Biblical Ambiguities: Metaphor, Semantics and Divine Imagery.* BRLAJ 4. Leiden: Brill, 2001.

Albright, W. F. "A Catalogue of Early Hebrew Lyric Poems (Psalm LXVIII)." *HUCA* 23 (1950–51) 1–39.

———. *Yahweh and the Gods of Canaan.* 1968. Reprint, Winona Lake, IN: Eisenbrauns, 1990.

Allen, Leslie C. *Jeremiah.* OTL. Louisville: John Knox, 2008.

———. *Psalms 101–50.* WBC 21. Nashville: Nelson, 2002.

Alonso-Schökel, Luis. "Hermeneutical Problems of a Literary Study of the Bible." In *Congress Volume, Edinburgh 1974,* 1–15. VTSup 28. Leiden: Brill, 1975.

———. *A Manual of Hebrew Poetics.* SubBib 11. Rome: Editrice Pontificio Istituto Biblico, 2000.

———. "Toward a Dramatic Reading of Job." *Semeia* 7 (1977) 45–61.

Alter, Robert. *The Art of Biblical Poetry.* Rev. ed. New York: Basic Books, 2011.

———. *The Wisdom Books: Job, Proverbs, and Ecclesiastes.* New York: Norton, 2010.

Andersen, Francis, and A. Dean Forbes. "'Prose Particle' Counts of the Hebrew Bible." In *The Word of the Lord Shall Go Forth: Essays in Honor of David Noel Freedman in Celebration of His Sixtieth Birthday,* edited by Carol L. Meyers and M. O'Connor, 165–83. Winona Lake, IN: Eisenbrauns, 1983.

Anderson, A. A. *The Book of Psalms.* NCB. Grand Rapids: Eerdmans, 1972.

Anderson, Bernhard W. "The Song of Miriam Poetically and Theologically Considered." In *Directions in Biblical Hebrew Poetry,* edited by Elaine R. Follis, 285–96. JSOTSup 40. Sheffield: JSOT Press, 1987.

Anderson, G. W. "A Note on Ps 1:1." *VT* 24 (1974) 231–33.

André, Gunnel. "'Walk,' 'Stand' and 'Sit' in Psalm 1:1–2." *VT* 32 (1982) 327.

Apple, Raymond. "The Happy Man of Psalm 1." *JBQ* 40 (2012) 179–82.

Aristotle. *On Rhetoric: A Theory of Civic Discourse.* Translated by George A. Kennedy. New York: Oxford University Press, 1991.

———. *Poetics.* Translated by G. F. Else. Ann Arbor: University of Michigan Press, 1970.

———. *Poetics I.* Translated by Richard Janko. Indianapolis: Hackett, 1987.

Auerbach, Erich. *Mimesis.* Garden City, NY: Doubleday Anchor Books, 1957.

Auffret, P. "Essai sur la structure littéraire du psaume 1." *BZ* 22 (1978) 26–45.

Bal, Mieke. *Reading "Rembrandt": Beyond the Word-Image Opposition*. The Northrop Frye Lectures in Literary Theory. Cambridge New Art History and Criticism Cambridge: Cambridge University Press, 1991.

Bartholomew, Craig G. *Ecclesiastes*. BCOT. Grand Rapids: Baker Academic, 2009.

Barton, G. A. *A Critical and Exegetical Commentary on the Book of Ecclesiastes*. ICC. Edinburgh: T. & T. Clark, 1908.

Barton, John. *Reading the Old Testament*. Rev. ed. Louisville: Westminster John Knox, 1996.

Bartor, Asnat. "The 'Juridical Dialogue': A Literary-Judicial Pattern." *VT* 53 (2003) 445–64.

Berlin, Adele. *The Dynamics of Biblical Parallelism*. Bloomington: Indiana University Press, 1985.

———. "Grammatical Aspects of Biblical Parallelism." *HUCA* 50 (1979) 17–43.

Beaton, Richard. *Isaiah's Christ in Matthew's Gospel*. Society for New Testament Studies Monograph Series 123. Cambridge: Cambridge University Press, 2002.

Beaucamp, E. *Le Psautire 1–72*. Sources bibliques. Paris: Gabalda, 1976.

Berger, Benjamin L. "Qoheleth and the Exigencies of the Absurd." *Int* 9 (2001) 141–79.

Black, Max. "Metaphor." In *Philosophical Perspectives on Metaphor*, edited by Mark Johnson, 64–82. Minneapolis: University of Minnesota Press, 1981.

Bloch, Yigal. "The Prefixed Perfective and the Dating of Early Hebrew Poetry: A Re-Evaluation." *VT* 59 (2009) 34–70.

Bourguet, Daniel. *Des Métaphores de Jérémie*. EBib 9. Paris: Gabalda, 1987.

Bovati, Pietro. *Re-establishing Justice: Legal Terms, Concepts and Procedures in the Hebrew Bible*. Translated by Michael J. Smith. JSOTSup 105. Sheffield: Sheffield Academic, 1994.

Bratcher, Robert G. and William D. Reyburn. *Handbook to the Psalms*. New York: United Bible Societies, 1993.

Brettler, Marc Zvi. *God Is King: Understanding an Israelite Metaphor*. JSOTSup 76. Sheffield: Sheffield Academic, 1989.

Briggs, Charles A., and Emilie G. Briggs. *A Critical and Exegetical Commentary on the Book of Psalms*. ICC. Edinburgh: T. & T. Clark, 1906.

Brogan, Jacqueline Vaught. "Simile." In *The New Princeton Encyclopedia of Poetry and Poetics*, edited by Alex Preminger and T. V. F. Brogan, 1149–50. 3rd rev. ed. Princeton: Princeton University Press, 1993.

Brogan, T. V. F. "Rhythm." In *The New Princeton Encyclopedia of Poetry and Poetics*, edited by Alex Preminger and T. V. F. Brogan, 1066–70. 3rd rev. ed. Princeton: Princeton University Press, 1993.

Brown, William P. *Ecclesiastes*. IBC. Louisville: Westminster John Knox, 2011.

———. *Psalms*. IBT. Nashville: Abingdon, 2010.

Brownlee, William H. "Psalm 1–2: A Coronation Liturgy." *Bib* 52 (1971) 321–36.

Buber, Martin. *Right and Wrong: An Interpretation of Some Psalms*. Translated by R. G. Smith. London: SCM, 1952.

Budde, Karl. "Das hebräische Klagelied." *ZAW* 2 (1882) 1–52.

———. "Poetry (Hebrew)." In *A Dictionary of the Bible Dealing with Its Language, Literature, and Contents, Including the Bible Theology*, edited by J. Hastings, 4:2–13. New York: Scribner, 1900–1904.

Bullough, Sebastian. "The Question of Metre in Psalm 1." *VT* 17 (1967) 42–49.

Caird, G. B. *The Language and Imagery of the Bible*. London: Duckworth, 1980.

Camp, Claudia V. and Carole R. Fontaine, eds. *Semeia* 61: *Woman, War and Metaphor: Language and Society in the Study of the Hebrew Bible*. Atlanta: Scholars, 1993.

Camus, Albert. *The Myth of Sysyphus and Other Essays*. Translated by J. O'Brien. New York: Vintage, 1991.

Carasik, Michael. *Theologies of the Mind in Biblical Israel*. Studies in Biblical Literature 85. New York: Lang, 2006.

———. "To See a Sound: A Deuteronomic Rereading of Exodus 20:15." *Proof* 19 (1999) 257–65.

Carroll, Robert P. *Jeremiah: A Commentary*. OTL. Philadelphia: Westminster, 1986.

Cassuto, U. *A Commentary on the Book of Exodus*. Translated by I. Abraham. Jerusalem: Magnes, 1967.

Cazelles, H. "אַשְׁרֵי *'ašrê*." In *TDOT* 1 (1974) 445–48. 1974.

Childs, Brevard S. *The Book of Exodus*. OTL. Philadelphia: Westminster John Knox, 1974.

Ceresko, Anthony R. "The Chiastic Word Pattern in Hebrew." *CBQ* 38 (1976) 303–11.

———. "The Function of Antanaclasis (*mṣ'* 'to find'// *mṣ'* 'to reach, overtake, grasp') in Hebrew Poetry, Especially in the Book of Qoheleth." *CBQ* 44 (1982) 551–69.

———. "The Function of Chiasmus in Hebrew Poetry." *CBQ* 40 (1978) 1–10.

Chatman, Seymour. *A Theory of Meter*. The Hague: Mouton, 1965.

Clifford, Richard J. *Proverbs*. OTL. Louisville: Westminster John Knox, 1999.

———. *Psalms 1–72*. AOTC. Nashville: Abingdon, 2002.

Clines, David J. A. "Job's Fifth Friend: An Ethical Critique of the Book of Job." *BibInt* 12 (2004) 233–50.

———. *Job 1–20*. WBC 17. Waco, TX: Word, 1989.

———. *Job 38–42*. WBC 18B. Nashville: Nelson, 2011.

———. "The Parallelism of Greater Precision." In *Directions in Biblical Hebrew Poetry*, edited by Elaine R. Follis, 77–100. JSOTSup 40. Sheffield: Sheffield Academic, 1987.

Cole, R. L. *Psalms 1–2: Gateway to the Psalter*. HBM 37. Sheffield: Sheffield Phoenix, 2012.

Collins. T. *Line-forms in Hebrew Poetry: A Grammatical Approach to The Stylistic Study of the Hebrew Prophets*. SPSM 7. Rome: Biblical Institute, 1978.

Coogan, Michael D. "A Structural and Literary Analysis of the Song of Deborah." *CBQ* 40 (1978) 143–65.

Craigie, Peter C. *Psalms 1–50*. WBC 19. Waco, TX: Word, 1983.

Creach, Jerome F. D. "Like a Tree Planted by the Temple Stream: The Portrait of the Righteous in Psalm 1:3." *CBQ* 61 (1999) 34–46.

Crenshaw, James L. *Ecclesiastes*. OTL. Philadelphia: Westminster, 1987.

Croft, Steven J. L. *The Identity of the Individual in the Psalms*. JSOTSup 44. Sheffield: Sheffield Academic, 1987.

Cross, Frank Moore, and David Noel Freedman. *Studies in Ancient Yahwistic Poetry*. 1975. Reprint, Grand Rapids: Eerdmans, 1997.

Culler, Jonathan. *Structural Poetics: Structuralism, Linguistics and the Study of Literature*. Ithaca, NY: Cornell University Press, 1975.

Culley, Robert C. "Metrical Analysis of Classical Hebrew Poetry." In *Essays on the Ancient Semitic World*, edited by J. W. Wevers and D. B. Redford, 12–28. Toronto: University of Toronto Press, 1970.

————. Review of *Studies in Early Hebrew Meter,* by Douglas Stuart. *CBQ* 40 (1978) 255–56.

Cullhed, Anna. "Original Poetry: Robert Lowth and Eighteenth-Century Poetics." In *Sacred Conjectures: The Context and Legacy of Roberth Lowth and Jean Astruc,* edited by John Jarick, 25–47. New York: T. & T. Clark, 2007.

Dahood, Mitchell. *Psalms 1–50.* AB 16. Garden City, NY: Doubleday, 1965.

————. *Psalms 101–150.* AB 17A. Garden City, NY: Doubleday, 1970.

Dailey, Thomas F. "And Yet He Repents—On Job 42.6." *ZAW* 105 (1993) 205–9.

Day Lewis, C. *The Poetic Image.* Clark Lectures 1946. London: Cape, 1947.

DeCaen, Vincent. "Theme and Variation in Psalm 111: Phrase and Foot in Generative-Metrical Perspective." *JSS* 54 (2009) 81–109.

Dell, K. "The Cycle of Life in Ecclesiastes." *VT* 59 (2009) 181–189.

De Moor, J. C. "The Art of Versification in Ugarit and Israel I: The Rhythmical Structure." In *Studies in Bible and the Ancient Near East,* edited by Yitshak Avishur and Joshua Blau, 119–39. Jerusalem: Rubinstein's, 1978.

Denham, John. *Cooper's Hill: A Poem.* London: Oxford University, 1709.

Dobbs-Allsopp, F. W. "The Effects of Enjambment in Lamentations (II)." *ZAW* 113 (2001) 370–85.

————. "The Enjambing Line in Lamentations: A Taxonomy (I)." *ZAW* 113 (2001) 219–39.

————. *On Biblical Poetry.* Oxford: Oxford University Press, 2015.

Dhorme, E. *A Commentary on the Book of Job.* Translated by Harold Knight. London: Nelson, 1967.

Dick, Michael B. "Legal Metaphor in Job 31." *CBQ* 41 (1979) 37–50.

Dresher, B. Elan. "The Prosodic Basis of the Tiberian Hebrew System of Accents." *Language* 70 (1994) 1–52.

Driver, S. R., and G. B. Gray. *A Critical and Exegetical Commentary on the Book of Job.* ICC. Edinburgh: T. & T. Clark, 1911.

Drury, John. *Painting the Word: Christian Pictures and Their Meanings.* New Haven: Yale University Press, 1999.

Dunn, James D. G. "Religious Experience in the New Testament." In *Between Experience and Interpretation: Engaging the Writings of the New Testament,* edited by Mary F. Foskett and O. Wesley Allen, Jr., 3–15. Nashville: Abingdon, 2008.

Eaton, J. H. *Psalms.* Torch Bible Commentaries. London: SCM, 1967.

Eidevall, G. "Spatial Metaphors in Lamentations 3:1–9." In *Metaphor in the Hebrew Bible,* edited by Pierre van Hecke, 133–37. BETL 187. Leuven: Peeters, 2005.

Eissfeldt, Otto. *The Old Testament: An Introduction the Apocrypha and Pseudepigrapha and also the Works of Similar Type from Qumran.* Translated by P. R. Ackroyd. New York: Harper & Row 1976.

Else, G. F. "Introduction." In *Aristotle Poetics.* Translated by G. F. Else, 1–14. Ann Arbor: University of Michigan Press, 1970.

Enns, Pete. *Ecclesiastes.* THOTC. Grand Rapids: Eerdmans, 2011.

Fabb, Nigel. *Linguistics and Literature: Language in the Verbal Arts of the World.* Oxford: Blackwell, 1997.

Farmer, Kathleen A. *Who Knows What Is Good? A Commentary on the Books of Proverbs and Ecclesiastes.* ITC. Grand Rapids: Eerdmans, 1991.

Finley, Thomas J. "The Waw-Consecutive with 'Imperfect' in Biblical Hebrew: Theoretical Studies and Its Use in Amos." In *Tradition and Testament: Essays in*

Honor of Charles Lee Feinberg, edited by John S. Feinberg and Paul D. Feinberg, 241–62. Chicago: Moody, 1981.

Fokkelman, J. P. *The Book of Job in Form.* SSN 58. Leiden: Brill, 2012.

———. *Major Poems of the Hebrew Bible: At the Interface of Prosody and Structural Analysis.* 4 vols. SSN 37, 41, 43, 47. Assen: van Gorcum, 1998 –2004.

———. *The Psalms in Form: The Hebrew Psalter in Its Poetic Shape.* Leiden: Deo, 2002.

———. *Reading Biblical Poetry.* Louisville: Westminster John Knox, 2001.

Follis, Elaine R. "The Holy City as Daughter." In *Directions in Biblical Hebrew Poetry,* edited by Elaine R. Follis, 173–84. JSOTSup 40. Sheffield: JSOT Press, 1987.

Forti, Tova. *Animal Imagery in the Book of Proverbs.* VTSup 118. Leiden: Brill, 2007.

———. "Bee's Honey—From Realia to Metaphor in Biblical Wisdom Literature." *VT* 54 (2006) 327–41.

Fox, Michael V. *Ecclesiastes.* Jewish Publication Society Bible Commentary. Philadelphia: Jewish Publication Society, 2004.

———. "Frame-Narrative and Composition in the Book of Qoheleth." *HUCA* 48 (1977) 83–106.

———. "Ideas of Wisdom in Proverbs 1–9." *JBL* 116 (1997) 613–33.

———. *Qoheleth and His Contradictions.* BLS 18. Sheffield: Sheffield Academic, 1989.

———. "Qoheleth 1:4." *JSOT* 40 (1988) 109.

———. *A Time to Tear Down and a Time to Build up.* Grand Rapids: Eerdmans, 1999.

France, R. T. *The Gospel of Matthew.* NICNT. Grand Rapids: Eerdmans, 2007.

Fredericks, Daniel C. "Chiasm and Parallel Structure in Qoheleth 5:9—6:9." *JBL* 108 (1989) 17–35.

———. *Coping with Transience: Ecclesiastes on Brevity in Life.* Biblical Seminar 18. Sheffield: JSOT Press, 1993.

Freedman, David Noel. "Another Look at Biblical Hebrew Poetry." In *Directions in Biblical Hebrew Poetry,* edited by Elaine R. Follis, 11–28. JSOTSup 40. Sheffield: Sheffield Academic, 1987.

———. "Archaic Forms in Early Hebrew Poetry." *ZAW* 72 (1960) 101–7.

———. *Pottery, Poetry and Prophecy.* Winona Lake, IN: Eisenbrauns, 1980.

———. "The Structure of Psalm 137." In *Near Eastern Studies in Honor of William Foxwell Albright,* edited by H. Goedicke, 187–205. Baltimore: Johns Hopkins University Press, 1971.

Freedman, David Noel et al. "דּוֹר *dôr.*" In *TDOT* 3 (1978) 169–81.

Friedman, N. "Imagery." In *Encyclopedia of Poetry and Poetics,* edited by Alex Preminger, 363–70. Princeton: Princeton University Press, 1965.

———. "Imagery." In *The New Princeton Encyclopedia of Poetry and Poetics,* edited by Alex Preminger and T. V. F. Brogan, 559–566. Princeton: Princeton University Press, 1993.

Frymer-Kensky, Tikva. "Pollution, Purification, Purgation in Biblical Israel." In *The Word of the Lord Shall Go Forth: Essays in Honor of David Noel Freedman in Celebration of His Sixtieth Birthday,* edited by Carol L. Meyers and M. O'Connor, 399–414. Winona Lake, IN: Eisenbrauns, 1983.

———. "The Planting of Man: A Study in Biblical Imagery." In *Love and Death in the Ancient Near East: Essays in Honor of Marvin H. Pope,* edited by John H. Marks and Robert M. Good, 129–37. Guilford, CT: Four Quarters, 1987.

Gammie, John G. "Alter vs Kugel: Taking the Heat in Struggle over Biblical Poetry." *BibRev* 5/1 (1989) 26–29.

Gemser, Berend. "The *Rib*—or Controversy-Pattern in Hebrew Mentality." In *Wisdom in Israel and in the Ancient Near East: Presented to Harold Henry Rowley by the Society for Old Testament Study in Association with the Editorial Board of Vetus Testamentum, in Celebration of His Sixty-fifth Birthday, 24 March 1955*, edited by M. Noth and D. Winton Thomas, 120–37. VTSup 3. Leiden: Brill, 1960.

Gesenius, Wilhelm. *Gesenius' Hebrew Grammar*. 2nd ed. Edited and enlarged by E. Kautzsch. Translated by A. E. Cowley. Oxford: Clarendon, 1910.

Gillingham, Susan E. *The Poems and Psalms of the Hebrew Bible*. Oxford: Oxford University Press, 1994.

———. *Psalms through the Centuries*. 2 vols. BBC. Malden, MA: Blackwell, 2008.

———. Review of *Major Poems of the Hebrew Bible: At the Interface of Hermeneutics and Structural Analysis*. Vol. 1, *Ex. 15, Deut. 32, and Job 3*, by J. P. Fokkelman. *JSS* 46 (2001) 153–55.

Gitay, Yehoshua. "A Study of Amos's Art of Speech: A Rhetorical Analysis of Amos 3:1–15." *CBQ* 42 (1980) 293–309.

Good, Edwin M. "The Unfilled Sea: Style and Meaning in Ecclesiastes 1:2–11." In *Israelite Wisdom: Theological and Literary Essays in Honor of Samuel Terrien*, edited by John G. Gammie et al., 59–73. Missoula, MT: Scholars, 1978.

Goldingay, John. *Psalms 1–41*. BCOT. Grand Rapids: Baker Academic, 2006.

Gordis, Robert. *The Book of Job*. New York: Jewish Theological Seminary of America, 1978.

Görg, M. "יָשַׁב *yāšab*; מוֹשָׁב *môsāb*." In *TDOT* 6 (1990) 420–38.

Gosling, F. A. "An Interesting Use of the Waw Consecutive." *ZAW* 110 (1998) 403–10.

Gray, George Buchanan. *The Form of Hebrew Poetry: Considered with Special Reference to the Criticism and Interpretation of the Old Testament*. 1915. Reprint, Eugene, OR: Wipf & Stock, 2002.

Gray, John. *The Book of Job*. Edited by David J. A. Clines. Text of the Hebrew Bible 1. Sheffield: Sheffield Phoenix, 2010.

Greenstein, Edward L. "A Forensic Understanding of the Speech from the Whirlwind." In *Texts, Temples and Traditions*, edited by Michael V. Fox et al., 241–58. Winona Lake, IN: Eisenbrauns, 1996.

———. "God's Golem: The Creation of the Human in Genesis 2." In *Creation in Jewish and Christian Tradition*, edited by Henning Graf Reventlow and Yair Hoffman, 219–39. JSOTSup 319. London: Sheffield Academic, 2002.

———. "How Does Parallelism Mean?" In *A Sense of Text: The Art of Language in the Study of Biblical Literature*, edited by Stephen A. Geller, et al., 41–70. Jewish Quarterly Review Supplement. Winona Lake, IN: Eisenbrauns, 1982.

———. "Two Variations of Grammatical Parallelism in Canaanite Poetry and Their Psycholinguistic Background." *JANES* 6 (1974) 87–105.

Groom, Susan Anne. *Linguistic Analysis of Biblical Hebrew*. Carlisle, UK: Paternoster, 2003.

Gruber, Mayer I. *Aspects of Nonverbal Communication in the Ancient Near East*. 2 vols. SPSM 12. Rome: Biblical Institute Press, 1980.

———. "The Meaning of Biblical Parallelism: A Biblical Perspective." *Proof* 13 (1993) 289–93.

Habel, Norman C. *The Book of Job*. OTL. Philadelphia, PA: Westminster, 1985.

Halle, Morris, and John J. McCarthy, "The Metrical Structure of Psalm 127." *JBL* 100 (1981) 161–67.

Hanson, K. C. "How Honorable! How Shameful! A Cultural Analysis of Matthew's Makarisms and Reproaches." *Semeia* 68 (1994[96]) 81–111.

Harrop, G. Gerald. "'But Now Mine Eye Seeth Thee.'" *CJT* 12 (1966) 80–84.

Hartley, John E. *The Book of Job*. NICOT. Grand Rapids: Eerdmans, 1988.

Harvey, Julien. *Le plaidoyer prophétic contre Israël après la rupture de l'alliance*. STR 22. Montreal: Bellarmin, 1967.

———. "Le *Rib*-Pattern, réquisitoire prophétique sur la rupture de l'alliance." *Bib* 43 (1962) 172–96.

Hauser, Alan J. "Judges 5: Parataxis in Hebrew Poetry." *JBL* 99 (1980) 23–41.

Hays, Richard B. *The Conversion of the Imagination: Paul as Interpreter of Israel's Scripture*. Grand Rapids: Eerdmans, 2005.

———. *Echoes of Scripture in the Letters of Paul*. New Haven: Yale University Press, 1989.

———. "Kerygma and Midrash: A Conversation with Luke Timothy Johnson and C. H. Dodd." In *Between Experience and Interpretation: Engaging the Writings of the New Testament*, edited by Mary F. Foskett and O. Wesley Allen, Jr., 105–26. Nashville: Abingdon, 2008.

Healey, J. F., and Peter C. Craigie, "Ugaritic." In *ABD*, 4:226–29.

Hecke, Pierre van. "Conceptual Blending: A Recent Approach to Metaphor." In *Metaphor in the Hebrew Bible*, edited by Pierre van Hecke, 215–31. BETL 187. Leuven: Peeters, 2005.

Helfmeyer, F. J. " הָלַךְ *hālakh*." In *TDOT* 3 (1978) 388–403.

Henle, Paul. "Metaphor." In *Philosophical Perspectives on Metaphor*, edited by Mark Johnson, 83–104. Minneapolis: University of Minnesota Press, 1981.

Hirsch, E. D. *Validity in Interpretation*. New Haven: Yale University Press, 1967.

Holladay, William L. "Hebrew Verse Structure Revisited (I): Which Words 'Count'?" *JBL* 118 (1999) 19–32.

———. *Jeremiah 1: A Commentary on the Book of the Prophet Jeremiah Chapters 1–25*. Hermeneia. Philadelphia: Fortress, 1986.

Holyoak, Keith J., and Paul Thagard. *Mental Leaps: Analogy in Creative Thought*. Cambridge: MIT Press, 1995.

Houston, Walter J. "Misunderstanding or Midrash? The Prose Appropriation of Poetic Material in the Hebrew Bible (Part I)." *ZAW* 109 (1997) 342–55.

———. "Misunderstanding or Midrash? The Prose Appropriation of Poetic Material in the Hebrew Bible (Part II)." *ZAW* 109 (1997) 534–48.

Hrushovski, Benjamin. "Note on the Systems of Hebrew Versification." In *The Penguin Book of Hebrew Verse*, edited by T. Carmi, 57–72. New York: Penguin, 1981.

———. "On Free Rhythm in Modern Poetry." In *Style in Language*, edited by Thomas A. Sebeok, 173–90. Cambridge: Technology Press of Massachusetts Institute of Technology, 1960.

———. "Poetic Metaphor and Frames of Reference: With Examples from Eliot, Rilke, Mayakovsky, Mandelshtam, Pound, Creeley, Amichai, and the New York Times." *PT* 5 (1984) 5–43.

———. "Prosody, Hebrew." In *Encyclopedia Judaica*, 13:1195–239. New York: Macmillan, 1971.

Huffmon, Herbert B. "The Treaty Background of Hebrew *Yada*." *BASOR* 181 (1966) 31–37.

Huizenga, Leroy Andrew. "Obedience unto Death: The Matthean Gethsemane and Arrest Sequence and the Aqedah." *CBQ* 71 (2009) 507–26.

Isaksson, Bo. *Studies in the Language of Qoheleth: With Special Emphasis on the Verbal System.* SSU 10. Stockholm: Almqvist & Wiksell, 1987.

Iwanski, Dariuz. *The Dynamics of Job's Intercession.* AnBib 161. Rome: Editrice Pontificio Istituto Biblico, 2006.

Jacquet, Louis. *Les Psaumes et le Cœur de l'homme: Étude Textuelle, Littéraire et Doctrinale.* Gembloux: Duculot, 1975–1979.

Jacobsen, Thorkild. *The Treasures of Darkness: A History of Mesopotamian Religion.* New Haven: Yale University Press, 1976.

Japhet, Sara. "Goes to the South and Turns to the North (Ecclesiastes 1:6): The Sources and History of the Exegetical Traditions," *JSQ* 1 (1993–94) 289–322.

Jakobson, Roman. "Grammatical Parallelism and Its Russian Facet." *Language* 42 (1966) 399–429.

———. "Linguistics and Poetics." In *Style in Language,* edited by Thomas A. Sebeok, 350–77. Cambridge: Technology Press of Massachusetts Institute of Technology, 1960.

Janzen, J. Gerald. *Job.* IBC. Atlanta: John Knox, 1985.

Jarick, John. "The Hebrew Book of Changes: Reflections on *Hakkōl Hebel* and *Kakkōl Zĕmān* in Ecclesiastes." *JSOT* 90 (2000) 79–99.

Jindo, Job Y. *Biblical Metaphor Reconsidered: A Cognitive Approach to Poetic Prophecy in Jeremiah 1–24.* HSM 64. Winona Lake, IN: Eisenbrauns, 2010.

Johnson, Luke Timothy. *Religious Experience in Earliest Christianity: A Missing Dimension in New Testament Studies.* Minneapolis: Fortress, 1998.

Johnson, Mark. "Introduction: Metaphor in the Philosophical Tradition." In *Philosophical Perspectives on Metaphor,* edited by Mark Johnson, 3–47. Minneapolis: University of Minnesota Press, 1981.

———. "Metaphor: An Overview." In *Encyclopedia of Aesthetics,* edited by Michael Kelly, 3:208–12. Oxford: Oxford University Press, 2014.

Joüon, P. *The Grammar of Biblical Hebrew.* 2 vols. Revised by T. Muraoka. Reprint. Rome: Editrice Pontificio Istituto Biblico, 2003.

Josephus. Translated by H. St. J. Thackeray et al. 10 vols. Loeb Classical Library. Cambridge: Harvard University Press, 1926–1965.

Kidner, Derek. *Psalms 1–72.* TOTC. Leicester, UK: Tyndale/Inter-Varsity, 1976.

Kirkpatrick, A. F. *The Book of Psalms.* 3 vols. Cambridge Bible for Schools and Colleges. Cambridge: Cambridge University Press, 1901.

Knowles, Murray and Rosamund Moon. *Introducing Metaphor.* London: Rouledge, 2006.

Koch, K. et al. "דֶּרֶךְ *derekh*." In *TDOT* 3 (1978) 270–93.

Kraus, Hans-Joachim. *Psalms 1–59.* Translated by Hilton C. Oswald. CC. Minneapolis: Fortress, 1993.

———. *Psalms 60–150.* Translated by Hilton C. Oswald. CC. Minneapolis: Fortress, 1993.

Kugel, James. *The Idea of Biblical Poetry.* New Haven: Yale University Press, 1981.

Kuhn, Thomas S. "Metaphor in Science." In *Metaphor and Thought,* edited by A. Ortony, 409–19. Cambridge: Cambridge University Press, 1979.

Kurylowicz, Jerzy. *Studies in Semitic Grammar and Metrics.* PJ 7. Wroclaw: Polska Akademica Nauk, 1975.

LaCocque, André. "Job and Religion at its Best." *BibInt* 4 (1996) 131–53.

Lakoff, George, and Mark Johnson. "Conceptual Metaphor in Everyday Language." *JPhil* 77 (1980) 453–86.

———. *Metaphors We Live By.* Chicago: University of Chicago Press, 1980.

———. *More Than Cool Reason.* Chicago: University of Chicago Press, 1989.

———. *Philosophy in the Flesh.* New York: Basic Books, 1999.

Lambrecht, Knud. *Information Structure and Sentence Form: Topic, Focus, and the Mental Representations of Discourse Referents.* Cambridge Studies in Linguistics 71. Cambridge: Cambridge University Press, 1994.

Landy, Francis. *Paradoxes of Paradise: Identity and Difference in the Song of Songs.* BLS 7. Sheffield: Almond, 1983.

Ley, J. "Origenes über hebräische Metrik." *ZAW* 12 (1892) 212–17.

Lichtenstein, Murray H. "Chiasm and Symmetry in Proverbs 31." *CBQ* 44 (1982) 202–11.

Limburg, James. "The Root ריב and the Prophetic Lawsuit Speeches." *JBL* 88 (1969) 291–304.

Liu, David J. "Parallel Structures in the Canon of Chinese Poetry: The Shih Ching." *PT* 4 (1983) 639–53.

Lohfink, Norbert. *Qoheleth.* Translated by Sean McEvenue. CC. Minneapolis: Fortress, 2003.

Longacre, Robert E. "Left Shifts in Strongly VSO Languages." In *Word Order in Discourse,* edited by Pamela Downing and Michael Noonan, 331–54. Typological Studies in Language 30. Amsterdam: Benjamins, 1995.

Longman, Tremper, III. *The Book of Ecclesiastes.* NICOT. Grand Rapids: Eerdmans, 1998.

———. "A Critique of Two Recent Metrical Systems." *Bib* 63 (1982) 230–54.

Loewenberg, I. "Identifying Metaphors." *FOL* 12 (1975) 315–38.

Lowth, Robert. *Lectures on the Sacred Poetry of the Hebrews.* 2 vols. London: Ogles, 1816.

Lunn, Nicholas P. *Word-Order Variation in Biblical Hebrew Poetry: Differentiating Pragmatics and Poetics.* Paternoster Biblical Monographs. Milton Keynes, UK: Paternoster, 2006.

Macky, Peter W. *The Centrality of Metaphors to Biblical Thought: A Method for Interpreting the Bible.* SBEC 19. Lewiston, NY: Mellen, 1990.

Magdalene, F. R. *On the Scales of Righteousness: Neo-Babylonian Trial Law and the Book of Job.* BJS 348. Providence: Brown University Press, 2007.

———. "The ANE Origins of Legal Impairment as Theological Disability and the Book of Job." *PRS* 34 (2007) 23–59.

Malul, Meir. *Knowledge, Control, and Sex: Studies in Biblical Thought, Culture and Worldview.* Tel Aviv: Archaeological Center Publications, 2002.

Martin, Wallace. "Metaphor." In *New Princeton Encyclopedia of Poetry and Poetics,* edited by Alex Preminger and T. V. F. Brogan, 760–66. Princeton: Princeton University Press, 1993.

Meyers, Carol L. "Lampstand." In *ABD,* 4:141–43.

———. *The Tabernacle Menorah: A Synthetic Study of a Symbol from the Biblical Cult.* Rev. ed. Piscataway, NJ: Gorgias, 2003.

Miller, Douglas B. "Qohelet's Symbolic Use of הבל." *JBL* 117 (1998) 437–54.

————. *Symbol and Rhetoric in Ecclesiastes: the Place of Hebel in Qohelet's Work.* SBLAB 2. Leiden: Brill, 2002.

Miller, Patrick D. "Meter, Parallelism and Tropes: The Search for Poetic Style." *JSOT* 28 (1984) 99–106.

Morrow, William. "Consolation, Rejection, and Repentance in Job 42:6." *JBL* 105 (1986) 211–25.

Mowinckel, Sigmund. *The Psalms in Israel's Worship.* 2 vols. Translated by D. R. Ap-Thomas. Nashville: Abingdon, 1962.

Muenchow, Charles. "Dust and Dirt in Job 42:6." *JBL* 108 (1989) 597–611.

Muilenburg, James. "Form Criticism and Beyond." *JBL* 88 (1969) 1–18.

Murphy, Roland E. *Ecclesiastes.* WBC 23A. Dallas: Word, 1992.

Negoiță A., and H. Ringgen, "הָגָה *hāgāh*." In *TDOT* 3 (1978) 321–24.

Newman, Louis Israel, and William Popper. *Studies in Biblical Parallelism.* University of California Publications. Semitic Philology 1.2 and 3. Berkeley: University of California Press, 1918.

Newsom, Carol A. *The Book of Job: A Contest of Imaginations.* Oxford: Oxford University Press, 2003.

Niccacci, Alviero. "Analysing Biblical Hebrew Poetry." *JSOT* 74 (1997) 77–93.

Nielsen, Kirsten. *There is Hope for a Tree: The Tree as Metaphor in Isaiah.* Translated by Christine and Frederick Crowley. JSOTSup 65. Shef-field: JSOT Press, 1989.

O'Connor, M. *Hebrew Verse Structure.* Winona Lake, IN: Eisenbrauns, 1980.

Oestreich, Bernhard. *Metaphors and Similes in Hosea 14:2–9 (1–8): A Study of Hoseanic Pictorial Language.* Friedensauer Schriftenreihe. Reihe A, Theologie 1. Frankfurt: Lang, 1998.

Ogden, Graham S. "The Interpretation of דּוֹר in Ecclesiastes 1.4." *JSOT* 34 (1986) 91–92.

————. *Qoheleth.* 2nd ed. Readings. Sheffield: Sheffield Phoenix, 2007.

O'Kane, Martin. "Interpreting the Bible through the Visual Arts." *Hebrew Bible and Ancient Israel* 1 (2012) 388–409.

O'Rourke, R. F. "Job's Final Response: A Cultural Interpretation." *JTAK* 30 (2006) 58–71.

Pardee, Dennis. "Ugaritic and Hebrew Metrics." In *Ugarit in Retrospect: Fifty Years of Ugarit and Ugaritic,* edited by Gordon D. Young, 113–30. Winona Lake, IN: Eisenbrauns, 1981.

Parker, Simon B. "Ugaritic Literature and the Bible." *NEA* 63 (2000) 228–31.

Patrick, Dale. "The Translation of Job xlii 6." *VT* 26 (1976) 369–71.

Perdue, Leo. *Wisdom and Creation: The Theology of Wisdom Literature.* Nashville: Abingdon, 1994.

Petersen, David L., and Kent Harold Richards. *Interpreting Hebrew Poetry.* Guides to Biblical Scholarship. Minneapolis: Fortress, 1992.

Pine, Red. *Poems of the Masters: China's Classic Anthology of T'ang and Sung Dynasty Verse.* Port Townsend, WA: Copper Canyon, 2003.

Philo. Translated by F. H. Colson. 10 vols. LCL. Cambridge: Harvard University Press, 1929–1953.

Plato. *Republic.* Translated by Desmond Lee with Introduction by Mellisa Lane. 2nd ed. London: Penguin, 1974. Reprint, 2007.

Pope, Marvin H. *Job.* AB 15. Garden City, NY: Doubleday, 1965.

Quine, W. V. O. "A Postscript on Metaphor." *CritInq* 5 (1978) 161–62.

Richards, I. A. *The Philosophy of Rhetoric.* 1936. Reprint, Galaxy Book, 1965.

Ricoeur, Paul. "Metaphorical Process as Cognition, Imagination, and Feeling." *CritInq* 5 (1978) 143–59.

———. *The Rule of Metaphor: Multi-disciplinary Studies of the Creation of Meaning in Language.* Translated by Robert Czerny. University of Toronto Romance Series 37. Toronto: University of Toronto Press, 1977.

Ritchie, Ian D. "The Nose Knows: Bodily Knowing in Isaiah 11.3." *JSOT* 87 (2000) 59–73.

Roberts, J. J. M. "Job's Summons to Yahweh: The Exploitation of a Legal Metaphor." *ResQ* 16 (1973) 159–64.

Robinson, Theodore H. *The Poetry of the Old Testament.* London: Duckworth, 1947.

Rousseau, F. "Structure de Qohelet 1:4–11 et plan du livre." *VT* 31 (1981) 200–217.

Samet, N. "Qoheleth 1:4 and the Structure of the Book's Prologue." *ZAW* 126 (2014) 92–100.

Savran, George. "Seeing Is Believing: on the Relative Priority of Visual and Verbal Perception of the Divine." *BibInt* 17 (2009) 320–61.

Scholnick, Sylvia Huberman. "The Meaning of *Mišpaṭ* in the Book of Job." *JBL* 101 (1982) 521–29.

———. "Poetry in the Courtroom: Job 38–41." In *Directions in Biblical Hebrew Poetry,* edited by Elaine R. Follis, 185–204. JSOTSup 40. Sheffield: JSOT Press, 1987.

Segert, Stanislav. "Problems of Hebrew Prosody." In *Congress Volume: Oxford, 1959,* 283–91. VTSup 7. Leiden: Brill, 1960.

Seow, C. L. *Ecclesiastes.* AB 18C. New York: Doubleday, 1997.

———. *Job 1–14.* Illuminations. Grand Rapids: Eerdmans, 2013.

———. "Poetic Closure in Job: The First Cycle." *JSOT* 34 (2010) 433–46.

Shea, William H. "The Qinah Structure of the Book of Lamentations." *Bib* 60 (1979) 103–7.

Shelley, John C. "Job 42:1–6: God's Bet and Job's Repentance." *RevExp* 89 (1992) 541–46.

Sherwood, Yvonne. *The Prostitute and the Prophet: Hosea's Marriage in Literary-Theoretical Perspective.* JSOTSup 212. Sheffield: Sheffield Academic, 1996.

Sievers, E. *Metrische Studien.* Vol. 1, *Studien zur hebräischen Metrik.* Leipzig: Teubner, 1901.

———. *Metrische Studien.* Vol. 1, *Studien zur hebräischen Metrik.* Zweiter Teil. Leipzig: Teubner, 1901.

Seybold, Klaus. "הֶבֶל *hebhel.*" In *TDOT* 3 (1978) 313–20.

Smith, Mark S. *The Origins and Development of the Waw-Consecutive: Northwest Semitic Evidence from Ugarit to Qumran.* HSS 39. Atlanta: Scholars, 1991.

———. "'Seeing God' in the Psalms: The Background to the Beatific Vision in the Hebrew Bible." *CBQ* 50 (1988) 171–83.

Stager, Lawrence E. "Jerusalem and the Garden of Eden." *ErIsr* 26 (1999) 183–94.

Stordalen, T. *Echoes of Eden: Genesis 2–3 and Symbolism of the Eden Garden in Biblical Hebrew Literature.* CBET 25. Leuven: Peeters, 2000.

Stuart, Douglas K. *Studies in Early Hebrew Meter.* HSM 13. Missoula, MT: Scholars, 1976.

Tollerton, David C. "Reading Job as Theological Disruption for a Post-Holocaust World." *JTI* 3 (2009) 197–212.

Thomas Aquinas. *Summa Theologiae I 1–13.* Translated by B. Shanley. Indianapolis: Hackett, 2006.

Thomas, Derek. *Proclaiming the Incomprehensible God: Calvin's Teaching on Job*. Ross-shire, Scotland: Mentor, 2004.

Tov, Emmanuel. *Scribal Practices and Approaches Reflected in the Texts Found in the Judean Desert*. STDJ 54. Leiden: Brill, 2004.

Tuell, Steven S. "Between Text and Sermon: Psalm 1." *Int* 63 (2009) 278–80.

Tsumura, David T. "Parallelism in Hebrew and Chinese Poetry." Paper presented at Conference of Philarchisophia. Xi'an, China 2007.

———. "Vertical Grammar of Parallelism in Hebrew Poetry." *JBL* 128 (2009) 167–81.

Utzschneider, H. "Job: An Aesthetic Theology of the Old Testament." *CTR* 8 (2010) 91–100.

Vance, Donald R. *The Question of Meter in Biblical Hebrew Poetry*. SBEC 46. Lewiston, NY: Mellen, 2001.

Van der Lugt, Pieter. *Cantos and Strophes in Biblical Hebrew Poetry: With Special Reference to the First Book of the Psalter*. Old Testament Studies 53. Leiden: Brill, 2006.

———. *Rhetorical Criticism and the Poetry of the Book of Job*. Old Testament Studies 32. Leiden: Brill, 1995.

Van Leeuwen, R. C. "Liminality and Worldview in Proverbs 1–9." *Semeia* 50 (1990) 111–44.

———. "Meaning and Structure of Hosea X 1–8." *VT* 53 (2003) 367–78.

Van, Seters, J. "The Creation of Man and the Creation of the King." *ZAW* 101 (1989) 333–42.

Van Wolde, E. J. "Job 42,1–6: The Reversal of Job." In *The Book of Job*, edited by W. A. M. Beuken, 223–50. BETL 114. Leuven: Peeters, 1994.

Vogels, W. Review of *Major Poems of the Hebrew Bible: At the Interface of Prosody and Structural Analysis. Volume 2; 85 Psalms and Job 4–14*, by J. P. Fokkelman. *CBQ* 63 (2001) 516–17.

Walton, John. *Ancient Near Eastern Thought*. Grand Rapids: Baker Academic, 2006.

Wallace, Howard N. "Garden of God." In *ABD*, 2:906–7.

———. *The Eden Narrative*. HSM 32. Atlanta: Scholars, 1985.

Waltke, Bruce K., and M. O'Connor. *An Introduction to Biblical Hebrew Syntax*. Winona Lake, IN: Eisenbrauns, 1990.

Watson, Wilfred G. E. *Classical Hebrew Poetry: A Guide to Its Techniques*. JSOTSup 26. Sheffield: JSOT Press, 1984.

———. *Traditional Techniques in Classical Hebrew Verse*. JSOTSup 170. Sheffield: Sheffield Academic, 1994.

Weber, Beat. "Toward a Theory of the Poetry of the Hebrew Bible: The Poetry of the Psalms as a Test Case." *BBR* 22 (2012) 157–88.

Weeks, Stuart. *Ecclesiastes and Scepticism*. Library of Hebrew Bible/Old Testament Studies 541. New York: T. & T. Clark, 2012.

Weiser, Artur. *The Psalms*. Translated by Herbert Hartwell. OTL. London: SCM, 1962.

Weiss, Meir. *The Bible from Within: The Method of Total-Interpretation*. Publications of the Perry Foundation for Biblical Research in the Hebrew University of Jerusalem. Translated by B. J. Schwartz. Jerusalem: Magnes, 1984.

Wenham, Gordon J. *Genesis 1–15*. WBC 1. Dallas: Word, 1987.

———. "Sanctuary Symbolism in the Garden of Eden Story." In *I Studied Inscriptions before the Flood*, edited by Richard Hess and David T. Tsumura, 399–404. Winona Lake, IN: Eisenbrauns, 1994.

Whybray, R. N. "Ecclesiastes 1.5–7 and the Wonders of Nature." *JSOT* 41 (1988) 105–12.

———. *Job*. Readings. Sheffield: Sheffield Academic, 1998.

Wilcox, Max. "The Promise of the 'Seed' in the New Testament and the Targumim." *JSNT* 5 (1979) 2–20.

Wiley, Henrietta L. "They Save Themselves Alone: Faith and Loss in the Stories of Abraham and Job." *JSOT* 34 (2009) 115–29.

Wilson, Robert R. *Prophecy and Society in Ancient Israel*. Philadelphia: Fortress, 1980.

Winsatt, William K., and Monroe C. Beardsley, "The Concept of Meter: An Exercise in Abstraction." *PMLA* 74 (1959) 585–98.

Winslow, R. "Meter." In *The Princeton Encyclopedia of Poetry and Poetics,* edited by R. Greene et al., 872–76. Princeton: Princeton University Press, 2012.

Wilson, L. "Artful Ambiguity in Ecclesiastes 1:1–11: A Wisdom Technique?" In *Qoheleth in the Context of Wisdom,* edited by A. Schoors, 357–65. BETL 136. Leuven: Peeters, 1998.

Wolters, A. M. "A Child of Dust and Ashes: Job 42:6b." *ZAW* 102 (1990) 116–19.

Wright, Al. "The Riddle and the Sphinx: The Structure of the Book of Qoheleth." *CBQ* 30 (1968) 313–34.

Yeats, W. B., ed. *The Poems of William Blake*. 1905. Reprint, London: Routledge & Kegan Paul, 1969.

Young, Gordon Douglas. ed. *Ugarit in Retrospect: Fifty Years of Ugarit and Ugaritic*. Winona Lake, IN: Eisenbrauns, 1981.

Zogbo, Lynell, and Ernst R. Wendland. *Hebrew Poetry in the Bible: A Guide for Understanding and for Translating*. New York: United Bible Societies, 2000.

Index of Subjects

Made in the USA
Columbia, SC
11 August 2020